CONQUERING INCEST:

My Life as a Trauma Survivor

E. Diane Champé

First published by Dog Ear Publishing
4010 W. 86th Street, Ste H
Indianapolis, IN 46268
www.dogearpublishing.net

ISBN: 978-145750-117-3

This book is printed on acid-free paper.

Printed in the United States of America

To Suzanne, the love of my life
To my therapist, thank you for your dedication to my recovery

"Even the helpless victim of a hopeless situation, facing a fate he cannot change, may rise above himself, may grow beyond himself, and by so doing change himself."

Victor E. Frankel

Man's Search for Meaning

Table of Contents

The Chambreaux Family

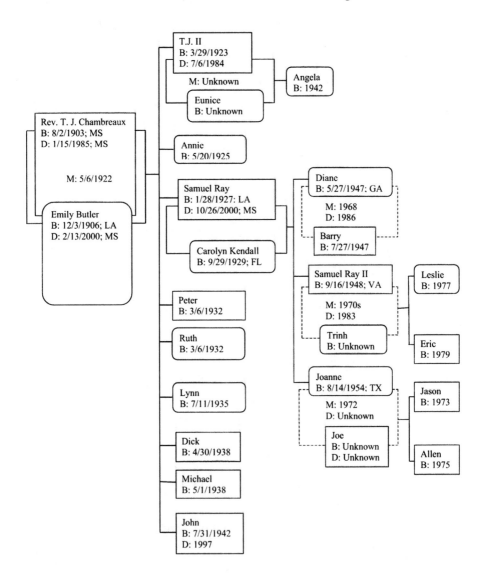

Rev. T. J. Chambreaux
B: 8/2/1903; MS
D: 1/15/1985; MS

M: 5/6/1922

Emily Butler
B: 12/3/1906; LA
D: 2/13/2000; MS

T.J. II
B: 3/29/1923
D: 7/6/1984

M: Unknown

Eunice
B: Unknown

Angela
B: 1942

Annie
B: 5/20/1925

Samuel Ray
B: 1/28/1927; LA
D: 10/26/2000; MS

Carolyn Kendall
B: 9/29/1929; FL

Diane
B: 5/27/1947; GA

M: 1968
D: 1986

Barry
B: 7/27/1947

Samuel Ray II
B: 9/16/1948; VA

M: 1970s
D: 1983

Trinh
B: Unknown

Leslie
B: 1977

Eric
B: 1979

Joanne
B: 8/14/1954; TX

M: 1972
D: Unknown

Joe
B: Unknown
D: Unknown

Jason
B: 1973

Allen
B: 1975

Peter
B: 3/6/1932

Ruth
B: 3/6/1932

Lynn
B: 7/11/1935

Dick
B: 4/30/1938

Michael
B: 5/1/1938

John
B: 7/31/1942
D: 1997

The Vincini Family

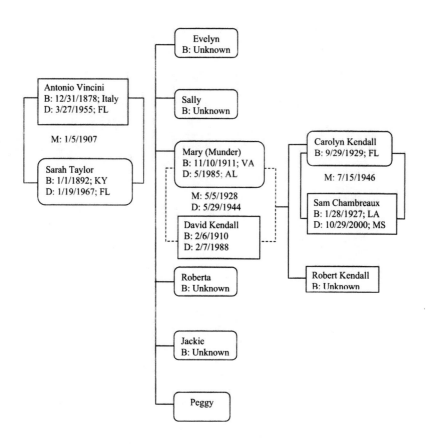

Evelyn
B: Unknown

Antonio Vincini
B: 12/31/1878; Italy
D: 3/27/1955; FL

Sally
B: Unknown

M: 1/5/1907

Carolyn Kendall
B: 9/29/1929; FL

Mary (Munder)
B: 11/10/1911; VA
D: 5/1985; AL

M: 7/15/1946

Sarah Taylor
B: 1/1/1892; KY
D: 1/19/1967; FL

M: 5/5/1928
D: 5/29/1944

Sam Chambreaux
B: 1/28/1927; LA
D: 10/29/2000; MS

David Kendall
B: 2/6/1910
D: 2/7/1988

Roberta
B: Unknown

Robert Kendall
B: Unknown

Jackie
B: Unknown

Peggy

Acknowledgements

Healing takes place within relationships. When you are abused and neglected as a child, you learn distorted ways of thinking and unhealthy methods of coping. It is only through the love and support of healthy people who care enough to guide you with compassion and professional skill that you overcome your trauma and become a fully functioning adult.

I was blessed to have had such people in my life.

I want to thank the following therapists for modeling appropriate care throughout my recovery: Christine Courtois, Ph.D., Joan Turkus, M.D., Trey Sunderland, M.D., Lynne Hazard, Ph.D., Myrna Alexander, Ph.D., and Alison Gartner, Ph.D. By receiving the highest of ethical treatment from therapists well-versed in the standards of care, I was able to overcome the trauma I endured.

I also want to thank Bethany Brand, Ph.D., for providing many opportunities for me to discuss my experiences and treatment with her college students.

Being fortunate enough to be hospitalized at the Psychiatric Institute of Washington in Washington, D.C., in their Center's Posttraumatic Disorders Program, made all the difference in the world during those times when my life was hanging by a thread. I am very grateful for the care I received on that unit.

Although I was fired from the Fortune 20 Company where I had worked for almost three decades, Amy Wind, Esquire and Philip Simon, Esquire successfully sued the Company on my behalf. Without them, I would have become homeless. Through their excellent legal support, they secured the financial resources which have enabled me to live a comfortable life. I am also greatly indebted to Stephen Ratliff, Esquire for his valuable assistance in his legal work regarding the publication of this book.

On a more personal level, three individuals have formed the core support for my overall well-being for over 30 years and continue as valued friends today. Hayden Constance was my professional mentor and a staunch supporter throughout my therapy. Her humor and practical support over the years helped me many a day to keep moving forward. She has been a true and loving friend. Kevin Whelan was always there to cheer me up and supported my arduous journey in any way he could, and for that I will be forever grateful. Peggy Peterson has been my rock of support in so many ways. She has been there for me, day or night, in every way possible, no questions asked. I would not be where I am today without her loving care. She has been a true blessing in my life.

I was fortunate to meet Suzanne at the end of my therapy when I could be the healthy partner she so richly deserves. I continue to grow and learn from her sensitive and loving guidance. With her, I am now enjoying the best years of my life.

Introduction

This is the saga of my recovery from child abuse and neglect that I suffered at the hands of my parents from 1947 to 1968, the first 21 years of my life. I was their captive for 7,665 days before I left home on my wedding day. My childhood and adolescence became consumed by my attempts to understand what I had done wrong.

When I left home, not having figured out the reason for their behavior, I thought I could put everything behind me and begin an entirely new life. I had no way of knowing how far-reaching the effects of their abuse would be. My parents' psychological torture set the stage for the rest of my life since they had brainwashed me into believing I was only allowed to act and think in a certain way.

The Fortune 20 Company I started working for in 1965 had very clear methods to follow. Having been indoctrinated from birth not to disobey any rules, I performed my professional duties in an outstanding manner.

Because my psychological programming as I grew up was reinforced by violence, my behavior in my marriage and during most of my career was that of a robot, dutifully performing my required functions in life, without questioning what I wanted or desired. My parents had been successful in not allowing me to grow emotionally or intellectually beyond the decision-making capacity of a child. Whatever my controlling husband or demanding supervisors asked became my immediate goal.

I worked diligently and within 12 years rose from one of the lowest jobs in the corporation to a management position. My marriage and quality of life improved greatly, and I thought I had successfully separated from my parents.

I was thriving for the first time in my life.

By 1979 I realized my husband's behavior was not normal. I began challenging his perceptions of household duties and intimacy issues. On the outside we seemed like the perfect couple. At 32-years-old we had a nice home; I was flying all over the country on business and stayed in the best hotels. What people didn't see was my marriage was in shambles.

I began therapy in 1981 hoping to get answers about how to make my marriage work and to deal with my abuse history. I had no idea what to expect. I thought it was a place where I could talk to an objective person about my problems, and we would come up with some solutions. I had no idea my past was totally intertwined with the present. I was also completely unaware that I had survived by developing about 20 personalities/alters.

I did not understand the concept of "psychological" work, nor did I realize the therapy process would center around my capacity to challenge and to be challenged, to be able to struggle with and to alter my entire belief system.

Even though the stress of my marital problems and intensive therapy presented monumental challenges, I continued working in an outstanding manner, and within only seven years I was in an upper management position.

Despite my valiant struggles to hold my life together, I experienced several new traumas, and the pain and rage from my child abuse burst into my consciousness. In the process, my entire world fell apart. I ended up spending 23 years in therapy and was hospitalized five times.

Without a doubt the greatest asset I had during my healing process was the unrelenting dedication of my psychologically healthy therapist. One of the most crucial aspects of my recovery was her modeling of appropriate behavior all along the way. The whole time I grew up, I kept thinking, *I don't know what I am supposed to do.*

By the way my doctor took care of her own needs she helped me learn the importance of appropriate self-care. She acknowledged when she was tired, mistaken, frustrated, and even when she needed to take a break. She helped me learn to pace myself with the traumatic material and recollections, and to turn my attention to other aspects of my life to gain sustenance, rather than focusing all of my energy on the past.

With my long exposure to corrective modeling with the same therapist, my comfortable lifestyle, and my capacity to integrate all the behaviors I was taught, I was able to work through my enormous trauma.

Even with all the support, extensive therapy and financial resources, I was 50-years-old before I stopped feeling the threat of being psychologically annihilated, a growing fear that if I followed my own conscience and spoke up about what I didn't like, my mind would completely shatter into total oblivion. It was not until I was 55-years-old that I finally stopped seeing the world through the eyes of a traumatized child.

My traumatic experiences had affected my entire life. Each and every incident of my parents' abuse contributed to how I viewed other people's behavior and how I felt about myself.

I have written this book to show the patterns of intergenerational abuse, the struggle to overcome the long-term impact of psychological torture, the lengths families will go to in hiding the *secret*, and the complete frustration survivors feel each time we confront what I call is society's "brick wall of denial."

Through my experiences you will see why child abuse and neglect is so destructive and the sheer perseverance it takes to separate the truth from the distortions. I hope to convey my history and the successful recovery process we used to overcome all the obstacles and to give hope to other child abuse survivors. I believe the hardest thing to do in life is to look at reality and then do something about it. This book is my way of doing just that.

Part 1

**Surviving the Trauma
1947—1968**

Chapter 1

Neglect and Molestation

The fight for my life started the day I was born on May 27, 1947, in Atlanta, Georgia. My arrival was not a blessed event in my mother's eyes. It was my misfortune to be born into the Chambreaux[1] family with all its rigidity and secrets. My parents, Sam and Carolyn Chambreaux, subjected me to enormous pain and suffering over the following 21 years to the point where I was on the brink of insanity. Their inner struggles became my living hell.

Sam had already been married and was in en route to a divorce at 18-years-old when he met Carolyn in Miami, Florida. His Navy enlistment as an aviation electrician's mate was almost complete at the end of World War II. At 16-years-old, Carolyn was so naïve, she told me years later she thought she could get pregnant by just kissing a man. They got married on payday, July 15, 1946, Sam in his Navy uniform and my mother in a beautiful, white gown with a long, flowing train. Carolyn's big dream was to travel all over America, but two days after their marriage ceremony Sam decided to get out of the Navy and move back to his hometown of Atlanta. She got pregnant one month later.

Carolyn was at first impressed with Sam's large family. His father was a well-known evangelist in a Pentecostal church. She soon learned, however, she was to be subservient "as the scriptures have instructed" to her husband and raise his children. This was not the exciting life she had envisioned.

---

[1] Pseudonym. All character names have been changed.

When I was born ten months later, we lived in a small apartment while Sam tried to start his own company building houses. He failed in that venture. So, after finding out Carolyn was pregnant again, he reenlisted in the Navy on March 2, 1948. With a wife and two children, Sam felt his best option for a secure future was with the military.

He was to report first to the naval base in Charleston, South Carolina, then his final destination at the Naval Air Station in Norfolk, Virginia. In less than two years, they had moved from Miami to Atlanta to Charleston to Norfolk. This nomadic lifestyle became a normal pattern for our family over the next 19 years.

When my brother, Ray, was born in Portsmouth Naval Hospital in Portsmouth, Virginia, the path of Sam and Carolyn's lives began to diverge markedly. Carolyn was 19-years-old with two demanding children only a year and a half apart. Her days were spent feeding, dressing and taking care of Ray and me, in addition to washing our clothes, our dirty, smelly, cotton diapers and Sam's Navy-whites by hand.

Although Sam, who would be 22-years-old in three months, had to get up early, walk three miles to catch a ride, and got home late every night, his days were spent around people his own age who were engaged in learning new skills aboard an aircraft carrier. He could escape the drudgery; she could not.

I, in the meantime, was not happy. I cried all the time and always wanted to be held. Carolyn resented the life she was now living and acted out her frustrations on me. She revealed many years later that she believed if I cried long enough, I would eventually shut up. At times, my mother gave me bottles with dirty water in them.

On October 21, 1949, Sam got orders to attend a 33-week training course in Memphis, Tennessee. We stayed with Sam's father, who we called Pappa, and his family. Carolyn had to contend not only with Sam's demands, but also with the watchful eyes of his parents.

Carolyn had not been home in three years. Somehow they found enough money for her to take the train to Miami to visit her mother, Mary. I don't remember the event, but I met her father, David Kendall, for the first and last time. After that visit, my mother never, ever mentioned her father or told us anything about our grandfather.

Ray and I started calling our grandmother "Munder" because we had trouble saying "Mother." Why we were trying to call her Mother, I don't know. When we went back to Memphis, I was irritable and fussy. Relatives informed me later in life that Carolyn was a cold person and wasn't particularly happy taking care of two kids. They also spoke about Sam's delight in saying he would lay me over his lap and pull my pants down to spank me, but he said it was so pretty, he just couldn't do it.

The war between my parents had begun. Carolyn was depressed but kept her silent rage to herself. After living through the Depression, he was all she had. She was confined within societal expectations of mothering two young children in the 1950s. Sam had had his fill of being controlled by his strict domineering parents, was determined to make a name for himself, and was not about to restrict his sexual appetites for anyone.

Ray and I developed an internal sense of being unloved from the very beginning. I showed my despair by crying and clinging to Carolyn. Ray was more temperamental and hard to control. Sam used to say, "When Diane was young, all you had to do was look at her, and she would cry. With Ray, the only thing he understood was the belt."

Sam's interaction with us was extreme. He was either physically gone for long periods of time or showed no healthy boundaries with us when he was home. This combination of parental neglect and abuse damaged both of us from the very beginning. Both Ray and I could only react physically and emotionally at this stage because neither one of us had the verbal skills to communicate our pain.

On May 2, 1950, Sam completed his training course and got orders to report aboard the U.S.S. Fabius in San Diego. We now had a standard routine when traveling. In the backseat of our black, oval-shaped Buick, my parents put boxes on the floor on one side. They then placed blankets on the boxes and the seat to form a bed for Ray and me to sleep on at night. During the day, we sat on the other side of the seat. This was how we traveled for the next two years.

We didn't have any toys or books but were expected to sit still the whole trip without saying a word. This enforced silence was cruel. I endured it from the ages of three to five and Ray from one to four. My reaction was to become very quiet and withdrawn, while Ray acted out, becoming even more of a handful. My attention was always focused outside the car window, watching the constant changes in scenery from the palm trees in Miami to the farms in Louisiana, the desert and immense heat in Arizona to the beaches in San Diego. Sam routinely pulled off on the side of the road and whipped Ray to make him conform. Carolyn, in the meantime, looked the other way. I had already learned at this early age that it was futile to seek reassurance from her. I just kept my emotions to myself.

When we arrived in California, our family moved into a small apartment in Del Mar near the railroad tracks. I used to love to hear the trains rumble by at night. It was very comforting for me.

On September 9th the Fabius sailed for points in Japan and Korea. Upon his return home, Sam received the Good Conduct Medal and was given permission to travel to Georgia to reenlist for another six years. I was four-years-old and remember seeing a photograph of Ray and me wearing Japanese pajamas he brought home as gifts.

As we traveled to Georgia, we stopped in Louisiana to visit with Mamma's (Sam's mother's) relatives. My great-grandmother, Grandma Butler, was outside chopping wood as we drove up. All the chickens were running around in the front yard of their one-story wooden house built on short stilts. Large fields lay behind a rail fence, and I could see a mule chewing some hay by the side of the house. My great-grandfather got up from his rocking chair on the front porch and came to greet us. Grandma Butler put the ax down and smiled a big, toothless grin.

Breakfast was great the next morning. I woke up early and watched my great-grandmother make biscuits, cut strips of bacon, boil grits, and cook fresh eggs she had gathered in the barn. Everything tasted wonderful except for the awful milk straight from the cow. I was used to a sweet taste. This was flat and a little sour.

Going to the outhouse was memorable too. I had never gone to the bathroom by walking down a path behind the house, opening a wooden door to a small enclosure, and trying to sit on a board with a hole in it. The smell almost gagged me. I don't remember what I wiped myself with because there wasn't any toilet paper, and as usual, I had to do this by myself without my mother's help.

That night after dinner, all of us sat on the front porch laughing and talking. One of my male relatives pulled me up onto his lap. While smiling and looking straight ahead, his hand moved slowly up my leg. His fingers inched inside my pants, but my squirming around didn't allow him to do anymore.

I jumped down, ran and hid.

I didn't run to my mother because her looks had always given me the message not to bother her. I didn't like being around my father, so I wasn't about to tell him. Shaking and afraid, I calmed myself the best I could. I was all alone with my distress and uncared for by family members.

The next morning we got into the car and continued our trip. After Sam completed his reenlistment paperwork and before returning to California, he drove to Miami and rented a small house near the old Orange Bowl Stadium.

On Sunday, Munder picked us up in her Chevy and took us to the same church where my parents had gotten married. Ray and I were walked to the pulpit on a raised platform and were told to sing one of Munder's favorite hymns. We really didn't want to get up in front of everyone, but as Brother Chambreaux's grandchildren, we did what we were told.

When Munder brought us home, Sam was getting ready to drive back to California as his month's leave was almost up. Before he left and while I was taking a bath, he told me to stand up so he could take a picture of me naked. I was embarrassed and only stood up after Carolyn got mad at me. I held the washcloth in front of my genitals and stood there stone-faced while he took my picture. Shortly afterward, he left and drove back to California.

Once Sam was back aboard ship, he was promoted to Aviation Electrician Supervisor and received a "Meritorious Mast" Commendation for his "leadership and devotion to duty."

I was, at four-years-old, becoming very confused. Munder, who I felt safe and secure with, adored me and wanted to show me off to all her friends. I loved that feeling but didn't see her very often. My mother never held me or comforted me in any way, which made me crave attention.

Sam's next assignment was as an instructor in Memphis, Tennessee. He first drove to Miami to pick us up, then on to Memphis and rented a small house.

After ten months, he was assigned for duty in Cherry Point, North Carolina. His younger brother, Peter, was in the military at Fort Bragg, which was about 150 miles away. Since this was an opportunity to visit one of his brothers he hadn't seen in a long time, we took a weekend trip to visit Peter and his family.

My parents, aunt, and uncle played cards until late in the evening. Ray and I were put to bed in their children's bedroom. I woke up in the middle of the night with Sam hovering over me trying to put his hands into my underpants. Carolyn came into the room, so he left. This is my earliest memory, at five-years-old, of her finding him in my bedroom during the middle of the night.

Sam's next duty station was the Naval Air Station in Jacksonville, Florida. We were only there for four months before he was transferred to Long Island, New York, for training on the F9F-6 aircraft. After driving up the eastern seaboard, Sam dropped us off with his parents at the parsonage in Kannapolis,

North Carolina. Pappa was the preacher at one of the oldest churches in the community.

I loved watching Mamma can vegetables and spending time in the upstairs bedroom with my uncles, Sam's younger twin brothers, Dick and Michael, eating popcorn and watching television. When Sam was through with his training, he drove down to North Carolina, picked us up, and we continued on to Cecil Field, Florida.

The following September I started the first grade at the Little Whitehouse Elementary School. By this time, I had only been living six years but had experienced great sadness, no stability, no real love or support from either parent, and sexual stimulation by my father and a great uncle. We had traveled 13,218 miles in our family car. Silent miles. Thousands of them. I was a very lonely and scared little girl.

Chapter 2

Sexualized Affection and Despair

Going to school opened a brand-new world for me. Once in school, I was with children my own age. We were given big thick crayons to put into our individual King Edward cigar boxes. I was extremely excited to learn how to read.

The most important aspect of all was that I felt 100 percent safe in school. When I walked into that large, solid brick building, it seemed like I was in a fortress. The teachers helped me learn things by being kind instead of being sarcastic like my mother.

At home, one of the few ways I had to distract myself was by watching television. A favorite show of mine was *Winky Dink and You* on Saturday mornings. My parents ordered the piece of green plastic I needed to put on the television screen. By using crayons, I could trace a path for *Winky* to get out of trouble. This was the only toy I had, so afterwards, I folded the green plastic ever so neatly and put it into the cigar box with my crayons.

In 1953 Carolyn got pregnant again, and Sam received orders to the Naval Auxiliary Air Station near Corpus Christi, Texas. On our way to Texas, we drove down dusty roads in Louisiana to visit Grandma Butler and some of my other relatives in their isolated farmhouses. While my parents were visiting in one part of the house, I wandered into another room and saw a very strange sight. In the middle of the room was a grown man in diapers in what looked like a large baby crib.

Someone came looking for me, and when they saw me standing, frozen in place, they said he was mentally ill, so that was where they kept him. I didn't know what to think. I just ran out of the room as fast as I could. Once outside in the yard, I tried to put what I had just seen out of my mind.

After dinner we left and continued on to Texas. We moved into a small house. All I could see in every direction was flat arid land. It seemed like we were out in the middle of nowhere.

Next door were the Henrys whose son, Billy, was my age. Ray was only five-years-old but still felt big enough to fight with him. One afternoon we heard Billy scream. We ran out to discover Billy lying on the ground holding his head with blood on his hands. Ray, who had hit Billy in the head with a brick, was becoming more wild and unmanageable. Not long after that incident, we moved to a small house closer to town.

I was finishing the first grade and got excited about the large tarantula I found in our backyard. I took a jar from the garage and prodded the tarantula with a stick until it climbed into it, then sealed the jar and poked holes in the lid. When I took it to school the next morning, without my mother noticing, all the other kids wanted to know if it was okay to touch it.

My teacher was impressed. Her favorable attention to something I had done made me feel very special. I craved that feeling. I needed it to counter all the loneliness I carried around most of the time. From that point on, school became an integral part of my sense of well-being.

In July 1954 when Carolyn was eight months pregnant, Ray was diagnosed with bulbar polio. He was one of the victims of the devastating epidemic that year. The type he had affected his spinal cord at the lowest part of his brain containing the nerve centers for breathing and circulation.

Death was a real possibility.

Two months shy of turning six-years-old, Ray was placed into an iron lung. This equipment changed the air pressure which forced his body to breathe. The doctors also had to perform a tracheotomy, and his whole left side was paralyzed.

Carolyn walked around with a scared look on her face yelling at me a lot. Sam was irritated with Carolyn and didn't come home from work until late at night.

I wasn't sure what was happening. I only knew Ray was very sick, and I couldn't be in the same room with him. Sam hoisted me onto his shoulders so I could see him through a window.

What upset me most was getting a gamma globulin shot. The needle was so big it felt like a pencil was being shoved into me. I had to sit on a pillow afterwards for a week. The number of shots was determined by how much you weighed. Carolyn needed three, and Sam got four.

Ray's recovery within a few months was called a miracle. The doctors said it was one of the shortest turnarounds they had ever seen. When he came out of the iron lung, he had to exercise his left hand. The doctors had a standing order that his water pistol was always to be filled. I'm sure the nurses loved that, but it was a playful way for him to work those muscles. The only sign of his previous paralysis was a slight weakness in closing his left eyelid all the way.

As usual I cried a lot. My parents decided to put me into their bed between them. Maybe that would calm me down so they could get some sleep. I woke up one night when my mother got up to go to the bathroom.

Sam pulled me close to him which felt comforting. He reached for my hand and wrapped my little fingers around something under the covers.

He asked, "Do you know what this is?"

It was big, long and felt soft and squishy. I tried to pull my hand away, but he held me tight.

He whispered, "It's my hot dog, but don't tell your mother. This is our secret."

He finally released my hand when Carolyn came back to bed. My body froze while my mind was overwhelmed. I felt like he had done something he wasn't supposed to do, but I understood I was to keep my mouth shut. Sam was 27-years-old. I was seven.

At this young age, I already felt like it was my responsibility to keep the peace between Sam and Carolyn. I was so lonely, I naturally hungered for the physical closeness and warmth of an adult, but I didn't like my father making me do things I didn't want to do. I yearned to be hugged and cuddled by Carolyn, but accepted that showing those feelings to her only pushed her away. To compensate I began living in a make-believe, happy world to escape the despair.

My sister, Joanne, was born in August 1954. Ray needed to be watched closely after getting out of the hospital, Joanne was a newborn, I was starting the second grade, and with Sam working all day, Carolyn asked Munder to come and help out. Things were much calmer when she was around.

Sam got a new set of orders on December 1st to attend a seven-month training course at the Naval Air Weapons School in Jacksonville, Florida. My parents agreed it would be best for us to stay with Munder while he was in school. Sam first drove us to Miami then left for Jacksonville.

I enjoyed very much being around my mother's relatives who were loud and carefree, and wherever my mother's family gathered there was always lots of fun with plenty to eat. I could always relax around them.

In Munder's home she had a second bedroom near the front of her small house where Carolyn and the three of us slept. During the day I either explored their musty garage or climbed the mango tree in the backyard. With a knife I got from the kitchen, I climbed up, got a mango for myself and had a nice treat. At night Munder bathed me in her bathtub with claw feet and showed me how Ivory soap floated in the water. Time spent with her was loving and fun. I finished the second grade with high marks.

Sam's next duty assignment was to report aboard the U.S.S. Lexington at the naval shipyard in Bremerton, Washington. After driving to Miami to pick us up, we left soon afterwards.

I was eight-years-old and emotionally closed down most of the time. For self-protection, I kept to myself. When I smiled, it was now fake, not innocent. My smile, I realized, kept people from asking me how I felt. Ray was six and a half. He also kept to himself but was still angry a lot. Joanne wanted attention in our closed car, but with nothing to do and no one to talk to, she screamed a lot.

This was our longest trip, 3,400 miles. Sam loved it. He woke us up in the middle of the night and said, "We're crossing the Mississippi!" and "We're driving down the main street of Dodge City, Kansas!" While this seemed like a big adventure to him, I was very lonely. I felt like I was in a prison on wheels.

At night instead of staying in motels, Sam usually pulled off on the side of the road. For some reason, my mother got in the backseat with Ray and Joanne and put me up-front with Sam. He would sit behind the wheel, make me lie on my back and put my head on his lap.

Everything seemed all right until one night I awoke to find his hand in my pants. This time it was different because he was touching me in a way that made me feel good. I couldn't help moving around because the warm feeling between my legs was so stimulating. I was afraid of getting into trouble. The only thing I could think of doing was to roll over on my side and pretend to be asleep. I believed I could fool him into thinking I had no reaction to what he was doing.

In reality I was very confused and felt guilty that I was doing something to make him act this way. I knew I couldn't say anything to my mother. I had to try and figure out on my own what was happening to me.

Very early in the morning, Carolyn got in the front seat. I got in the back and rolled up into a ball as close to the door as possible. As we got back onto the highway, Sam looked and smiled at me in a way that said, "This is between me and you."

I didn't like being treated this way. I didn't feel good about myself, but I had no idea how to stop him or get help. My solution was to push what happened to the back of my mind, tell myself it happened in a place we were leaving, and focus on my new life in a new city. That's the best coping mechanism I could come up with as an eight-year-old.

After we arrived in Bremerton, everything was unpacked. I went outside to be by myself. I climbed a grassy hill behind our house and entered the woods. As the sun gleamed through the trees, I marched as if I were a soldier, true to a mission and intensely focused. Rocks, twigs, old dead tree stumps, nothing escaped my notice. It seemed so important to me now to start identifying and memorizing my surroundings. I had learned my world wasn't safe. I couldn't be carefree because too many times Sam had caught me unawares and was sexual rather than playful. And Carolyn seemed to watch my every move as if I were doing something wrong. I was constantly on guard and stressed out.

Sam reported aboard the Lexington and sailed for Japan. I started the third grade but knew no one. I tried to fit in the best I could. I felt angry and envious but accepted the fact we would soon move again, so I kept to myself.

When the Lexington returned to its home port, Sam came home, and we did what we had done since the day I was born, got into the car and traveled to a faraway location, this time to the San Diego Naval Air Station.

My parents rented a small house in Imperial Beach. Their social life went into high gear. Up until that point, Sam had either left us with relatives while he was gone or was only home a short time before leaving on another duty assignment. Now that he was not at sea, he frequently brought his friends home and partied hard with them.

I watched as my parents cut up lemons, limes, and oranges, set the booze out, put the card table up, and sorted out records to dance to later in the evening. Couples came over, and all I could see was dancing, drinks being filled, and everyone laughing at each other's dirty jokes.

One night as I peered out my bedroom door into the semi-dark hallway, I saw my father embracing and kissing another woman. Although I had never noticed much affection shown between my parents, this was someone outside our family. My heart hammered against my chest as I very quietly closed the door. I didn't understand why my father sneaked around and did things like that with me and now with this strange woman. It made me even more afraid to be alone with him. As much as I hated Sam's sexual overtures toward me, this was our private game. Seeing him kiss a strange woman totally confused my understanding of our relationship. I wasn't his only secret.

Behind our house was a short fence with overgrown weeds on the other side. The minute I got outside, I ran for that fence, jumped behind it and pretended I was on a secret mission. My job was to be on the lookout for the bad guys and warn the others before they got hurt. I crouched down behind the fence, made it my intention not to be noticed by anyone in the house, all the while analyzing my surroundings. I was convinced I could some-how make myself invisible just by wishing it so, and no one could find me or hurt me.

During this time my father started singing this song to me:

"Don't save your kisses, pass them around.

You'll soon find my reasons are logically sound.

Who's going to know that you passed them around

A hundred years from today?"

While he sang, he tried to put his hands into my pants. I always pulled away from him, ran and hid.

Sam got orders to go to sea again, this time on the U.S.S. Essex. Before he reported onboard and went to sea, my parents moved once again, this time to Navy housing in Cabrillo Heights, California.

I felt comfortable with the neighborhood boys and started acting out what I had been taught at home. A neighborhood boy and I found two large pieces of cardboard. As we lay down in the middle of the large yard in front of the apartment buildings, we pretended the bottom one was a bed and the other a top sheet.

"This feels good," we said as we held each other and ran our hands over each other's body.

"Hey! What are you doing down there?" a woman yelled from a second-story window. "Come here right now!"

The boy jumped up, ran away and left me to face her alone.

"What were you doing?"

"Playing," I said.

I didn't know this woman, but since she was in the same unit we lived in, I knew she would tell my mother. I didn't want her to know I was angry at her for interfering with me doing what I wanted to do. I waited all day for my mother to say something to me, but she never did.

On another beautiful day, several kids I was playing with tried to guess each other's last name. "I know," I said proudly. "It's on your mailbox."

Just inside the front doorway to each apartment building was a row of mail slots with the tenants' last names across it. A boy raced me across the lawn to see who could reach the apartment building first. Being the first to arrive, I stopped outside the building to catch my breath. The boy was trying to get inside before me and ended up pushing me through a plate glass window. Lying face down in the glass, I turned over to see a one inch gaping hole on the top of my left forearm. At first I was curious. I didn't feel any pain. I thought it was odd that I could bleed and not hurt. Then I saw the flesh inside and became frightened.

Running to my apartment, I pressed the open wound together with my right hand. As soon as my mother looked at my injury, she became hysterical. She didn't know what to do and had to go next door for help. Someone came over to check me out then drove us to the hospital. Knowing I needed stitches while holding my skin together, I consoled my mother and told her I would be fine. On the inside, I resented having to take care of her and wished she could make some effort to comfort me.

Balboa Naval Hospital was cold and frightening. I never said a word even after looking at the child sitting next to me with a crochet needle stuck through his middle finger into the palm of his hand. Another child had his thumb bandaged, but it was soaked in blood. He kept crying and saying, "Please don't let them cut it off." I watched the other mothers and fathers put their arms around their kids and tell them they would be okay. Meanwhile, I sat silently while my mother read a magazine.

My mother did not protect or comfort me at all. I didn't understand, but accepted it and hated her all the more.

I was now very familiar with pain, anger, abandonment and fear. Since no one ever sat down and explained anything to me, the only place I felt safe was within my own mind. In there, I could shut off my feelings and pretend I lived in a happy world.

When Sam came home, he took leave and drove us back to Miami to visit Munder. After another 3,000 mile silent-trip and pulling into her driveway, I couldn't wait to run to Munder's arms. It was so good to see her.

When I was around Munder, I could relax. When she took me to church, she gave me a dime tied into one corner of a handkerchief so I would have something to put into the offering plate. Most importantly, she was the only person I ever saw stand up to my father.

When he was mad at me Munder would say, "Oh Sammie, leave her alone."

Before leaving for California, I held onto Munder as long as I could. Sam seemed relieved when I finally got into the car, then sped away as fast as he could.

Chapter 3

Experimentation and Initiation

On our way back to California, we stopped in Snakeville, Mississippi, for a brief visit with Mamma and Pappa where he was currently preaching. My father rented a small house, and since there were only three rooms, Ray, Joanne and I slept on a bed at the foot of my parents' bed. I heard them making moaning sounds during the night.

In the morning in an ashtray next to their bed, I found a small, round, rolled up rubber object I had never seen before. It had gooey stuff all over it. I wouldn't dare ask my parents what it was out of fear they would become angry at me for asking a stupid question or being nosey.

In February 1957 Sam drove us back to San Diego as he was still stationed at the Miramar Naval Air Station attending schools. This time we lived in an apartment in Claremont. The Henrys, who we had met in Corpus Christi, Texas, lived nearby.

One day our mothers went shopping and left Billy with me in our apartment. We went into my bedroom and pulled down the window shade.

"Let's do what grownups do," I said. "First we'll take our pants off then you lie on top of me."

"What do I do?" he asked.

"You stick your thing in me and go up and down."

At ten-years-old he didn't have an erection, and not knowing that that was necessary, I remembered saying to myself, *what's the big deal? There is nothing to this.* We decided to just hold each other. The car screeched as it came into the driveway. We quickly put our clothes on and sat on the bed. Opening the bedroom door with a scowl on her face, my mother asked, "What have the two of you been doing?"

"Reading," I replied.

"With the window shade drawn?"

I was both angry at her for disturbing us and afraid to say anything. I just sat there and stared at her. My skills of ingenuity and deception were developing, something I had learned all too well from my father.

In September 1957 I started the fifth grade, and in November Sam moved us to a duplex in Chula Vista. That Christmas, which is one of the few I remember, I got a bicycle. To me it meant freedom. When I went racing around the neighborhood, I felt alive, a feeling I yearned for but seldom experienced.

We also got a small record player on which I played a 45 record from the movie, *The Inn of the Sixth Happiness*. When I saw it on television, I closely focused on Ingrid Bergman as she stood up for young girls who were having their feet bound tightly to look attractive for men. She said, "Is there not one woman who loves her daughter enough to unbind her feet?"

Hearing this, a young woman rushed forward and unbound her daughter's feet. Ingrid Bergman stood up to the men and said, "To obey any man unquestionably is wrong." That made a deep impression on me, but who would stand up for me?

From January 18-30, 1958, Sam was in school in San Diego and then traveled to Newport, Rhode Island in March for 16 weeks of instruction for Officer Candidates School. On August 14th he received his commission to Ensign, got his third Good Conduct Medal and proceeded afterwards to the Naval Amphibious Training Unit in Coronado, California, for two weeks.

In May 1958 I turned 11-years-old. The whole time Sam was gone I was able to relax. I didn't have to keep looking over my shoulder. I got up early many mornings that summer and took Ray with me as I walked to the community swimming pool. We never had any problems when we were together. I had to feed Joanne, however, before we left because Carolyn made it my responsibility to take care of my four-year-old sister every morning.

When Sam came home in September, I steered clear of him. I now knew the looks he gave me didn't mean he was happy to see me. He just wanted to feel my body. Shortly afterward, he left home and reported onboard ship. He was gone for seven months performing local operations.

Once more I could relax. I started the sixth grade at Chula Vista Elementary School and was in the Girl Scouts. Even though I was active, I never had any friends or anyone to talk to. I was shy and felt dirty about myself. Everyone else always seemed to be having a good time. I was never allowed to express my feelings at home, so I certainly wasn't going to open up to strangers. I never felt like I fit in anywhere. I continued to be a very lonely and sad little girl, living by my mother's constant refrain:

"Children are to be seen and not heard."

My eternal, internal lament was, *I don't know what I'm supposed to do.*

I decided I would learn what people expected of me and then would perform to the best of my ability. When watching television and people in the movies, I imagined I was in the starring role and figured out how to conduct myself by watching them. I made a promise to myself that no matter how other people treated me, I would NEVER treat them the way I had been treated. I couldn't bear to see the pain on their faces.

While at sea, on January 10, 1959, Sam's commanding officer wrote in his fitness report:

> *For an officer of his rank, Ensign Chambreaux is excep-tionally mature. He has a fine military and moral character.*

The school wanted to show a film to girls about the menstrual cycle, but they required my parents' written permission, not knowing that at 12-years-old I had already been introduced to my genitals by my father for most of my life. As I watched, I felt the subject odd, not because it discussed changes within a woman's body, but that they were discussing it so openly. I didn't understand everything, but I wasn't going to talk about it at home.

Just before graduating from sixth grade, after putting the dinner dishes away one night, Ray, Joanne, and I were told to go to our bedroom because my parents were going to have a party. We played records on our record player for awhile and then were told to go to bed.

All three of us slept in the same room. My twin bed shared the same wall as the living room which allowed me to clearly hear what my father was playing on the stereo. Ray and Joanne slept on bunk beds a few feet away.

Sam had been to Japan many times and was raving about the sexual music he could find. My heart started beating faster as I listened to noises I had never heard before. I felt a strange tingling all over my body which was new to me. It only heightened my experience.

"Wait until you hear this," Sam said excitedly.

First there were soft drumbeats.

boomp BOOMP boomp bat tat tat tat

Then a woman's heavy breathing.

oooohh! Ooohh! ooohh!

A man started grunting.

OOOOGG Ah! OOOOGG Ah! OOOGG Ah!

This kept repeating itself.

boomp BOOMP boomp bat tat tat tat

OOOGG Ah!

It kept getting louder and louder until the man gave a loud Ahhh! The woman was whimpering. Everyone was laughing, but

I couldn't figure out what was so funny. The rhythm of the drums was stimulating, and I could feel the excitement of the party. When they started playing other records, I fell asleep not having really understood what I had heard.

Sometime during the night, I woke up and discovered my father had carefully lifted the cover from my bed and was gently trying to pull my pants down. They were caught somewhat, so he put his hand softly into my pants, touched me very lightly, and pushed my underpants down from the inside.

I was scared to death.

He began rubbing his moistened finger very gently on my clitoris. The whole time I kept my eyes closed, trembling with fear. He put his lips on mine and gently opened my mouth with his tongue.

What the hell was going on?

I thought I heard a faint noise, and apparently so did Sam because he carefully laid the covers back down and left. It wasn't long, though, before he was back. I had not budged an inch.

This time he lifted the covers, gently opened my legs and started kissing me between my legs. *Why was he doing this to me? Where was my mother?* When he covered me back up and left the room, I was totally disoriented, frightened and alone.

The next morning nothing was said, and my father acted as if nothing had happened at all. This was my initiation into becoming a teenager.

My behavior was now becoming distinctly different. I watched everyone's moves, listened very intently to what was said and didn't miss a trick.

When playing outdoors, I slinked around buildings and crouched low to the ground. Once again I felt like I was on a secret mission. It seemed like I lived in a different world than everyone else. I believed it was critical for my survival to be keenly aware of my surroundings so I could anticipate bad things that might happen to me.

I stayed outdoors until it got really dark. After I took my bath at night and put on my pajamas, I would lie on the floor in front of the heater vent until time to go to bed. By lying on the floor, I was in full view of everyone. Only at the last minute would I go to my room.

I had to constantly dodge my father. He got a big kick out of grabbing at my developing breasts all day. He would wait behind doors to grab me then would laugh as he pawed me.

He always whispered to me, "Diane, don't ever hate me. I'm trying to teach you something."

Sam was 6'1" and weighed about 200 pounds while I was 12-years-old and probably weighed about 90 pounds. I was at his mercy both physically and psychologically.

I felt totally empty. There was no sincere warmth, no feelings of privacy or safety, no one willing to notice my despair or do anything about it. I knew the only person I could depend upon was me, so I habitually isolated from others. I felt it was the safest thing to do.

The year was 1959 and my parents started packing all our things repeating the one constant in my life, moving to another city. This time we went to Treasure Island in San Francisco. While Sam attended a Damage Control course, we lived in a Quonset hut near the water for his 10 weeks of school.

After Sam completed his course, we drove to Chula Vista where I started the seventh grade at Chula Vista Junior High School. His ship sailed on August 10th for Kobe, Yokosuka, and Okinawa.

As usual, I looked forward to the times he was gone so that I could relax. On my long walk to school I would sing:

> *"The Lord is good to me, and so I thank the Lord,*
>
> *For giving me, the things I need,*
>
> *The sun, the rain, and the apple seed,*
>
> *The Lord is good to me."*

Some of our teachers said they were going to show us how to dance which made me very excited. I felt part of a group doing something pleasurable but safe.

As we stood in long rows in the gym, we were shown how to fox trot and bop to *A Summer's Place* and *Shimmy, Shimmy Cocoa Puff*.

This was fun and a strange new experience for me. For the first time, I was doing something socially with people other than my immediate family. I didn't talk about it much with my mother, but from then on I loved listening to popular music. It became another outlet for me to escape my surroundings. I never danced at home, though, particularly around Sam.

Ray's interest turned to body-building. He admired George Reeves, the Superman who was on television from 1953 to 1957. Sam always laughed about Ray's interest and in 1959 threw Ray's dreams in his face by saying that George Reeves was such a powerful man, and yet he blew his brains out. Ray was 11-years-old.

Ever since Ray had polio, Carolyn always spoke up and defended him—something she never did for Joanne or me. Ray's need for love and belonging was constantly thwarted, however, by a father who continually put him down in an attempt to render him powerless.

In May 1960 after Sam came home, he drove us to Miami to visit Munder. I spent the last week of the seventh grade at Robert E. Lee Junior High. On his way back to San Diego, he stopped in Snakeville and dropped us off in a garage apartment near Pappa's church, and then drove west for another deployment.

After his ship arrived back in San Diego on December 16th, Sam was given a month's leave before having to report onboard the U.S.S. Nantucket[2]. He immediately left for Snakeville to pick us up.

Before going back to California, Sam moved us to Thibodaux, Louisiana, into a garage apartment next door to his older brother,

---

[2] Fictitious ship name

T. J., and his family. When I met my cousin, Angela, we hit it off immediately. We were so much alike, nothing could separate us.

I was 14-years-old and she, at 18, was my very first friend. She and I joined the rest of my cousins in playing canasta and hearts all summer, climbing in the barn, and having a great time.

Angela and I slept in the same bed and cuddled like sisters. This was the first time I felt safe and secure at night in bed. I never thought it could be like this with another human being.

I received a letter from Sam dated July 4, 1961, which was quite disturbing. He wrote:

Dear Diane and Ray,

In about two weeks I'll be home. It has been a long time since we've been together for any length of time and I am very glad that I will get to be home most of the time from now on.

You're possibly wondering why I'm writing this kind of letter. I feel that both of you are old enough, and smart enough, to be told of the things that will be expected of you for the next few years.

I want you to read this letter when there is nothing else on your mind. Read it well and believe every word because your feelings, your privileges, your punishments and your future living conditions depend on how you take this letter and how you react to it.

You aren't minding as you should. If you were smaller children it would be a simple matter to spank you and tell you not to do it again. Since you are older you should be warned first, but only this once, then, if you continue to act as before, punishment is in order.

One of the most important lessons in life is to learn to be obedient. I cannot allow my feelings to get in the way and neglect you to the point that I will let you do as you please.

The fact that I am going to spend many thousands of dollars on your education does not mean that I love you. The fact that I am going to train you right, even if it hurts you, does.

In the future in any and all situations where you know that you have done wrong, you will be whipped severely.

If you love me and your Mother then do us the favor of not hurting our feelings by having to punish you.

I have told you all of this because I am coming home in just two short weeks. I wrote you this letter not to scare you but to let you know that I love you and want you to have the chance to do the things you know to do. Take the rewards. They are much better than the other.

Love,

Daddy

Love? That was an unfamiliar word in the Chambreaux home. When Sam's ship arrived back in San Diego, he left on August 22nd to pick us up in Louisiana. Before reporting to his next duty station, he took us to Snakeville to visit his family. We stayed with Mamma and Pappa.

One weekend Mamma and Pappa invited several of Sam's siblings and their families to have a picnic and to camp-out near a lake. When it was time to go to bed, my mother announced she was going to sleep in the car because she did not like sleeping on the ground. I don't know where Ray and Joanne slept, but Sam put our sleeping bags next to each other a slight distance from the rest of the family. I was uncomfortable about it but felt I had no choice. None of the other family members said anything or acted like this was odd, even though I was 14-years-old.

After it got really dark and all was quiet, I felt the warmth of his body cuddling mine. That felt good. I was very lonely and starved for attention. What I didn't like was his hands trying to probe my body. This night was no different from the others, but somehow I managed to prevent any direct contact by staying bundled up in my sleeping bag. He did his best to rub me all over, but my constant moving around stopped a lot of it.

The next morning I climbed the highest tree I could find. Everyone kept trying to coax me out of it, but I was frozen. This was a safe place, and I didn't want to leave it. I eventually came down only to get into the car, go back to the Chambreaux's while my parents got the rest of their things and stayed a few more days before we left. That night I woke up from a nightmare thinking I was dying. I went to my mother for comfort, but she said I was acting silly and told me to go back to bed.

Around this time, Pappa's dog had some puppies. We were allowed to pick one to take with us. Sam named her "Joson" which he said was Japanese for "little girl."

We were now on our way to Jacksonville, Florida, where I would start high school. By this time I had traveled 31,094 miles in our family car.

Chapter 4

Mind Explosion

In Jacksonville, we moved into a small house and waited for our possessions to arrive in the moving van. I started the ninth grade and began trying to make friends. In the past I was usually quiet and studious, but I discovered that being a class clown drew more attention in a good way, and was a faster route to friendship.

With Carolyn's silent encouragement, Sam's behavior steadily grew worse. Once while we were at a neighbor's house having a picnic, my mother mentioned she wanted my father to go home and get some more food. She wanted me to go with him. I tried my best to convince her I didn't want to go, but she insisted. As soon as the car doors closed, his hands were all over me. I hugged the door handle, but he had no problem reaching me. Upon our return, I couldn't wait to bolt out of the car and hide.

My parents bought a home in Atlantic Beach around November 1961, and for the first time, we lived in something decent. We each had our own bedroom.

I had been given a diary at Christmastime and began writing in it.

January 3, 1962

Got a "talking to" from Daddy today and was told to start doing what Mama says, and is getting a little sterner than I thought.

January 12, 1962

Mrs. Strickland was talking today about when was the right age to start dating. She said when you were ready, you would know. She said some parents don't let them date until they are 16. That's what Mama & Daddy said. But if I start acting grown up & all I might get to this year. At least I'll be 15.

The following night I woke up and discovered Sam completely naked with his left foot on the floor and his right foot by my left ear. He was trying to put his penis into my mouth!

It tasted awful, and he was hurting me. I could taste what seemed like salt coming out of it. I pushed with all my might to get him off of me. My heart was pounding and my mind racing. Either I knocked him off balance or he just changed his mind. All 220 pounds of him forced my legs open. He got on top of me and forced his penis into my vagina. It felt like he was ramming a baseball bat up me. As this was happening, I looked to my right toward the bedroom door and saw Ray standing there watching the whole thing.

I don't know how I was able to get him off of me, but he finally got up and left the room. As best I could I walked bent over to the bathroom, locked the door, and sat crying as blood dripped into the toilet. The next morning, as usual, nothing was said.

With that rape, my mind exploded. I had held it together the best I could for almost 15 years. I was in shock, my body was cold, and I felt like a rag doll with no feeling whatsoever. I had been successfully conditioned to remain silent by both parents. I was attacked in my own bedroom by my "authority figure." With no one to comfort me, I walked around in a stupor, but something told me to record the event in some way.

January 14, 1962

It's 10:00 now & I can't write long. Last night, Daddy did it again, only this time it was even worse. All of my friends came over today and we played marbles.

In order to keep functioning, I pushed the memory of my rape and my feelings about it deep into the recesses of my mind, just as I had done with all the other painful memories.

Ray had turned 14 the previous September. Throughout his young life, he had experienced his own forced conditioning to be silent, and now had not only witnessed sexual molestation but also severe violence. His aggressive behavior got worse. He kept getting into fights at school which was embarrassing to my parents who disliked having to meet with his teachers and the principal.

Ray often pretended he was going to bed at night, would lock the bedroom door, and then would climb out the window to meet his friends. One night, Sam went to a party but came home early and caught Ray in the act of leaving the house. Sam caught up with him, forced him into the house, and beat him unmercifully.

Around this time, Sam pulled himself together and went out to sea for about a month. I tried to focus on schoolwork to get some normalcy back into my life. This was a welcome relief for me. It allowed me to settle my jangled nerves and not have to worry every night when I went to bed. A new experience, though, presented a different aspect of sexual behavior for me.

February 19, 1962

Well, it finally happened. I got kissed by a boy for the first time. Jay came over & we were playing softball. He had to go home, so he rode me on my handlebars to the dirt ditch. He stopped & we walked around it then got behind a big sand dune. He kept talking and then he kissed me. After that he kissed me once more. I sure was nervous on the way home because a boy had never kissed me before.

I was completely confused. Even though I liked his attention, the teenage boy kept pushing me to meet him after school for more kisses. I cut off from him after a few weeks because his behavior reminded me too much of Sam.

In early May Sam got orders for Charleston, South Carolina. When we drove away from Atlantic Beach, I felt severely depressed. For the first time, I'd spent an entire school year in one location and had made lots of friends. I was tired of never having a permanent home. I had also been sexually assaulted and traumatized by my father. Now I had no choice but to ride in a car with him for over 250 miles to our next destination and pretend everything was fine. Ray had been beaten a lot and had to sit there with his mouth shut too.

Joanne, who was almost eight-years-old, had traveled all over America by car, had not bonded with our parents or her siblings, and had witnessed Sam's many violent outbursts. Carolyn was just as neglectful with Joanne as she was with Ray and me.

At first, we lived in a small house. I started talking and playing with a boy in the neighborhood which made Sam jealous. One night after everyone had gone to bed, I was lying on the floor in front of the television while Sam was sitting on the sofa. I noticed him getting up and felt my body freeze. He laid down behind me then started feeling my body. I tried to tell him I didn't want to do anything with him, so he started telling me things he thought would be comforting.

"You know how I have always told you I was trying to teach you something?" he asked.

As I nodded he said, "That wasn't true. I just fell for you."

It was incredulous to hear, and he thought nothing of it.

He added, "You don't have to worry about getting pregnant. I got myself fixed." As he raised his body over mine, I passed out.

On June 1st the Navy promoted Sam to a full Lieutenant. We moved into Captain's quarters on the naval base because the person who was supposed to live there had other arrangements. I actually had a bed, a chest of drawers and dresser all my own. The only problem was my bedroom door wouldn't lock, so I was continually on the lookout for my father.

In October 1962 things got pretty tense as President John Kennedy spoke on television about issues with Cuba. I tried hard to understand what was going on in my personal world. Even though my father was the Security Officer for the Charleston Naval Base during the Cuban Missile Crisis, he was still sexually molesting me every chance he got.

I started perfecting a poker face. They could abuse me, but I would never give them the satisfaction of knowing how they made me feel. I told them very little about myself or what I thought. It was a self-preservation technique, but also a good way to vent my rage. I was determined to win this war at all costs, but on my terms. At different times the abuse was so bad I couldn't hide the pain, but I tried anyway. I always said to myself, *they will never break me*, but I had no idea the considerable damage they were causing.

I made up my mind my life was miserable and would never get better. Since we were told we would be moving again soon, I didn't even try to make any friends at school. I mostly went to the movies on the base. It only cost ten cents, and I could totally lose myself in whatever was on the big screen. I was also safe there.

Sam took leave the beginning of March 1963 to move us to Norfolk, Virginia, his next duty station. His orders stated he was the Prospective Commanding Officer of an LST (a flat-bottomed vessel to land troops and cargo on open beaches) in the Atlantic Reserve Fleet.

When we left Charleston I continued to use the only coping mechanism I knew, the same one I had used for the last 15 years, which was to not think about the trauma I had endured, pretend like it had never happened, and shove the enormous pain deep into my mind so I could continue to function.

Chapter 5

Trauma and Near Death

This trip was the 28th time we were packed into the car, traversing a sizeable portion of the country and moving into a new home. I was near the end of the 10th grade. As I sat in my usual spot in the back seat, I thought about my experiences and all I had learned about my parents and grandparents to try and figure out why Sam and Carolyn treated me like they did.

Pappa was born in Meadville, Mississippi in 1903. When he grew up, husbands did all the thinking, speaking and decision making for the family. Women were raised to move from their father's house to their husband's.

As a young man, he was personally drawn to the church. He, along with his parents and siblings, would travel for days to the "camp meetings." Big tents were erected, and the preacher would electrify the audience to whet their thirst for salvation.

Men with a talent for self-promotion who were physically fearless and valued rigid obedience had the qualities to do well in the evangelical movement. Pappa identified strongly with these characteristics and decided he, too, would become a preacher.

After living a number of years in Meadville, he moved to Louisiana where he eventually met Mamma. Her childhood on the farm was harsh. She lived in a shack with no electricity, and everyone slept in one room with little privacy. With precious little schooling, her home life was the only one she knew.

When Pappa came along, this charismatic 6'4" 250-pound man with a commanding voice, high native intelligence, and a sense of purpose, it was like life itself came alive for Mamma. Swept off her feet, Mamma jumped at the chance when he asked her to marry him.

Mamma and Pappa wed in 1922. He joined the Church[3] and soon became a successful preacher. The Church had rigid standards; it did not believe in dancing, drinking, wearing jewelry, or smoking.

Pappa wanted to do well as a leader, therefore, he believed it was critical that he set an example for other families to follow in the area of strict obedience. His loud booming voice, along with the stinging snap of his belt strap in the wood shed, ensured that his children were ruled by an iron hand.

By the 1940s Pappa was a high Church official in Atlanta. His reputation had spread throughout the Southeast. By the time I was born in 1947, there were nine children in my father's family—Sam being the third eldest.

Munder's parents were completely different. Her father, Antonio Vincini, had sailed to America from Italy in 1903 and found a job in the coal mines in Kentucky. He married Munder's mother in 1907 and moved their family to Miami in the early 1920s.

Munder, the third eldest, grew up in a boisterous household with five sisters. She was a loving and kind person who was also attracted to the Church. She married Carolyn's father in 1928 and divorced him near the end of World War II when Carolyn was only 14-years-old. It was a momentous decision to end a marriage in those days, but Munder's strong character and religious faith enabled her to part ways with an adulterous husband.

Knowing these few facts made me believe Sam was following Pappa's example in ruling our home under a system of rigid obedience. I still didn't understand Carolyn's behavior though. She was not protective or strong like Munder. It would take me a

---

[3] A Pentecostal denomination which will simply be called the "Church."

long time to understand why Carolyn was so neglectful and hateful toward her children.

We arrived in Norfolk in March 1963. With his increased responsibility in the military, Sam started getting more brazen in his behavior. I would come home from school to find him walking around in his undershirt and jockey underwear holding a glass of straight scotch and eyeing every move I made. The older I got, the worse he behaved; he still wanted me to sit on his lap like I did when I was a little girl.

The increasing stress of having Sam around more often manifested in physical symptoms that plagued me. I almost always felt sick to my stomach, and large fever blisters popped up on my mouth. When Carolyn took me to the Little Creek Naval Base Dispensary on several occasions, she and I were dismissed with a simple, but erroneous diagnosis, that I had the flu.

My siblings were fixtures in my life. I rarely interacted with them. Ray and Joanne fought all the time, so I just kept to myself. Carolyn had little to do with me. Sam, on the other hand, had to be the center of attention.

When I saw my parents' cutting up lemons and limes, putting out the Jim Beam, Cutty Sark, and vodka, I knew it was time to set up a babysitting job if at all possible. It was great if I could, because it meant that I would spend the night at whosever house I babysat. If not, I would sit in my bedroom listening for the stairs to creak, knowing he was coming to make out with me during the party.

When I'd see him at my door, my heart would stop and my body would freeze. I'd gently push him away because I didn't want to make him mad while he tried unbuttoning my blouse. He would say things like, "Can't I ever?" or "It's okay if you tell me you like it."

Incredulously, I'd look at him and tell him I didn't like it, but that never stopped him. Then Carolyn would always call out from the bottom of the stairs, "Sammie, are you up there?"

"Yes, Carolyn," he'd answer and slowly get up and leave. At other times, he threatened to divorce my mother if I said anything. These intrusions left me in an extremely hypervigilant state. I'd just hold myself for the rest of the night and pray he wouldn't come back.

Ray continued to act out, refusing to do his schoolwork as he should, and getting into fights at school. This, of course, was a threat to Sam's career because a military person was looked down upon if he couldn't keep his own family under control.

On May 2, 1963, Sam had an Amphibious Shakedown Training at Little Creek Naval Station. His Commanding Officer wrote:

Runs a taut, happy ship; handled himself superbly under very difficult conditions during the exercise; strongly recommended for promotion.

In the fall of 1963 I started the 11th grade. I was not allowed to join any clubs or belong to any groups. This had been Sam and Carolyn's way of keeping me isolated the whole time I grew up. I accepted it as normal. I made the most of it by learning new subjects and making people laugh.

During the night my father was still creeping up the stairs, entering my bedroom and putting his hands under the blankets until I would wake up finding him rubbing my breasts or genitals. Joanne slept in the same bed, but that didn't deter him. I pushed him away each time until he slinked out of the room back downstairs.

To protect myself, I began sleeping in the family room closet. After everyone was asleep, I crept downstairs as quietly as I could and hid in the closet knowing he wouldn't find me there. I slept a little, then, before everyone got up in the morning, I quietly sneaked upstairs and got back into bed. Needless to say this was very exhausting, but safe.

From February 27-June 30, 1964, Sam was involved in various training exercises. Home life continued to deteriorate.

Once while we were eating lunch, Ray was outside mowing the lawn. He must have accidentally run over something because the lawn mower came to an abrupt stop. My father jumped out of his dining room chair. We all froze as we watched him run out the door.

He shoved Ray toward the house. When he got to the screen door, Sam turned Ray to face him and hit him in the face so hard he knocked him clean off his feet. Ray landed on the dining room floor. My father then picked him up and started pushing him toward my parents' bedroom.

My mother pleaded for him to leave Ray alone.

He said to her in an angry voice, "Carolyn, either leave me alone or I will take him out to the woods and beat him."

She backed off. I don't know where Joanne went, but I hurried upstairs and sat on my bed while listening to Ray whimper as he was being beaten.

You could hear my father all the way upstairs yelling that if Ray cried out, he would be beaten harder. By now I was in complete shock and hated my life.

Ray had become too much of a threat to my father's career, so Sam and Carolyn signed their consent for Ray to enlist in the Army even though he was only 16-years-old. After all, Sam said, he himself had left home when he was sixteen.

From June 1964 to July 1965 Sam focused on his new assignments with deployments to the Dominican Republic and other ports along the Eastern Seaboard. Having eliminated a major problem in his life, he could now concentrate on his work.

My nerves were shot. I was so upset that, along with the incessant fever blisters, the whites of my eyes turned blood-red. I was nauseated all the time and continued to make several trips to see Navy doctors who prescribed a lot of medicine which did nothing at all.

During the fall of 1964, when I was 17-years-old, I woke up in the middle of the night with Sam once again trying to put his penis into my mouth. I struggled to push him away. This time he was so angry at me he put both of his hands around my throat and began choking the life out of me.

I could hardly breathe!

I fought him with all my might and somehow got away and out of bed. I rushed to the bathroom and locked the door. My heart was pounding. I kept saying to myself, *I want to be with my mother.*

After a few minutes, and not knowing whether he was standing outside the door or not, I slowly unlocked the door and opened it.

No one was there.

I didn't want to wake anyone up (that's how brainwashed I had been not to call out for help), so I didn't turn on the light. I walked down the stairs as quietly as I could. As soon as I got to the bottom of the stairs, an arm came out of nowhere, flinging me against the wall as I was being strangled again by my father.

I let out a yell. At that point the dining room light came on with Carolyn asking what was going on.

Sam said, "I heard something."

I looked at her and said I was having a nightmare and wanted to sleep with her. We all three walked to their bedroom.

I wasn't thinking clearly when I climbed into the middle of their king-size bed. My mother was on my right and my father on my left. In the darkness while in their bed, my father tried to fondle me.

I started saying, "I want up."

Carolyn got out of the bed, turned the lights on, looked at my father and said, "Sammie, let her up." She had to tell him twice.

I got out of bed and went back to my room.

Even as flagrant as that had been, my mother did not try to protect me in any way and, as usual, the next morning, nothing was said. It was as if nothing out of the ordinary had happened at all. I was in total shock that Sam's undeniable acts were being ignored. I continued to shut down. I felt like a zombie.

Sam's rage was so out of control, he almost killed me. I thought I was going to die. Even with all the defensive maneuvers I had tried: finding babysitting jobs, staying outdoors, sleeping in the downstairs closet or on the bathroom floor with the door locked, nothing worked. My mind was imploding.

On Christmas Day 1964 I was so sick I could not walk. I had hives from the top of my head to the bottom of my feet. They were even in my ears.

My father carried me to the car and drove to the Little Creek Naval Base Dispensary. He had to carry me in because I still couldn't walk. We sat in the waiting room for an hour, the only two people on Christmas Day.

He finally got mad and demanded to see a doctor. I was taken in for an examination and, as usual, was told I had the flu. More medication was prescribed. Sam carried me back to the car and drove home. I went to bed and dove further down into my inner world in an attempt to escape reality and my surroundings.

A few nights later while working on my homework in my bedroom, I heard Carolyn yell, "Sammie, don't!" There was the sound of metal-on-metal. He had cocked his Navy issued .45 pistol. It took little imagination to envision what he was about to do. At 17-years-old, I went downstairs and into their bedroom.

Carolyn was very distressed in a self-protective mode with half her head under the sheets. He was sitting on the side of the bed with his cocked pistol pointed at his head. I walked over to him. With my presence there, he put the gun away. I went back upstairs totally convinced he was at a point of actually killing someone. Who that might have been was the only uncertainty.

The next morning, as usual, nothing was said.

My father went out to sea to get away and wasn't home for my high school graduation, which was more than fine with me. With my school years now at an end, I had traveled 31,783 miles in our family car since the day I was born.

I wanted to go to college in the fall, but it was up to me to make the money to pay my tuition. I had already started working for a Fortune 20 Company at an entry-level position in March 1965.

On July 23, 1965, Sam's Commanding Officer wrote:

> *Lieutenant Chambreaux is a soft-spoken officer with a natural ability for fine ship handling. He accomplished his missions in direct support of the Army during the Dominican crisis in an outstanding manner.*

Shortly after starting college in September 1965, I met two young women I really liked—Sandy and Ellen. We talked on the phone a lot, went to the beach and drive-in movies together, and had a wonderful time. On Christmas Eve, Sandy had a party at her family's home. One of Sandy's friends, Jeff, brought along an old friend of his, Barry.

I was quickly drawn to him. Home for the holidays from the University of Richmond, Barry was 6'2" with sandy-colored hair, attractive, and very well-mannered. I felt very comfortable around him. In fact, when I went home, I said to myself, *this is the person I am going to marry*. Somehow I just knew.

From January 7 to May 18, 1966, Sam was transferred to the Commander Amphibious Group Two. On March 16th GEMINI VIII was launched. Sam was in charge of navigating one of the aircraft carriers assigned to the rescue mission. His superiors were grooming him for further advancement.

I was still in college and working for the Company (as it was called). Barry and I started dating immediately. He drove back and forth from Richmond every weekend he could. During the summer we went to the beach, the movies, and had parties with

Sandy, Ellen, Jeff and the people they were dating. This was a whole new life which I loved. Sam stopped everything sexual with me from the moment I started dating Barry. His career was too precious for him to jeopardize a confrontation with someone outside the family.

I continued to correspond with Barry during our separations. On October 3rd I wrote:

> *Dear Barry:*
>
> *Ray wrote each of us, Mama and Daddy, Joanne and I, and we were real glad to hear from him. He wrote me not to tell Mama but he's been taking a karate course and can now break two inch concrete blocks with his hands and stop a man 27 different ways.*
>
> *Miss you!*
>
> *Love,*
>
> *Diane*

Ray was 18-years-old, had been in the Army for two years and nothing had changed. He still had a penchant for fighting and violence.

Sam and Carolyn did not seek outside help for their individual problems nor support for their three children. They both sanctioned violence to solve problems; we were not taught healthy conflict resolution skills. It was drilled into our heads that our needs and wants meant nothing, and we all three were made to feel totally worthless.

Ray learned that physical aggression made him feel powerful. Joanne resorted to verbal aggression to get her needs met, while I continued my conditioned role of putting everyone else's needs above my own by sealing off my emotions. Sam and Carolyn stayed in denial most of the time so she could hang onto her man and he could excel in his career.

Chapter 6

Escape to a New Life

By the fall of 1966 I had fallen in love with Barry. We had been dating for a year, spent a wonderful summer together, and got along great. Barry wasn't pushy with me. We held hands and kissed a lot, but that was it. I had never dated before but was pleasantly surprised to get so much affection from someone who was not crude or demanding. I began opening up to him a lot more when we were together and in my letters.

December 2, 1966

Barry,

You have changed me a great deal in some respects. Before, I had many thoughts with no one to talk to. I learned from an early age not to trust anyone, especially men, the hard way. No girl should ever have to go through the fear and humiliation I have.

I have been put in positions in the past where I haven't had anywhere or anyone to turn to. I told you about me and Daddy because I love you and want your trust and respect so very much.

Love,

Diane

December 6, 1966

Dearest Barry,

For five or six years, I have been accustomed to sneaking, hiding, and forcing my feelings. I have been so scared that many times I have prayed to God that I wouldn't have to go through another ordeal every night. You say these are our lives and you don't like past experiences to interfere. I understand that, but I can't just shut five years of my life out. I have had to push Daddy away my whole life. What was I to do or say? I was just a kid. I got to the point where I couldn't stand to be near him or for him to touch me.

When you ask me if I know what frustration means, know that frustration has been my experience through Junior High and High School. I've had to put on a false front all the time, to appear as though I loved Daddy, just to keep the household halfway sane. And all the time I wrestled and fought and ran to stay away from him.

To be able to sleep through the night without waking up with him on top of me. To be able to come home from school like a normal child and share all I had accomplished with my family. Well, that was someone else's childhood, not mine. And yes, I know what frustration is all about.

Love you,

Diane

Christmas 1966 was the happiest Christmas ever. I had spent a whole year with someone who really cared about me, excelled at my first year in college, made some great friends, and, for the first time in a long time, felt hopeful. We initially discussed waiting to marry until after we both graduated, but were so much in love we wanted to get married the following summer.

The one issue that made me curious about Barry was his parents, Bill and Betty. It took a long time before he introduced me to them or showed me where they lived. Their beachfront home in Ocean View, in an older part of Norfolk, was pretty run-down. Bill was loud and crude. Betty smiled a lot, but I could tell Barry didn't feel comfortable around her.

Barry's mother's side of the family had been more prominent in the community, but they had all passed on. The dark secret was that Betty had had mental illness problems in the past. When Barry was 10-years-old, Bill took him to Norfolk General Hospital to visit her. They locked the door behind him after he went into her room, which scared him a great deal.

Perhaps this conflict in Barry's early life drew me closer to him. We decided to go ahead with our plans to get married and told both sets of parents.

In early January 1966 Sam put in for a transfer to Jacksonville, Florida and on February 25th we left Norfolk. Barry was with me the few days before we left. I found it difficult saying good-bye but knew we would be together for the Easter holidays. When we pulled out of the driveway, I looked at him as long as possible before he was out-of-sight. Sam drove off quickly just like when we left Munder's when I was a little girl.

After a month in Jacksonville and listening to my parents' constant messages about finishing college before I got married, I wrote Barry about postponing our wedding. I had been too conditioned by Sam and Carolyn to think clearly about my own needs.

I was jumping up and down with joy, though, when I met Barry's plane during Easter vacation. He was excited to see me and loved the car I had bought, a British Racing Green MGB. We put the top down and drove home. I took time off from work, and we were gone most of the day every day. St. Augustine was fun with its local history, old jail and fort. I packed picnic baskets when we spent days at the beach, and we danced in the local hot spots at night. My life was definitely changing for the better.

Sam and Carolyn's bedroom was at one end of our ranch house while mine and Joanne's were at the other end. Joanne slept with me during Barry's visit, so he used her room. My parents' bed was situated in such a way that Sam could lie in bed, look out the door and watch everything.

When we came home late at night, and as we walked to our respective bedrooms, I looked toward my parents' room. I watched the embers glow as Sam took a long drag on his cigarette, just to make sure I knew he was watching me.

After Barry flew back, I knew I loved him but had ambivalent feelings about whether to get married that summer as we had planned or to finish college first. Several events occurred over the following months which made my decision for me.

Barry and I continued to stay in close contact. We decided I would drive to Norfolk to visit with our friends which would also give us more time together. After Sam saw how in love I was with Barry, it bothered him a great deal.

April 21, 1967

Barry,

I want to be near you and am really looking forward to April 30th. Daddy has some feelings, though, about not letting me go.

A little at a time, Daddy has started drinking again. By this I mean a beer or two here and there. And tonight when I came home from work, Uncle Bob, Aunt Nancy and my cousins who you met, were here. Right now they are all playing cards and having a good time.

In the kitchen there is an empty bottle of rum and a garbage bag full of beer cans. Daddy is acting silly like he always used to.

Logically, I don't feel there is much cause to worry, but I worry anyway. Barry, if I have to go through all that again— I won't go through it, college or no college.

I'm a nervous wreck as it is. I'm so glad I have a lock on my bedroom door. At least I can go to sleep and not worry. I miss you.

Love,

Diane

April 26, 1967

Barry,

I have talked it over with Daddy and I plan to fly up.

The last thing in this world I want is to hurt you. While I am in Norfolk, I won't be able to see you. This was the main condition for whether I could go up there at all.

Love,

Diane

When I went to Norfolk, I stayed true to my word and didn't see Barry. My friends were so happy to see me and gave me the determination to put a transfer in at work as soon as I got home. I felt bad about hurting Barry, but Sam had conditioned me too well not to disobey him.

Right after I got home, I put a transfer in to move back to Norfolk. I wasn't going to go through all of that again, worrying about Sam and what he wanted.

I was fed up with how I felt living with my parents and made up my mind to leave.

At first, Sam said I couldn't take the car.

I said, "My name is on the title. You co-signed it. As long as I make the payments, there is nothing you can do about it." I went to the grocery store, got boxes, and started packing my things.

I told Carolyn I had put in my transfer and would be leaving as soon as it came through. I don't know how I got the courage to stand up to them.

A couple of weeks later, Sam came to me and asked that if we were going to get married, would I please consider getting married at home, and to see if Barry could come down for Christmas. I was floored. He also stopped drinking. I withdrew my transfer and waited to see if things would change.

On July 27th Sam's Commanding Officer wrote:

> *LT Chambreaux has proven himself, in a relatively short period, to be an asset to this command. His leadership ability is considered excellent. Although LT Chambreaux has been onboard for only three months, he appears to be qualified and is therefore, recommended for promotion to LCDR.*

In the meantime, Barry had barely written me that summer. By October he had written about three letters. Not having him in my life felt unbearable, so the middle of October I called him while on my break at work and asked, "When do you want to get married?"

He didn't know.

I said I would call him back when I got off at midnight. I did call him, and he said we could talk about it. I asked him to come down for Christmas. The next day I wrote him a letter.

October 18, 1967

Barry,

I feel I have grown up so much just in this short period of time. You know all about the relationship between me and Daddy and I'm glad I could talk to you about him. He has always resented any boy who showed affection toward me and I believe he always will. I've learned to accept this even though it is very hard.

I love you.

Diane

Barry and I started talking more on the telephone and decided to get married the following June. He took the train down for the Christmas holidays to see me.

On December 24th at a beautiful beach location, Barry asked me to marry him and gave me my engagement ring. Sam was mad as hell when we got home because we were late for dinner. I started crying and ran out the back door. He always had to mess up everything.

When I left Barry at the train station for his trip back to Richmond a few days later, I cried harder than I had ever cried before. I wanted to be with him and away from my life of hell with Sam and Carolyn.

Over the next few weeks, Barry and I exchanged lots of letters about our wedding plans. Sandy was going to be my maid of honor and Jeff his best man.

Coincidentally, Ray wrote about his wedding plans to a Vietnamese woman he had met in Vietnam. He didn't say much other than he didn't care if the family approved of her or not.

After Barry went back to Richmond, I focused totally on our wedding and finally leaving home. Barry, Sandy and Jeff flew down the day before our wedding. Mamma and Pappa drove down from Mississippi so he could perform the marriage ceremony. Munder, Barry's parents, sister and grandmother also attended.

We said our good-byes to everyone after our reception, got into the MGB and left. When we drove out of the church parking lot, it felt like a hundred tons had lifted from my chest.

I was free.

I was in love.

All I wanted to do was enjoy the rest of my life. For awhile I was very happy, but the impact of my sexual abuse hit me so hard later in life, I almost killed myself. For now, I focused on building a new life with my husband and was determined to become a great success at the Company.

Part 2

Awakenings Before the Storm
1969—1983

Chapter 7

Sickening Revelations

A few months after my wedding, Joanne turned 14-years-old and started the ninth grade. With Ray and me married, Sam totally devoted himself to his career. On April 4, 1969, his fitness report read:

> *LCDR Chambreaux is a highly capable and aggressive officer whose performance during this period has been outstanding in all respects. He is fair but firm in his dealings with subordinates. His personality is pleasing; he has a keen and active sense of humor and is a definite asset to morale.*

As Sam's career continued to soar, I was beginning my new life. Late in the afternoon on the second day after our wedding, Barry and I entered the quaint town of Richmond, Virginia. He had rented a tiny one-bedroom apartment for us in a rundown neighborhood.

That fall after we moved to a larger apartment, Barry started asking me politely if he could take pictures of me in my underwear. He bought one of the new style cameras which shot small Polaroid pictures. For the almost three years we had known each other, Barry had never demanded or forced me to do anything I didn't want to do. He wanted the pictures to carry around with him in his wallet. Since the film was developed at home, I went along with it even though I felt uncomfortable. This reminded me of the time Sam took a picture of me in the bathtub as a little girl.

Many times we had very little to eat, but Barry requested that I fix him breakfast in bed every morning before I left for work.

His first class wasn't until 10:00 AM, but as a newlywed, I wanted to please him. I was so traumatized after what I had lived through at home, I didn't mind doing these things.

Barry never yelled at me or said a harsh word. As long as he held me and put up with my craving for attention, I did everything he wanted. At that time I didn't know there were different ways of controlling people other than being violent or neglectful like my parents.

One of the methods he started using almost immediately was to monitor everything I ate. He was obsessed with how I looked. I weighed 135 pounds when we got married, but he felt I was overweight. I was allowed to have an egg, two pieces of bacon, a slice of toast and a glass of milk for breakfast. For lunch, I ate diet Jell-O and diet cookies. No dinner. And I had to exercise every night. My head was splitting from my intense hunger pains, but I had been so conditioned to obey others, I followed his every desire. Any sign of withdrawal of emotional support on his part made my anxiety go sky-high. When we drove to Jacksonville to visit my parents at Christmastime, I weighed 125 pounds. Barry was very happy.

We lived on the $60 per week I made because Barry liked his freedom too much to find a part-time job, therefore, we lived at a subsistence level. I had to wash our clothes by hand by putting them in the bathtub with some soap powder because we couldn't afford the Laundromat.

After working in an entry-level position for four years, never missing a day of work, and winning lots of awards, I was promoted to a customer service representative position. Wow. An 8:30 AM to 5:00 PM job with my own desk and more money. Barry was also happy about my accomplishment.

During our first year of marriage, I noticed he was obsessed not only with how I looked but with his own physique as well.

One night while lying in bed, Barry told me his father had sexually molested him. He was sodomized often as a young boy. That was all he would say. This news made me very sad. Although

Barry was 6'2" with a large build, he was not physically aggressive like his father. It took me a long time, though, before I saw the full impact of just how much his father had emasculated him.

On January 20, 1969, Richard Nixon was inaugurated as the 37th President. Five days later the Paris Peace talks finally began as a means to end the Vietnam War. The war, however, wasn't winding down as predicted. In March, he secretly ordered the bombing of Cambodia. Sam's career took a sharp turn. Instead of him becoming a Commander of a Naval recruiting station, he got orders for Vietnam.

Sam left in March 1969 for four months of intensive Counter-Insurgency Pre-Deployment training at the Naval Amphibious Base in Coronado, California. Carolyn told us he was taught what to do if captured. When Sam arrived in Vietnam, he was assigned as the Senior Advisor to one of the Commanders of the Vietnamese Navy on the Mekong Delta.

While Sam was overseas, Barry and I talked about our future. I saw great possibilities for myself at the Company, but Barry was not doing well at college. He talked about going into the military. I mentioned this to Carolyn to see what Sam thought.

Within a month and without any further discussion, Carolyn informed us Sam had arranged everything. Barry would enlist in the Naval Air Reserves in Norfolk to serve two years active and four years inactive. Barry agreed and signed up as soon as his 1970 spring semester was over.

When he began his monthly reserve obligations and had to leave for the weekend, I was almost hysterical. Before he could leave, Barry had to calm me down in the bedroom while a fellow reservist waited in our living room. My insecurities began to surface more and more the longer I was away from Sam and Carolyn. Over time, though, I began to gradually hold myself together and not fall apart each time he left.

We drove to Norfolk in June for Barry to begin boot camp. I would be on my own for the first time in my life. My friends at work reassured me of their support and agreed we would stay busy.

The whole time Barry was in boot camp, my thoughts focused on fulfilling his wishes of being physically desirable when he came home. Neither one of us knew how much our sexual abuse had stunted our development.

The lovemaking between us was childlike since neither one of us had dated others before marriage or had healthy sexual experiences. There was a distinct difference, though, in our sexual needs. The more I felt secure, the more I opened up with my intimacy. Barry needed more visual stimulation.

He got excited when he took us to the drive-in for Russ Meyer's violent films like *Vixon*. I watched these super-stacked babes with insatiable libidos and was totally turned off. Barry actually got more excited watching these movies than making love to me. I told myself these were Barry's fantasies which caused no harm because he was still very gentle with me and loved me. I wrote to him often while he was in boot camp.

July 9, 1970

Barry,

Guess who I got a call from as soon as I got home today? Daddy. He got home around 5:30 P.M. yesterday and said it was great to be home again with all the comforts.

Diane

Shortly thereafter, Sam got new orders to serve as the Commanding Officer for naval recruiting in another state, something he really wanted.

Barry's orders were to report to the Admiral's staff as their one and only yeoman (clerk-typist). We packed our few belongings into our trailer and moved to the upstairs of a small house in Norfolk. I transferred as a customer service representative-specialist which I was promoted to before we left. We now had two steady incomes. Life was looking good.

My office was in downtown Norfolk, so I rode two buses to and from work. Barry drove to the naval base for his Monday through Friday 7:00 AM to 4:00 PM job. Sam was right. It was an enviable position for an enlisted man.

Around the fall of 1970, my job was being relocated to a brand-new office building in Virginia Beach. The Marketing Department was co-located in the same building, thereby influencing the career path I eventually chose.

We accepted Sam and Carolyn's invitation to visit them at Thanksgiving. I didn't look forward to the trip but wanted to spend time with Joanne. We arrived to find them living in a very expansive home with enormous rooms, nothing like what I grew up in. It was two stories with a carriage house in the back. The kitchen alone was as big as our apartment.

I was emotionally and psychologically distant from Sam and Carolyn. My poker face was back on the minute I walked through the door. Although it had been two years since I had left home, the minute I was in my parents' presence, I clammed up. This was an ingrained self-protective technique that I was not ready to relinquish.

I wasn't about to disclose that Barry was starting to find me in the middle of the night either in the closet or hiding under the kitchen table. I didn't understand what was happening and didn't want them involved in my personal business.

What made my skin crawl, though, was the newspaper clipping Sam showed me. It was a picture of him in his uniform holding a little girl with a cleft pallet. The article gave him glowing reviews about his procurement of medical care for children while in Vietnam. I felt sorry for her and revolted by him. By the look on his face and the way he held her on his lap, I was sure he had gotten his sexual needs met with that little girl and perhaps other children.

In the spring of 1971, Barry started going to the enlisted men's club to take pictures of topless dancers. He was excited when he showed me the 8 x 10 glossies he took of their bare breasts from the waist up. I wasn't happy with his new hobby.

"I'm only taking pictures, and I am showing them to you," he said. "I'm really not doing anything wrong." Barry then informed me he had invited one of the dancers to our apartment so he could take pictures of her on our bed. I was told to leave the apartment so I wouldn't make her feel uncomfortable.

I acquiesced, leaving him alone at the designated time, but called from a shopping mall and said I was coming home. The woman didn't show up. Once again, I swallowed my anger. I could not jeopardize losing his affection or disrupting our relationship.

On May 20, 1971 Sam's fitness report read:

LCDR CHAMBREAUX has exhibited outstanding management and judgment in meeting his command responsibilities. During this reporting period, LCDR CHAMBREAUX was presented the Bronze Star with Combat Distinguishing Device, the Navy Combat Action Ribbon and the Vietnamese Armed Forces Honor Medal 1st Class for his meritorious service performed in Vietnam. He also received commendatory letters from the Chief of Naval Operations and the Commander of Naval Forces, Vietnam. He is fully capable of assuming increased responsibilities and is recommended for promotion.

The following month Joanne, who was 17 at this time, called and wanted to visit us. A few days after she arrived, I mentioned I was going to get a pizza and asked her to come along. While driving home, she announced a shocking surprise. Sam had started sexually molesting her shortly after I got married.

I hit the roof. I always told myself I would rather him continue hurting me than ever harm her. It never dawned on me that if he had molested me, why wouldn't he abuse her as well?

I stormed into the house, gave the news to Barry, and told Joanne she wasn't going back. Next, I called home and informed them of the same thing. My instructions were simple and direct: They were to ship her clothes to Norfolk with whatever else she needed, along with the money we would need because we didn't have enough to support her. Sam wanted to know why. I said I was sure he already knew, and we didn't have to spell it out for him. Barry talked to him next.

Sam announced, "I'm coming up to get her."

"Go right ahead," Barry replied, "and the Security Officer from the base will be here to greet you." That shut him up. They followed my orders precisely.

Within a few months after starting the 12th grade, Joanne began dating Joe. She excitedly shared with me her plans to marry him. At 17-years-old and on such short notice, I didn't feel it was the right thing for her to do. When I expressed my reluctance, she calmly told me Sam and Carolyn said they would pay for her wedding if she came home.

I was in shock. I stood up to them for her. I took her in. Sam mailed tickets for Joanne and Joe. They were gone within a week.

When I got home from taking them to the airport, I fell to my knees dumbfounded. I had tried to protect her, gave her a safe, loving place to live until she could get on her feet, and this was how she repaid me? I didn't even hear whether or not Joanne graduated from high school. We stayed in touch by phone, but it wasn't the same.

During the Thanksgiving holidays, my phone rang. Carolyn called from Sam's office at the recruiting station. He had a gun and was going to kill himself. I felt both shocked and enraged. He said he couldn't go on and felt bad about what he had done to me. This was the first time he had talked openly about his abusive behavior toward me in front of Carolyn.

Unbelievably, Carolyn asked me to talk sense to Sam, expecting me to be the voice of reason. I complied. All I could think to do was to calm him down, reassure him everything would be all right, and tell him to go home. That seemed to work. After I hung up, I shook all over. I was glad Barry was there to hold me. I didn't want to go through any more trauma alone as I had done the whole time I grew up.

The next morning, with new resolve, I called their house.

Carolyn answered the phone. I asked if Sam was nearby and she said, "Yes." I asked her to go to another phone. When she picked up the extension, I made my stand: "Don't either of you try to write me, call me or see me ever again. I have my life to live, and I've had it with you two. You are not going to ruin my life anymore."

Carolyn said, "I don't see what I have done."

"You are absolutely right," I replied. "You never did a thing." I quietly hung up the phone and felt immense relief.

After 21 years of sexual, emotional and physical abuse, and now a continuation of Sam and Carolyn's psychological enmeshment in my life, I set myself free. Or so I thought at the time. I told myself they were both dead. Not only did I split off my memories of them, and the remembrances and feelings of anger, shame and fear associated with those recollections, but I also erased Sam and Carolyn from my mind, as if they had never existed at all. It was as though whatever space they occupied in my mind had vanished.

It took me months to pull myself together, but the knowledge that I would never be around Sam and Carolyn again was empowering. I began to feel more confident. It showed in my work as I once again started receiving awards. Barry's active duty would be complete the summer of 1972. We began making plans about what we would do next with our lives.

Sometime in the fall of 1971, Ray flew to my parents' home with his wife, Trinh. To have Joanne, Joe, Ray, Trinh, Sam and Carolyn all under the same roof, no matter how big the house, would have created an extremely tense situation. Joanne and Joe moved back to Norfolk, renting a small house about two blocks from his parents. Ray drove to Norfolk soon afterwards so we could meet Trinh.

Ray had changed in the eight years since I had last seen him. He was stockier with a moustache and half his index finger was missing. Oddly, he smiled when he explained that he had gotten it caught while working with some machinery. Ray was proud of the fact that so tightly could he control his feelings he didn't cry out in pain when it happened. In fact, Ray reported that he calmly picked up his finger and drove to the hospital. They couldn't save it, so he watched as they sewed the end of it up.

"Didn't that hurt?" I asked.

"Not at all," he said with a sneer on his face, narrowing his dark-brown eyes into a cold stare.

Trinh had long black hair, was a little over 4' tall and spoke broken English. We had trouble understanding each other. They didn't stay long. It would be seven years before I would see them again.

In March 1972 Joanne became pregnant. She and I agreed to move on and focus on the new baby. I met her in-laws, went to her baby shower, and helped any way I could. Jason was born in January 1973.

In the meantime, Sam faltered at work. He couldn't keep up the charade any longer and received a deflating fitness report. He immediately put in for retirement.

After Barry finished his active duty in June, he decided to go back to Richmond and complete his degree. I was doing very well at work and didn't want to move again. We struck a compromise. He began commuting on a part-time basis.

I felt like we could finally focus on building a better life for the two of us. I was tired of all the pain and suffering I had been through and wanted to move on.

Chapter 8

Turning Points

In September 1972 Barry started his tri-weekly trips to Richmond for classes on Mondays, Wednesdays, and Fridays. Barry had a trust fund that paid for his tuition and books, so at least that was taken care of.

Sam put everything he had into retiring with an outstanding record. With no one living at home except Carolyn, he devoted 100 percent to his job. On April 1, 1973, his fitness report read:

> *LCDR CHAMBREAUX has performed his duties as Commanding Officer of this Navy Recruiting District in an outstanding manner. As this is the concluding report on fitness for LCDR CHAMBREAUX, it is only appropriate that it clearly indicates his superior management and professional abilities that are complemented by his intelligent and forceful approach to enlightened leadership. The Navy loses a fine officer and gentleman who has distinguished himself over a long and dedicated career.*

In 1973 my career took a big leap. The Marketing Department was enlarging, and from what I observed about their non-management positions, I knew I could do the job. After passing an initial assessment, I was flown to Northern Virginia for testing and interviewing. With my intense focus on the matter at hand, acute attention to detail, ease of grasping complex concepts, and outstanding rapport with people, I was accepted and promoted into marketing.

I was ecstatic.

I kissed the customer service representative job good-bye and eagerly jumped into becoming the Company's top performing marketing representative.

In May 1974 Barry graduated from college. I talked to managers at the Company and was able to get him an interview with the Marketing Department. He passed all tests and was hired. Now we worked together in the same office. With a very large increase in our incomes, we were actually able to buy a new home. Life was looking good. Really good.

Barry still exerted control by watching everything I ate and badgering me to exercise. I never weighed more than 135 pounds, but even then, I was made to feel like I was very fat. With everything else looking so positive, I kept my mouth shut and did as he said. I was 24-years-old but still terrified that if I made Barry angry, all we had worked for would disappear. I deemed it best to keep quiet and do as he said.

I began to see ways in which Barry's behavior was patterned after his father's. Bill put whatever money he had into his boat. Barry put most of our money into sports cars. We had two cars and a motorcycle but no new furniture or pictures on the walls. Everything we had came from second-hand stores. I still cooked all the meals, cleaned the house, washed the clothes, and cut the grass while he watched television.

Even though Barry was a big man at around 200 pounds, he was very insecure. He worked out incessantly. He went to the Norfolk Police Department and managed to get a concealed weapons permit. Shortly afterward, he came home with a .38 revolver and shoulder holster. From then on, anytime we went motorcycle riding, he carried his concealed gun under his jacket—just in case. I said I didn't like it at all, but he did it anyway.

During 1975 and 1976 Barry and I were totally concentrated on our careers. We visited his family, and Joanne had another son she named Allen. My parents moved to Snakeville, Mississippi, about 1,000 miles away.

Ray got out of the Army at some point and enlisted in the Navy. We got a letter from him with a Hawaii postmark.

January 31, 1977

Barry and Diane:

How's it going? We're doing fine here. The 1977 GUN DIGEST has a big article on the Automag. I suggest you read that as it will tell you more than I could send you. As far as handguns go I don't hunt with them. I'm saving up money now for the only two firearms that I want. They are both custom made and will cost almost five-thousand for both of them. One is a bolt action rifle and the other an over and under shotgun. After that I won't need anymore. I have a '22', a 7mm magnum, a S&W 41 mag, a Model 12 Winchester 12 ga shotgun, and about 12 knives. The two custom's that I'm ordering are a Champlin bolt action in 378 weatherby caliber and an Itaca MT 6 12 ga.

Oh, well, that's about it here.

Ray

Ironically, Ray and Barry had bonded because of their shared need to prove their masculinity, their belief in controlling their wives, and their goal in arming themselves with guns, giving them added protection from the "bad guys."

In 1977 the Company started investing a lot of time and money into the Marketing Department, and I had positioned myself as one if its key players. All my hard work had paid off. I was finally promoted to management as an Account Executive, but was informed the job was in Northern Virginia.

In October we packed our belongings and moved to Herndon, Virginia. Leaving Norfolk behind proved to be symbolic. That would be the last time Barry and I were happy. Our marriage went downhill from there.

We bought a two-story, three-bedroom home. This abundance was unbelievable coming from our meager beginnings. My new boss, Mark, was wonderful. He was the epitome of a people-person who got the job done.

As an Account Executive within the new organization, I was the team leader. Mark saw my potential and backed me 100 percent. He used my account planning and selling techniques as examples to follow. I became a role model. I had responsibility for the retail market and since most retailers were headquartered in New York, Mark and I flew there often. We stayed in the best hotels, conducted our business meetings and flew home. I was on cloud nine.

For the first time in my life, at 30-years-old, I felt confident and stable. I had adopted the Company as my family. I met Elizabeth when we moved north and liked her from the start. She soon became one of my confidants and a good friend.

Meanwhile, Barry became very depressed. No longer was I behaving as I had in the past. I still did all the housework and yard work, but I no longer needed to cling to him for support. He was becoming Mr. Diane Champé. While I advanced, he remained non-management, which didn't help matters. I once again talked to our superiors, and through my urging, he was promoted to management.

Around the house Barry withdrew considerably. He didn't want to go anywhere and seemed angry all the time. He never discussed what was bothering him and denied there were any problems.

On April 19, 1979 my evaluation as an Account Executive read:

> *Her decisions regarding strategy and account involvement have been very good. Diane's leadership is reflected in other AE's respect for her judgment in strategy and proposal preparation. In summary, she possesses outstanding leadership qualities. She is rated Ready Now for Promotion to the Next Level.*

Although I was excelling at work, my relationship with Barry was getting worse. Because he was so depressed and emotionally distant, we didn't share the warmth we had in the past. Our sex life was almost non-existent and there was a lot of unexpressed anger. We both had great jobs, a beautiful home, and my career was taking off. I didn't want to jeopardize anything, so just like when living with Sam and Carolyn, I closed my eyes, pretended I lived in a happy world, and kept moving forward.

I was now in charge of retail accounts for four states. I traveled a lot to New York, New Jersey, Atlanta, and other places around the country. In my off-hours, I partied and made many new friends.

On the home front, I found it very distressing that Barry would not open up, trust me, or work with me on our problems. He never expressed his anger directly, but rather threw tools in the garage or drove recklessly. He also withdrew from me emotionally. When I put my arms around his waist, instead of leaning down to kiss me, he tapped my back so I would let go. We no longer cuddled in bed. And sex was primarily focused on getting his needs met with total disregard for my desires. The more he acted like that, the less I wanted to be around him. It became a downward spiral.

This was driving me up the wall for two reasons. One, I could not understand why he was acting this way. Two, his behaviors were becoming identical to what I grew up with: denying reality, acting like he did nothing wrong but implying something was wrong with me, and withdrawing emotionally and psychologically. I felt like I did when living with Sam and Carolyn.

By 1979 Barry was in a full-blown depression. Nothing I said or did helped the situation. He became more withdrawn and drove like a maniac.

One morning, our phone rang. It was Ray. He got our number from Joanne who was now living in Ohio. Ray said he was having a hard time financially, and wanted to know if we could help. I said I would and flew to his home in Jacksonville, Florida.

By this time they had two children, Leslie and Eric. Their situation was more urgent than he had let on. In fact, they were one step ahead of the law. Ray had not paid his bills promptly—or owed too much, and very shortly the police would be coming after him to put him in jail. Trinh told me they needed $2,000. I called Barry who sent them a check for the entire amount.

His next duty station was in San Francisco. With Trinh's urging, he first drove up the coast to stay with us a few days, then continued to Snakeville to see my parents before traveling on to California. Trinh confided to me in her broken English, "You not like rest of family."

I said, "You're right."

During my brother's visit I started witnessing behaviors I didn't like. He didn't bathe often and was very sloppy. Leslie was only two-years-old, but already he had her acting like a robot. He was very strict about when she could speak and how she should sit. Ray was reenacting the same behaviors Sam used on us when we were that age. He continually said, "Papa King, Mama Queen, and you belong to me." Eric was only a few months old.

Barry, as insecure as he was, admired my brother. Ray still got into fights, even in the Navy. He showed Barry all kinds of ways to strike someone and kill them, like hitting them in the neck with a sharp jab of his knuckles. Barry ate it up. Ray also said if he were ever double-crossed, he wouldn't kill the person. Instead, he would break every bone in their body so they would remember him the rest of their life. After sharing these violent fantasies with my husband, Ray collected his family and left town. It didn't take long before Barry was back into his depression.

I was out-of-town a lot. During these trips I kept bumping into another manager named Paul. He also handled retail accounts but in another state. We were thrown together at the retailer's annual convention held each January at the New York Hilton in Manhattan. He was tall, well-built, good looking and lots of fun.

When out on the town at night, we tried to see who could tell the most jokes to everyone. He grew up in New York, so he was also very cocky and full of himself. I couldn't wait to see him again.

On my many trips to New York, Paul was always there. After our business meetings, the same crowd got together, had dinner and danced until 2:00 AM, only to get up early and put in a full day's work the next day. It got to where I didn't want to go home to Barry.

On one trip in January 1980, Paul walked me to my room. When we got there, I turned and said good night.

He said, "I'm coming after you."

I pointed to my wedding ring and said, "I am married."

He was married, too, but still wanted me.

I said, "No. Good night."

After flying home, I tried to find fun things Barry and I could do together. He just sulked, didn't want to go anywhere, and didn't want to talk about it. The next trip to New York was the turning point in my marriage.

I went dancing with Paul and our friends. The music was great, the disco lights glittered, and I was in heaven. While dancing, Paul and I bumped the lower parts of our bodies together. And then it hit me full force. Never in my life had I ever felt like that. I had to stop dancing. I was aroused in a way I never thought possible. When we went back to our table, it was all I could do to contain myself. Paul was sitting next to me and had ordered strawberries and whipped cream. He was doing all sorts of things suggestively with his tongue while licking the whipped cream. I was becoming more stimulated as each minute ticked by.

When the evening ended, we walked ahead of the others. He stopped, held me in his arms and kissed me. I told him I had never kissed or even made love to anyone other than my husband. I was overwhelmed.

After our taxi dropped us off at the Hilton, Paul and I walked to a quieter area. The inner conflict between right and wrong, compounded by all the excitement, was more than I could endure. I announced that I was going to my room and left him there. The next morning I flew home.

Barry was still withdrawn and depressed. At work the next day, I called Paul and told him I was flying up the following week and wanted him to spend the night with me.

He asked if I was really sure that was what I wanted.

I said, "Yes."

I took the shuttle from National to LaGuardia airport and told the taxi driver, as I had done so many times before, "Take the Holland Tunnel to the New York Hilton."

Around 5:30 PM my hotel phone rang. It was Paul. He asked me, again, if I was sure this was what I wanted.

I responded, "Yes."

After I invited him into my room, we kissed and sat down. My hands were ice-cold. I was very nervous.

He said, "I've never seen you nervous about anything."

"I've never done this before."

He looked at me and suggested we go to dinner. While at an Italian restaurant, Paul tucked his napkin under his chin and said, "Ummm."

All I could think of was his tongue and the whipped cream.

About halfway through the meal he looked at me and said, "Let's dance a little."

We left and went to our favorite nightspot. We weren't dancing two minutes before I looked at him and said, "I'm ready."

In the taxi ride back to the hotel, we passionately kissed each other. As we undressed in my room I said to myself, *what in the hell have I gotten myself into?*

Once we started making love, however, everything changed. I had never experienced anything like that with Barry. This was my introduction into adult sex, and it blew my mind.

When we went to work the next day, I could not concentrate on anything said in the meeting. Paul and I did not get an opportunity to be alone together before I left, but all we had to do was look at each other and smile. From that first magical night together, we called each other every day at work. We were madly in love and couldn't get enough of each other.

Early March Ray sent me a copy of a letter Sam had addressed to him.

February 28, 1980

Dear Ray,

I have some things to say to you, Diane, and Joanne. The same words are meant for each of you but I cannot write or phone any of you. I'm not asking you to convey my words to Diane or Joanne, but if they should ever ask, I would appreciate it if you would just read my letter to them.

If you do not care to read my letter, stop here and return it to me. Then I will know not to write again.

Love

Daddy

March 2, 1980

Dear Diane and Barry, Ray and Trinh, Joanne and Joe,

I love each one of you. I pray that God will give you peace of mind, happiness, and material success. I ask for forgiveness for my failures, and give you my promise that I will not interfere in your lives.

Seven years ago I came face-to-face with myself. I realized then, for the first time, that I had a sickness of mind and body called alcoholism. By the Grace of God, and with the help of other people afflicted with the same disease, I have been able to face life and accept responsibility for my actions. I bear my shame in silence, and have admitted to God, myself, and another human being, the nature of my wrongs. One thing remains for me to do, and that is to make amends to the people I have hurt. I stand ready to do that for each of you. I will ask your

forgiveness in person, in writing, or by phone, anytime, any-
where. All I ask is the opportunity to do so.

I love you,

Daddy

After reading his letter, I called Ray and told him to give Sam this message: "You can fool some people some of the time, but you don't fool me one bit. Stay the hell out of my life."

He wasn't drunk the entire 21 years I lived at home, or when he raped me, or each time he tried to put his hands between my legs when we were alone in the car. I screamed out loud, "I've had it with you!" I was going to live my life from now on the way I wanted to, and no one was going to stop me.

Chapter 9

Disgusting Family Behavior

In 1980 several major events occurred which helped me better understand myself and the significant people in my life. The insights I gained furthered my resolve to take control and do what was in my best interest.

Throughout most of the year, Paul and I were madly in love. We had romantic interludes all over the country. After a full day of work, we ate at the best restaurants, then went to our hotel room and made passionate love.

When I was with Paul, I felt totally comfortable. He was funny, supportive and encouraged me to express myself like I had never been able to before. We were a perfect match. Paul was sensitive, loving, and not threatened by my abilities. We were on the same level professionally and shared a fun-loving zest for life.

I confided in Paul my reservations about Barry, our marriage and where it was headed. I also talked frankly about my childhood. I usually cried a lot when these subjects came up because my feelings of frustration, anger, loneliness, and pain overwhelmed me. This was the first time I had been able to express these deep-seated emotions without being ridiculed or put-down.

In the summer of 1980, I started to crack. Paul made it clear he was not going to leave his wife, and my life with Barry was hell. I couldn't imagine giving up my relationship with Paul, but I also couldn't continue this double life.

I sat crying in his office in New York City only nine months after our love affair had started, and told him I had to cut off our relationship. By that time, too many other events had crashed down upon me, making my life almost unbearable. If he was not going to leave his wife, I couldn't take it anymore.

During my flight home, it hurt so much I felt like someone had cut my heart right out of my chest. Paul did not want us to end our relationship, but I told him I couldn't keep up the charade. I felt I was dying inside and had to bring some stability back into my life. We continued to bump into one another sporadically after that, but our relationship was never the same.

Meanwhile, Barry's behavior was becoming more irrational. Once while we were on our way home, he tried to pass a car in front of us just before our exit. He didn't make the turn off, so he just floored the accelerator. The speedometer hit 70 mph, 80 mph . . .

"Barry, slow down."

85 mph . . .

"Barry, slow down."

He looked at me and said very calmly, "No."

90 mph . . .

"Barry, slow down!"

He finally pulled over to the side of the road and told me to drive. When I asked him later why he did that, he said, "It's all over with now. Why are you bringing that up?"

I said, "Because you scared the shit out of me."

"Well, it's over now, Diane. Forget about it."

"Barry, we've worked so hard to get where we are. We need to talk about what's going on. I want you to tell me what I do wrong or what you want me to change."

"There's nothing wrong, Diane."

"Sure there is. What do I do wrong?"

"Nothing."

I got up and left the room. I couldn't believe all this was happening. Once more I felt desperate, lonely and confused.

Barry and I decided it would be nice to take a break and visit Ray and Trinh in San Francisco. We enjoyed taking everyone to dinner, going to the zoo, shopping with Trinh and the kids, and having a BBQ. I felt I had some family again.

When Barry was around Ray, he perked up. After we flew home, Barry suggested we move to San Francisco to live near them. The idea appealed to me. It had been three years since my promotion, and I saw this as a means of starting new somewhere else where we could hopefully revitalize our marriage.

Mark, my manager, wanting the best for me, resisted my request for a transfer. He told me all my friends were in Virginia. He did not have a high opinion of Barry, and suggested I think hard about whether I would be moving for my best interests or just trying to please Barry.

I asked Mark to push hard to get me promoted to give me a reason to stay. He was successful. I was promoted and moved into the ranks of middle management. Needless to say, I was once again higher than Barry professionally, but I knew I deserved it and was proud of myself. Barry started sinking deeper into his depression.

While we were in San Francisco, Ray had said Pappa was probably dying. His heart wasn't healthy. I had not seen Mamma and Pappa since our wedding in 1968, so I told Barry I was going to Snakeville.

I called my grandparents' house and Mamma answered. "Hi," I said. "I know Pappa has been ill. I would like to come see both of you if that is all right."

"That would be fine," she said. "Tell me, Diane, why haven't you been home in 12 years?"

"I'd rather not discuss it. It's personal."

"You can tell me," she said. Again, I told her I'd rather not.

"Diane, I'm 74-years-old and have heard everything. You can tell me."

"I don't want to talk about it."

Out of the clear blue, she asked, "Diane, is it incest?"

I almost dropped the phone. After saying, "Yes," we didn't get to finish our conversation because Pappa picked up the extension.

She said, "I've got to go now," and hung up the phone. I was in profound disbelief. Why would a 74-year-old grandmother ask about incest out of thin air? I was dumbfounded.

Not too long after that, I called John (my favorite uncle and the youngest of their nine children). I mentioned why I was coming, and he also wanted to know why I hadn't been home in so long. I told him the truth. My shocking revelation was met with dead silence on the other end.

"My brother did that to you?"

"Yes," I replied simply.

"And I always thought the Chambreaux shit didn't stink," he said.

Gwen, his wife, told me later Uncle John was so sick after hearing my disclosure, he had to go to bed. It was astonishing for me to hear a normal reaction to my very abnormal upbringing.

They picked me up at the airport, and the next night we met with my father's brother, Michael, and his wife, Nelly, at a local coffee shop. I hugged each of them and told them I was very happy to see them. After eating, John mentioned we could all go to his house. Michael and Nelly asked if it would be all right if I rode with them. I said, "Sure."

Michael drove, I sat upfront, and Nelly got in the backseat. Looking at Michael's profile as he drove in the dark took my breath away because all the Chambreaux boys looked alike. I felt like I was in the car with Sam. Michael immediately wanted to know why I hadn't been home in so long.

Once again, I said I didn't want to get into that. He continued to press me for an answer. "All right. Your brother sexually molested me from as young as I can remember until I left home."

Michael said dryly, "Diane, we all must learn to forgive."

I said, "Michael, how would you like a cock shoved down your throat at 14-years-old?"

Nelly gasped but said nothing.

"Also," I continued, "I find it pretty interesting people had to have known, but did nothing to stop it. I'm even wondering if it happened today while I'm here, would anyone help me?"

There was no response.

After we got to John's house, nothing more was said about it. The next day John and Gwen took me to see my grandparents. When Mamma opened the door, I looked her straight in the eyes and felt awkward. When we went inside, Pappa gave me a big hug. I felt better being around him.

For lunch, we had a lot of vegetables from their garden. It reminded me of those days long-ago in Louisiana when my relatives had to be pretty self-sufficient living in the country, and it tasted great. After everyone had eaten, Pappa went to the family room but was still within hearing distance.

The phone rang. It was Michael wanting to talk to me. I saw everyone hold their breath. They just sat there silently as I picked up the phone.

"Diane," he said, "I've been thinking about what you said last night, and people do make mistakes."

"This was more than a mistake," I said.

"Well, your father manages the airport, and when he came here, it was in the red. It is now in the black."

These people are insane, I thought. I don't remember the rest of the conversation, but when I hung up, they were all looking at me. They could see I was visibly shaken, but didn't say a word.

Gwen looked at Mamma and said in her Mississippi southern drawl, "Mu-ther, what shoul' we do with the chik-ken salad?"

Boy, this was par for the course. No one comforted me or asked what was said. I ran out the backdoor to a big tree in the farthest corner of the yard and cried my heart out. This was just like when growing up. Let's pretend nothing happened, and above all else, protect the Chambreaux name.

As I walked back toward the house, I saw Pappa coming out the backdoor. The others had their noses pressed to the kitchen windows with their eyes wide open, wondering what would happen next. I sat down on the top step. As he sat down next to me he asked, "Is there anything you want to tell me?"

Here was my grandfather with a weak heart. I said, "No."

He asked me again, "Is there anything I need to know?"

I told him, "No," again.

After that, I got up, went inside, and asked John and Gwen to take me to their house. I packed and left the next day.

Before flying home, I flew to Louisiana to visit my cousin Angela who I had not seen since I was 14-years-old. We reminisced about that great summer long ago.

I then confided in her about my abuse. She said her father, T. J., had sexually molested her too.

When I told her Ray had seen Sam rape me, Angela said her younger brother Charlie had witnessed her abuse. She also mentioned how another aunt and uncle had either watched or participated in her abuse.

I flew home with a new understanding of the level of distorted thinking and perversion that existed within the Chambreaux family. Two of Reverend Chambreaux's sons were pedophiles. It was just as sickening listening to Angela's story as it was remembering what I had gone through. I started wondering how many other aunts and uncles were child molesters. Incest doesn't start happening in a family for no reason. Sam had molested and raped me. Ray could have been sexually molested as well. I didn't know. But with the abuse he suffered as a child, I saw how miserably he was now treating his own family.

Joanne was an emotional and psychological mess. She could barely function on her own. At some point, she and Joe had divorced, so she moved to Snakeville with her two children and relied on Carolyn and Sam for support. At times over the years, she entreated me to "make up" with them so we could all be a happy family. For my part, I longed for her to break the psychological hold Sam held over her. I tried to convince her to leave his sphere of influence, but she never could.

My new job became effective January 1, 1981. It was a staff position where I developed strategies and tactics for two industry segments covering four states. I supported an entire region of Account Executives. Mark's superb managerial style had helped me believe in myself.

My new boss, Patricia, was another godsend. She was very funny, knowledgeable and empathetic. Over time I found myself telling her about my past and could not get over her level of sensitivity.

While my marriage was falling apart, she supported me. I worked my butt off, but some days she would come into my office, pick up my pocketbook, and tell me, "Go home. You need a break." I was blessed to have worked for both Mark and Patricia.

Professionally, I was performing the best I had ever been. I was a highly respected manager and worked hard to meet our corporation's goals. I was determined that just because my home life was horrible, my reputation within the Company would stay intact.

Ray called at the beginning of February to borrow money for a truck as theirs no longer worked. He said, "I'll dig ditches if I have to, to pay you back."

We mailed him a check and flew out there for a long weekend. Ray picked us up in his shiny, new red truck.

Barry and I sat in the backseat as he drove home. It was wonderful seeing Trinh, Leslie and Eric again. Leslie was three-years-old and Eric a little over one. However, Ray's body odor was so bad I thought I would throw up. When we got to their two-bedroom duplex, I scrambled out of the car as fast as I could.

Ray was a disgusting person in every way. We watched as Trinh waited on him hand and foot while he sat like a big fat toad. His hair was greasy, and he didn't brush his teeth. I was appalled.

He was also very proud of his hand-carved knives framed and displayed of all places, on his bedroom walls. The largest one he nicknamed "Baby Doll." Ray showed Barry and me the AK-47 under his bed. He proudly demonstrated to Barry the expandable nightstick he used as a Navy investigator when interrogating people.

Barry ate it up. I was amazed he was still in the Navy.

After we got home from that visit, Barry's behavior deteriorated. He became more violent. I tried to tiptoe around his flashes of anger, but I felt ever more resentful. Living like this reminded me more and more of how I grew up.

One day while washing some dishes in the sink, I could hear Barry in the shower moaning very loudly like he was wounded. He got out of the shower and yelled, "Why isn't there any hot water?" I said I had recently washed some clothes in the washing machine, but if he could wait about 15 or 20 minutes, it would be hot again.

He looked in a kitchen drawer, pulled out a large knife, and went downstairs. When he came back up, he announced, "There, that will never happen again," and got back into his cold shower.

Barry had "fixed" the problem in a fit of rage by cutting the water hose leading to the washing machine. Then he went back to shower. I heard more moaning as he finished his bath in ice-cold water. I couldn't believe it. It wasn't until years later in therapy that I understood his passive aggression.

Shortly thereafter, the crowning incident of dysfunction occurred. It was more than I could take. While I was driving us home one weekend Barry said, "Pull over."

"What for?"

"Someone threw a rock at our car."

"Barry, we are going 60 mph. I didn't see anything, but if something did hit the car, it was probably from a car in front of us."

"Stop the car and back up." he commanded.

So I did.

There was nothing or no one to be seen. When we got home, he ran up the stairs to our bedroom. After following him, I watched him load his .38 pistol. I asked, "What are you doing?"

"We're carrying this in the glove compartment from now on."

"Oh no, we're not," I said.

As he slammed the barrel of the gun into a small cloth suitcase I had left on the bed, he screamed, "You have nothing to say about it!" and then went downstairs to put it in the car.

I went to my car and drove off. I calling Denise, a co-worker, from a pay phone and went to her home. After I calmed down, I called Barry. No answer. I called several times, still no answer. I told my friend I was going home and had no idea what I was walking into.

When I got home, his car was in the driveway, and he was in the family room watching television. He called out as I opened the door, "Hi Honey."

I asked him why he hadn't answered the phone.

"I just didn't feel like it," he said.

"Are you trying to drive me insane? Don't you know how much that upset me about the gun after all I went through growing up?"

Barry replied, "It's okay. It's over now."

I went upstairs and went to bed. The next morning I put the gun into my car and went to work. I was trying to figure out what to do with it when my phone rang.

"Where is it?" Barry asked. I told him I had it.

"Well, I'll just go to the credit union, get some money and buy another one."

"Don't worry," I said. "I'll bring it home."

I didn't sleep well that night and said very little to Barry.

The next day after he went to work, I packed my clothes, got into my car and left. Denise said I could move in with her. I called him and told him I needed time to myself and to leave me alone.

Shortly after I left Barry, he started calling me constantly, begging me to come home. I kept reiterating my need for time alone to work things out. This went on all summer. Late in August he told me he that he needed back surgery.

"Don't worry," he said. "The ambulance will bring me home, and people at work will bring food over."

It worked. I was there when he had his surgery and moved home shortly thereafter. I was livid, but I went home. One of the things we agreed upon was that it would be nice if Trinh and the kids were with us. Since he was practically immobile, she could help him during the day while I was at work. I would take over once I got home.

We flew them out from California, but everything was strained. Barry and I were angry at one another. I tried to explain to Trinh that I had just moved back home, so it would take some time for Barry and me to work things out.

I loved Trinh like a sister and was sorry she had to go through this. Trinh started confiding in me about her own marital problems. She always wanted to learn to read and write English, but Ray continually thwarted her efforts.

One night when we were talking, I told her about my childhood. I read some passages to her from *Father-Daughter Incest* by Dr. Judith Herman. She looked at me and said, "I think Ray is doing that to Leslie."

I froze. "Why do you say that?" I asked.

"He does things I don't like. He had her in the bathtub with him, and she was soaping him up while his thing was sticking up."

"Yes," I gasped. "He is doing the same thing. Did he do anything else?"

"Sometimes I find him holding Leslie over his head. She has everything on except her underpants."

I almost threw up. I couldn't believe this was happening.

I was appalled and enraged.

Leslie was only four-years-old.

With Ray out at sea, I couldn't do anything about it. I was very upset. I told Trinh it was definitely wrong, and I would help her any way I could.

One night it was raining very hard, but I needed a break. I decided to go for a drive. Trinh asked if she could go with me. After driving awhile, I pulled into a shopping mall so we could continue talking. Suddenly she asked me, "When you and Ray were growing up, did you do sexual things together?"

I said I could remember when we were very young, we looked at each other, but that was it. "Why?" I asked.

"Because Ray and Joanne did."

My mind exploded.

"Ray told me they took turns making each other come."

I started the car and was driving wildly. *This can't be true*, I kept thinking. I was crying and in shock. "Let me get this straight and get it all out at once. Did Carolyn and Ray have sex? What else did these sick bastards do?" Trinh said that's all she knew.

When I drove into my driveway and turned off the ignition, Trinh screamed, "I hate the Chambreauxs' guts!"

We went inside, and I was so distraught I just sat by myself for a long time. Eventually, I got up and carried my heavy load of sorrow to bed.

The next day, my number one concern was finding help for Leslie.

I called everywhere. Finally, after talking to someone at Children's Hospital, I was told, "You have got to talk with this woman." They gave me her name and phone number. We continued our conversation a bit, and she said again, "You have got to talk to this woman."

Before I could call her, however, Trinh very abruptly announced she was going back home. I didn't understand why. She kept telling me she had to leave. I took her and the kids to Baltimore-Washington International airport and waved goodbye.

Once again, my life was a complete mess, no matter how hard I tried to escape my past. From this point on, it got progressively worse. I would spin out of control for another 20 years before I could finally begin to emerge from the accumulation of lifelong torment.

Chapter 10

Professional and Family Crises

To get the support I needed, I decided to call Dr. Maria Anderson, the therapist highly recommended by Children's Hospital.

I thought if she's that good, she can help me.

When I asked for an appointment, she welcomed me with these words, "You've called at a good time. I am just starting my practice."

At our first meeting, her introductory comments set the stage: "If we should decide to work together, we will meet here temporarily. I am presently making arrangements to meet my clients at the home of a colleague with whom I co-lead group therapy sessions. I would like to know more about what you are looking for and the issues you are seeking help with."

After relating my abuse history she said gently, "It is important to listen to your feelings and honor them. I can say this. I have my Ph.D. in psychology with a specialty in incest and have been working in this field for the past nine years. It will be your decision, but we will proceed in a way that is most helpful for you." I felt I was finally with someone who could help me.

In December 1981 Patricia called me into her office and said she had been given a new assignment in another department. She then surprised me by saying she had selected me as acting District Manager because of the outstanding work I had done in spite of all my personal problems. I would do her job until an official replacement could be found. The prospect of this appointment left me feeling overwhelmed but very happy. I started my new job highly focused and with a burst of enthusiasm.

Mark, my former manager, met with Patricia and me to review requirements for the field. In the meantime, I attended Division-level staff meetings. I was preparing marketing plans for the region with stringent deadlines to meet. All of this was a bit heady. Eating at restaurants like Tavern on the Green after conducting business meetings in New York was a far cry from having to wash our clothes by hand in the bathtub.

When meeting with Maria, I felt apprehensive and unsure of myself. I told her about my marital problems, my visit to Snakeville and my brother. She stressed that with everything going on in my life, it was important we take it slow as we worked on my therapy material. I usually got very quiet and didn't say anything. Whenever any feelings started to well up, I clamped down immediately.

Exerting ironclad self-control had been the only way I had managed to keep my sanity all those years, so allowing a crack in this façade of non-feeling was frightening. I had never met anyone like her in my life. My instincts told me she was genuine, but trusting from the heart was practically impossible.

Just three months into my new job, on March 23, 1982, I flew to Norfolk for a presentation. The conference center manager approached us and said, "Mark is dead."

"That isn't funny," I said.

"I'm not kidding."

Mark was only 37-years-old. I was numb and in shock. We agreed to go ahead with the client presentation, but afterwards, everyone broke down.

The next day I met with Maria and told her about Mark's death. "Why don't you let the tears come?" she asked.

"Because I don't cry," I said defiantly.

"But, Diane, I can see your heart is breaking."

I clammed up. A week later on April 1st, I was asked to take Mark's former position.

My environment shifted dramatically. I was responsible for a $78 million revenue stream. I left my staff position and ended up reporting to a totally insensitive woman. It was rough rallying the troops, but it helped that they knew I was hurting as much as they were.

Maria wanted me to talk about my feelings. "This must make you very angry," she said.

"I don't get angry," I responded.

"In some ways Mark's death is another abandonment for you," she continued. I stared blankly ahead. "Can you write how you feel?"

In big letters I wrote, I DON'T FEEL ANYTHING.

She then suggested it might be helpful if I joined the group therapy sessions she was running with her colleague for incest survivors. I reluctantly agreed.

In my first group session there were five other women. It was very strange to meet people who had experienced what I had. As I looked at the other women, I thought, *all of us have carried this terrible secret all our lives, and now we are in the presence of other people we don't know and are about to talk about it openly.* I hardly said two words. I just tried to take it all in.

In my next individual therapy session with Maria, I talked about my marriage.

"It's important that we pay attention to your feelings. It's remarkable how you have stood up after all this. What do you need right now?"

"Just be there for me as I sort this all out. There are times when I feel I need to call you, but I don't want to bother you."

"You worry about that needlessly," she said softly.

I was amazed but worried where all of this was heading. To actually sit and talk about my past abuse and present-day emotional upheaval with someone as reassuring as Maria caused another type of conflict. I wanted so much to share my feelings, but my past experiences had been filled with pain. Once again, I felt all twisted up inside.

I told Maria and the other survivors in the group I was going to confront my brother. I said I went through 21 years of torture, and no one had helped me. I wasn't about to let that happen to Leslie.

Barry and I flew to San Francisco. It was late when we got to their home. Around lunchtime the next day I said, "Barry, why don't you take Trinh and the children to the shopping mall and get them something? I want to talk to Ray about a few things." I had already gotten Trinh's permission to confront Ray about his behavior with Leslie.

After they left I asked, "What's this I hear about you and Leslie?"

"What do you mean?"

"You know exactly what I mean."

"Has Trinh been talking to you?"

"Yes, she sure has," I said directly.

"As I told Trinh, I'm only trying to teach Leslie things."

"Oh really. That's what Daddy used to always tell me. Don't you find that interesting?"

"I'm not my father's son!"

"It escapes me. What were you trying to teach her as she was soaping you up in the bathtub while you were having an erection?"

"That was an accident." I noticed he didn't deny it.

"Okay. What were you teaching her when Trinh found you holding Leslie over your head, and she had no underpants on? I'm confused."

"I'm trying to teach her about sex; that it is not dirty."

Looking him straight in the eyes I asked, "At four-years-old?"

"Look, as Leslie grows older you will be able to talk to her about anything but sex. I will do that," he said rather dryly.

"Wrong," I exclaimed. "Whether you like it or not, I'm not looking away from this, and this will not continue."

"Oh really," he said as he raised his eyebrow.

We both got up and went to separate rooms. When Barry and Trinh got home, they could tell from the look on my face I had talked to Ray.

Flying home the next day, I was very proud of myself but annoyed at Barry. He didn't confront Ray man-to-man or tell Ray he supported me because he idolized Ray and wanted to remain friends with him. I was becoming more bewildered at my husband and everyone in my family. More and more, I just wanted to be left alone.

My new boss, Olive, was not like Mark or Patricia. She bought the corporate line that yelling at people made them work harder.

I forced myself to put everything personal out of my mind. It had been extremely painful visiting Mark's wife, discussing his death benefits knowing she was eight months' pregnant, going through his desk at work, and consoling everyone. I made a commitment to myself that his (our) group would make our yearly objectives.

I talked to Trinh's attorney over the phone and corroborated her testimony about Ray's abuse growing up, my molestation as a child, and my discussion with Ray. When Ray went out to sea, Trinh began divorce proceedings. I believed this situation would work out for the good.

Once I was back in my therapy sessions, however, I felt like I was crumbling.

Many times I found myself thinking about running away. When I was with Maria, I kept going into trances which took awhile to pull out of them. I was feeling mass confusion and frustration. My values, sense of self-worth, and identity all seemed to be up for grabs. The slow picking away at my defense structure, while at the same time trying to maintain some sense of control, was maddening to me.

I needed to scream. I felt like I was going mad.

Both my mind and body were fucked with during my growing years, and I was constantly on guard to see if anyone was trying to fuck me now.

I believed if I allowed Maria into my psyche with her knowledge of my defense system, and if she began to use me, put me down or betray me, I would feel like self-destructing.

When I felt close to my pain, I cried inside, *please don't hurt me again*.

What had allowed me to survive and keep functioning all those years was to keep my emotions split off and my mind compartmentalized for certain functions. My work in therapy was slowly tearing down those carefully constructed walls, and it scared me to death.

Whenever I spaced out, Maria would get a very puzzled look on her face and would work hard to bring my attention back into focus. My spacing out was starting to happen more frequently. When I was in group therapy, it got worse. As each person started telling their stories, I tuned out. I felt like I was in my own self-contained unit with a giant steel wall surrounding me. No one was getting in.

The end of October 1982, Barry said it might be best if we separated. The one thing he needed from me the most was for me to lose weight.

Nothing had changed. I only weighed 150 pounds but to him, I was a blimp. I made a deal with him. I said if I lost 20 pounds by December 31st, he would agree to go into therapy. At first he balked, but when I said I would have to lose 20 pounds in two months, he accepted my challenge. I told myself I would lose those pounds if I had to starve to death. It was worth it to me for him to get professional help and hopefully save our marriage.

By January 1, 1983, I weighed 130 pounds. Barry found a therapist and started seeing him right away, our group at work had been very successful the previous year, and I believed my life would finally be less stressful.

On April 1, 1983, Olive gave me my performance evaluation for the previous year. It stated:

> *Diane has a strong positive impact on those who work for her. They look up to and follow her willingly and form strong loyalties to her. She has the potential to be a strong leader of her peers.*

Even with all the problems in my marriage, finding out about Ray and Leslie, confronting Ray, coping with Mark's death, and being in therapy, I still persevered and performed in an outstanding manner on my job. I inherited this characteristic from Sam— the major difference being I didn't abuse other people to manage my emotions or make me feel better.

Maria and I had been working together for about 18 months. She gently prodded me to open up, trust her, and allow myself to start feeling some of those pent-up emotions.

I revealed to her that over the past month during the dark rainy nights, I had had thoughts of driving into the Cabin John Bridge railings. Other times I thought about taking a butcher knife and stabbing myself in the heart. I was going off the deep end.

When I started remembering my past, my body felt cold, just like when I laid prepped for surgery. It was a cold, tingly sensation. When I felt this coming on, I tried very hard to block my feelings. I had a scary premonition that if I allowed my feelings to come up, I'd explode.

As far back as I could remember, I had always minimized my feelings and forged straight ahead. I was finding it extremely difficult to keep that attitude, especially in group therapy.

When someone or several of them began discussing their pasts, that cold feeling would come over me again. I would try to concentrate on what they were saying, but I would begin to feel sick, and it would be all I could do to maintain control of myself.

Their discussions triggered memories of my living at home. There was no dignity. I was something to be diddled with. When I now had nightmares, I could taste his salty, pulpy penis.

The following month Ray started writing to Barry and me about his divorce proceedings. What he wrote was more disturbing than I could have ever imagined. I was glad I had Maria and my friends to lean on through the horrible months that were about to unfold.

Chapter 11

Brotherly Love

Ray was extremely upset after receiving notification that Trinh was filing for divorce. His first letter to us was dated May 5, 1983.

Barry and Diane:

I believe we should share our lives and be a family, but I also believe we should be ourselves. There are certain things I believe in and nothing anybody can do will change that. Anyone that tries to push me or change me either directly or indirectly through someone else will see things they shouldn't see. I believe in War, Killing, Honor and Pride. I am a Warrior and always will be. Everyone keeps trying to get Trinh to make me a Priest. It won't work. No one but Trinh has seen me in War. I am a killing machine and we both know it. I know that Diane's views of love and sex were distorted when she was very young. Maybe still are, but my views are different.

First of all (these are my and Trinh's thoughts) sex, the human body, children, and love are beautiful. Killing, Violence, Drugs and hate are obscene. Trinh and I walk around our house with no clothes on and will continue to do so. I will not teach my children that sex is Filth. I will not teach my children that Trinh and I hid and did something we were ashamed of so we could have children. I'm not a sex pervert.

We love our children and they love us. I would not lie to them or hide things from them. Whenever I want to grab Trinh between the legs, I'm going to. I'm not going to hide my love of Trinh for any reason. I think other people are distorted. I think that if Diane can get rid of the thought that if I walk in front of my children with no clothes on that I'm a sex maniac, she will be okay. When Diane can tell the difference between me, Trinh, Leslie, and Eric's love for each other and Sam and Diane's distorted world, we will truly know each other.

I'm a superior warrior and I have astronomic morals, whether you can believe it or not. I should have been born in the 1600's when warriors were looked up to.

I responded with immense anger.

Ray:

I got your nice letter a few weeks ago and have purposefully waited to answer it so that I could calm down. I'd like to begin by responding to certain statements you made.

1. *"There are certain things I believe in and nothing anybody can do will change that. Anyone that tries to push me or change me either directly or indirectly through someone else will see things they shouldn't see."*

   Who do you think you are? Do you think that because people have feelings, emotions, or reactions different from yours that you can bully people and threaten them? I am not some jerk on the street—I am your sister, in case you have forgotten. For your information, I have only encouraged Trinh to stick with you and work things out. What you confuse with a naturally growing, adjusting and relating in a relationship is a perceived threat to you personally, so you just start lashing out. Well, find someone else to beat up on.

2. *"No one but Trinh has seen me in War. I am a killing machine and we both know it."*

   Is that something you're proud of?

3. *"I know that Diane's views of love and sex were distorted when she was young. Maybe still are. But my views are different. When Diane can tell the difference between me, Trinh, Leslie, and Eric's love for each other*

*and Sam and Diane's distorted world, we will truly
know each other."*

*What a joke. Please, don't insult my intelligence. For
me to even respond to that, somehow gives it credibility,
but again, I cannot allow myself for one minute to let
you believe I buy into that hogwash. I do not have a distorted view. Remarkably, even though I was mentally
and sexually abused, I am extremely healthy, more so
now that I have been in therapy and can honestly face
the pain and suffering I endured. You ought to try it
yourself sometime, but you see, it takes a strong person to
do that, not a weak one.*

4. *"After I come back from this cruise, I won't discuss the
   past or sex anymore."*

   *Just like I said before, if everybody doesn't jump when
   you say jump, then it's their tough luck.*

5. *"Trinh and I walk around our house with no clothes on
   and will continue to do so."*

   *That's interesting because when I read this to Trinh, she
   didn't agree with it. A second point is obviously you are
   not concerned with what is best for Leslie or Eric because
   after a certain age they probably would prefer not to see
   their mother and father walking around nude. The
   point is they have no choice in the matter.*

6. *"I'm a superior warrior and I have astronomic morals."*
   *Does that mean you respect other human beings, like
   your wife and children (forget what I think), or that
   everyone must think and do as you say or suffer the consequences?*

*As you can see from my responses, you really pissed me off.
Now that I've gotten all of my anger out by writing you, I hope
we can discuss what the real problems are. I meant everything I
said though, even though it wasn't worded too tactfully.*

Diane

As a last ditch effort to put some life back into our marriage, Barry and I took a two weeks' vacation for our 15th wedding anniversary and sailed to London on the QE II (Queen Elizabeth Two). It didn't solve our marriage problems, but I was still determined to fight for it, especially since Barry was now in therapy.

After we got home, we received several letters from Ray. Some of the things he said were quite disturbing. After reading his letters, I was becoming more frightened, disoriented and confused. In the past I had channeled enormous amounts of energy into manipulative and defensive behaviors. Now that I was starting to confront issues head-on, I was amazed at the intensity of the struggle.

My anxiety heightened as I let my defenses down. This uneasiness was associated with allowing me to feel what was happening rather than rationally dealing with it in a detached manner. The struggle appeared to center around how I could balance that.

I was soon to be promoted to an upper-level management position at a new division in the Company with more responsibility and a significant pay raise. The division's Director was highly impressed with my record of achievement and had written the job description specifically to recruit me.

Once again we received a bundle of letters from Ray. His comments continued to be alarming.

July 22, 1983

There is something I should tell you. I kept Trinh caged up these past years because I was trying to make her a good woman. When she came to the States she had the same knowledge as an American six-year-old. I wanted her to be an independent, free thinking woman, not a slave, even though it may have looked that way. I guess I'll just act like her father or brother now.

July 22, 1983

I am going back to being what I was in the war. No one was able to hurt, bother, or trick me then. I was totally uncaring. Maybe I should have never tried to become civilized.

I want Trinh to know I will "never" pass on to Eric or Leslie my love of war, guns, or a walled mind. I want them to be normal healthy children with a better chance than I had.

Over the next month we continued receiving letters from Ray as he tried to accept the inevitable. His life as he knew it was over.

July 28, 1983

I have been really pushing myself, my mind, back into my way. I am going over my code continuously in order to redo my mind. I am starting to feel myself come back. I have begun to flow again. Don't think I'm withdrawing as I'm not. I am coming out.

BUSHIDO

I researched the word "Bushido." It described a Samurai's code and way of life in Japan between the 9th and 12th centuries. Death was not feared because they believed in reincarnation. Their ideals of love, honesty, self-control and stoicism were highly valued. A true warrior showed no pain or joy.

July 31, 1983

If anything has happened to my family, I will probably become very violent when I get home. I'm very afraid of doing that as I'm good at it. If some sick lawyer is messing up her mind, God help him. If I have to wait for years, I'll get him. I will never let someone stick me in the ass and get away with it again. If you are able to find out who the lawyer is, you should tell him to walk lightly.

My Chief here has taken me off any cases. A doper came in the other night, and when I got through with him (he wanted to fight), I had broken his arm and they put stitches in his mouth. Lucky for me the Chief covered it up. So I don't have to worry about that for awhile. I hadn't felt that kind of anger since Vietnam. I hope it doesn't surface again.

Even when I was growing up, I have never encountered this much stress. I walled off my mind, but the fear of Eric and Leslie being hurt is an almost equal force against me. Right now I wish

I had never been a Green Beret in Nam or had to carry around the knowledge of destruction that I have.

After reading those letters, I felt disgusted and angry. He was in absolute denial about how his behaviors were affecting his wife, children and me. I saw the enormous damage inflicted by Sam and Carolyn, the pain, rage, and helplessness he must have felt as a child, as well as his distorted thinking that had evolved as a result of his abuse. I had no idea where this was heading, but I didn't trust Ray one bit.

His letters also reminded me of my father, how Sam had equally tried so hard to convince me our "shared love" was beautiful. The common belief of many child molesters is that they are punished by society because they have a special love for children. They believe their behavior is misinterpreted, so their actions have to remain hidden. The reality they won't face is that child molesters isolate children and use their youthful bodies to ease their adult frustrations and excite passions. Children are an easy target because they aren't smart enough to humiliate or challenge their molesters.

I was becoming more aware of how much I was suppressing my rage. It was still vitally important, in my mind, to keep my true feelings "invisible" to remain safe. I had no idea the degree to which Sam and Carolyn had conditioned me to remain silent to cover up their crimes. This became more obvious during the following year.

Chapter 12

Falling Apart

The end of August 1983 Ray's ship docked in Norfolk. He called to see if we could drive down to see him before he went home. While Barry was talking to him on the phone, Ray asked to speak to me.

I looked at Barry with a disgusted look on my face and said, "I have nothing to say to him."

Barry told Ray he would drive to Norfolk the next day. When Barry came home a few days later, he informed me we were getting a divorce.

I became extremely depressed. I had worked so hard for so long to hold my life together in spite of what had happened in my childhood, but circumstances kept pulling me down. Barry's mind was made up, so I looked for a divorce attorney. The strain was becoming too much. My mind was reaching its breaking point.

I had worked my ass off for 17 years to make a success of myself. I was about to begin an exceptional new job the first of the year, and my life was falling apart. I tried to find out why Barry had made such an abrupt decision after seeing Ray, but as usual he wouldn't reveal his motives or feelings.

During the month of September, I focused on wrapping up my duties in my current position at work and began thinking about dividing up our personal property at home, but it was becoming increasingly difficult for me to concentrate on anything.

In therapy, I was fearful about confronting as directly as possible incidents of my past and showing Maria the level of terror I felt. Since this was never allowed in the past, I had no idea how it would come out or what her reactions would be.

I asked myself, *what would it be like to act like a child in front of her*? I would never know unless I did it.

At nighttime the pressure started building in my head. I felt like taking a knife and slicing. I felt like vomiting. I told myself, *I should win the Academy Award for Best Actress of the Year.*

It seemed like the emotional part of me was taking over the rational side, and I didn't have much strength to fight it. I wanted to beat on my father's chest and knock the shit out of my mother. I couldn't stand being around Barry any longer.

I felt like Sam, Carolyn and Barry were devouring me, and I couldn't keep them away.

At our next therapy session, Maria said she had been talking to a psychiatrist, and she felt medication would help my depression.

"I can take care of myself," I said. "I'm not taking any drugs."

Speaking slowly now, Maria asked, "What would it be like to let go of some of that pride?"

"What are you talking about?"

"You have had to shoulder the pain and anger for a long time and have done remarkably well, but now when you are feeling so low, it might help to take something that will make it easier for you to cope."

"I can take care of myself."

"Remember when we talked about different ways of being in control?"

"Yes."

"This is one of them. It is a way at looking at what you need right now and finding ways to help. We can discuss it further next time."

I agreed to give it some thought.

During the month of October something just snapped inside of me about Barry. I said to myself, *you can go to hell, you fucking bastard.*

I found an attorney, we signed a property settlement, and he moved out. I was completely torn apart. My heart was ripped to shreds.

When I attended group therapy, my spacing out was getting much worse. Almost always, at the beginning, as soon as anyone started talking, I was in another world. Maria motioned to the other women she needed to assist me.

"Diane, where are you?"

I stared at her blankly. It usually took about 10 to 15 minutes before I could refocus back into the room. Since I didn't feel it was fair to the other women when this happened every session, I quit group therapy.

What scared me was that I was beginning not to care anymore.

When I got home, Trinh called to tell me she was separated from Ray but was allowing the kids to stay with him on occasion. That just blew my mind. She didn't think it was a problem.

At my next therapy session with Maria, as soon as she started talking about Leslie, my pupils dilated and I was completely in another world. She got a very concerned look on her face.

It was almost as if I were under water. I could see what was going on, but my hearing level had dropped. Try as she might for the rest of the session, she could not get me reoriented back to the present.

We were still meeting in the basement of her colleague's townhouse. Since I was in a trance when my session ended, she went upstairs to greet her next client. She came downstairs to check on me periodically. After the client left, I was still disoriented. It had been two hours. Slowly, my level of anxiety and terror dropped enough for me to regroup and drive home.

The Christmas holidays arrived. With my heightened pain, memories of Christmas 1964 loomed in my head when Sam had tried to kill me. Elizabeth invited me to spend Christmas Day at her home. Maria was glad she had made the offer because in my frame of mind, it would not have been good for me to be alone.

Maria spent the rest of December demonstrating relaxation techniques and talking about something called a "safe place." She said we really needed to take it slow and get through the holidays safely.

I agreed. My new job was starting on January 2nd. I wanted to be in a good frame of mind. Maria was going to be out-of-town over the holidays but gave me a phone number to reach her.

I spent most of Christmas Day with Elizabeth and her family. It was very hard for several reasons. Although Elizabeth was a very dear friend of mine, being with her family brought the loss of my family and husband to the surface. It was good, though, to be around people who loved and cared about me.

By early evening I was ready to leave. I told Elizabeth I would go to bed as soon as I got home, and the next day I would feel better.

The minute I got home, the phone rang. It was Barry. He was in Norfolk with his family, and with a very chipper voice wanted to wish me a Merry Christmas.

"I have a niece and nephew here who want to say hello to you," he said without asking me how I felt.

"Barry, I don't want to talk to you or your family."

He started getting upset with me, so I slammed the phone down. I immediately got the largest butcher knife I could find out of the kitchen drawer, sat down at my kitchen table, put the point of it on my chest and said to myself, *just one quick thrust and it's all over*.

The only thing that stopped me was I knew I could call Maria. I didn't want to ruin her Christmas, so I told myself I would go to bed and call her the next morning.

About mid-morning the next day, I called and asked to speak to her. When I told her I had almost killed myself the night before, there was dead silence on the other end as she paused for a moment. She asked why I didn't call the night before. I said I didn't want to upset her on Christmas Day.

After she spent some time making sure I was all right, she said she was going to be home in a few days and wanted to see me. I had started having therapy sessions with her in a detached building at her home because she was in the process of getting an office lease.

The day after she returned home, I walked up her driveway and knocked on the door. When she opened it, she gasped at how I looked. The circles under my eyes were so dark, I looked like a raccoon.

It was so good to see her. After doing some relaxation exercises, she said she was leaving again for a week but had called Andrew (my psychiatrist). He agreed to see me the following night at his home in Washington, D.C.

Although I felt my anxiety rising knowing she was leaving again, I calmed down because I liked Andrew a lot. I felt very comfortable working with him. Maria gave me a big hug before I left and said she would be thinking about me.

I met Andrew around 6:30 PM. He asked a lot of questions to assess my level of depression and thoughts of suicide. Seeing that I was pretty despondent, he asked, "Can you assure me that when you go home you won't hurt yourself?"

"No," I responded with a lot of pain in my voice.

"Then you will have to go into the hospital. I have privileges at a local hospital, so I will be your attending doctor. Can someone take you there?"

I called Elizabeth. She immediately told me how concerned she was and agreed to help me. I asked her to meet me at my home so I could pack some clothes after which she could drive me to the hospital.

Elizabeth was very soothing and helped me realize this was for the best. She stayed until I was checked in and told me to call her anytime I needed.

After being walked to the ward, they locked the door behind me and showed me to my room. I sat down on my bed and said to myself, *I am supposed to be starting my brand-new job in two days, and here I am in the psychiatric ward.* I shook my head and bawled my eyes out.

After I calmed down, I went to the big open Day Room to inspect my surroundings. On the wall was a poster for a movie to be shown: *Raiders of the Lost Ark.* With an extremely despondent look on my face, I asked the nurse when the movie was going to start.

"Oh, that was last week," she said matter-of-factly. But tomorrow is New Year's Day. We are going to have turkey and ham for everyone. I slowly walked back to my room. *Why me?* I kept asking myself. I hated myself, my family, and the whole world. I never knew a person could be in so much pain.

Part 4

The Ugly Truth Comes Out
1984—1986

Chapter 13

Evil Exposed

Being hospitalized in a psychiatric ward meant I had now reached a new level. I didn't know what to expect. I waited all day for the turkey and ham the nurse had promised. We got New Year's fixings all right—turkey and ham lunchmeat. The next day I watched as the staff brought in leftovers and started cutting them up in front of us in the Day Room. We were told they were making a casserole. I thought it was ridiculous.

"I want a hot meal from the kitchen," I said, looking at the other patients. "Don't you want a hot meal?"

Speaking in unison they answered, "Yeah, we want a hot meal from the kitchen too."

I was immediately pegged as a troublemaker.

On January 2nd I called my new manager from a pay phone. "Hi Al. This is Diane. I'm sorry to say I am in the hospital and won't be reporting to work for a few weeks. No, I don't want any visitors. I'll call the Company medical department and explain everything to them. I'm sorry. I'll keep in touch." When I hung up the phone, I was livid that my career was in jeopardy because of having to deal with the ramifications of my abuse.

Since I was in a general psych ward, no one was trained in child abuse issues. I was angry and frustrated. My anger was both misinterpreted and ignored. They didn't understand it was progress for me to vent my anger instead of directing it at myself.

I told my story to four nurses. They sat there attentively and asked things like, "Why didn't you confront your mother as a child?"

The rage in me was building. I learned that slamming my fist into my pillow helped.

Brenda, a co-worker brought my mail. In it was a letter from Barry.

> *You have a lot of good friends who understand as much as possible. They all find you worthwhile, as a boss, co-worker, companion, and friend. You are getting their help, and I am glad. On an intellectual level, I know you are searching and trying to resolve the pain, hate, and guilt from the past the best way you know how. Keep working through your doctors and friends. The time in the hospital, I pray, will be good for you and give you a different view, allow new insights, and let you get out some of the rage within you. Don't stop trying.*

Who in the hell was this person? Where was this person who I had longed to hear express himself and who I tricked into going into therapy? The only thing that had changed was others now knew his presence wasn't wanted and was harmful to me.

One night when I woke up sweating with my heart pounding after a flashback, I went to the front desk and said I needed to speak to a nurse. We went to a small room. I explained when this happened, what helped me the most was to hold my hand and help me stay in the present. The nurse looked at me and said, "I don't care what your therapist says, when you are in here, you do what I say."

I looked at the phone on a table nearby and told her angrily, "Get Dr. Anderson on the phone right now!"

"You can call her?" she asked.

"Get her on the phone!"

She dialed the number and Maria answered. I immediately felt like a frightened child. Maria talked me through what had happened then told me she would see me in the morning. I was able to go back to sleep.

The next day I wanted to take a shower, but there were no towels. When I asked for one at the nurse's station the nurse said, "Use one of those sheets on the floor to dry off with."

I said, "I'm paying $450 a day and can't get a towel?"

She just looked at me and started writing in my chart. This is the type of care I received the whole time I was there. It was so terrible, it worked. I was enraged and told Maria I would do anything she wanted. I would smash Styrofoam cups, yell, beat my pillow, whatever.

The only good thing was the constant stream of visitors I had from my old division at work who showed me how much they cared about me, and Elizabeth called every day.

I was finally able to leave the hospital on January 28th, but could only go back to work half-days for a week. I stayed with a friend, Angie. One night the phone rang. Angie said Trinh had tracked me down and wanted to talk to me. When I got on the phone she said, "Diane, the children are safe!" She then started to tell me about her troubles with Ray and the kids.

I immediately went into one of my trances and didn't hear what she said. After we hung up, I asked Angie to call her back and explain I had just gotten out of the hospital. I told her to ask Trinh to please write me a letter because I had to take it slow for awhile.

When I went back to work, I told Al where I had been and why. I didn't want any secrets. I said I was better and plunged right into getting on top of my assignments. I thought things would be easier for me when I started working with Maria again, but that wasn't the case.

I was still experiencing intense rage. During the day I could manage somewhat to keep the lid on, but when I was with Maria, I felt like exploding.

Maria and I both agreed I needed a fun vacation. Two girl-friends and I decided to spend a week in sunny Jamaica. I had a blast. It was great to go to a totally different environment, lie in the sun, and take a break from all my troubles. It was good I did because when I got home, I was hit with yet another shock.

The second week in April I received a large package of documents from Trinh with a cover letter telling me about her life over the last year and particularly the past six months.

On January 15, 1984, my daughter, LESLIE, age six related to me a number of sexual experiences she had had with her father on her visitations with him. I immediately contacted my attorney and then made reports to Child Protective Services and the police department.

I phoned Ray from the police department because he had been calling us several times to find out when I would bring the children back to him. The police overheard the entire conversation. He asked me when he would be able to start his therapy as if I had to make the arrangements for him. You know how he can cry and assume the attitude of a beaten dog.

I allowed him to phone the children and to see them briefly on his way home from work. Not only did he become gradually more pressing by suggesting more freedom with the children, after all he now recognized his sickness and was willing to be cured, but he was also cunningly instilling in the children's minds that if I had not left him, this would not have happened. Not only did Ray insinuate I had to let him come to my place to see his children, he also asked Leslie why she had spoken, giving up "their secret." In the mediation interview, Ray spoke as if he recognized his faults and would do anything to repair things.

Before moving to Ojai [California] with my new husband, Tom, the Detective who was investigating the case, interviewed Leslie.

Her father had made her aware that through her talking he might have to go to jail, and she was feeling very guilty about that because she did not want to hurt her father.

New details, more revolting than ever, started coming out of Leslie. This was it. He had done everything except fuck her. He was too clever for that. Instead he was manipulating her mind so that she would gradually turn into a sex-hungry robot. Tom and I had recently taught her the correct anatomical words to use, when describing what happened, by using a child-appropriate book.

I wrote back to the Detective and relayed my conversation with Leslie.

"Mummy, you remember the first day you took us (Leslie and her brother Eric) to Daddy's house? That night Daddy first stuck his finger in my butt. Many times he played with my vagina, rubbing it with his finger or licking it with his tongue when Eric was asleep. Daddy often gave me sweets and gum so that I would be a good girl. He told me to kiss his penis which was hard and big. It was difficult for me to get it in my mouth. Sometimes there was that cream, and I cried because I did not want it in my mouth."

Daddy said, "Well, you want to be a good girl like Mummy, don't you? You are beautiful and have long black hair like Mummy, and you look so much like her. Don't you like that?" I said "Yes," and then Daddy told me you liked it very much and if I wanted to be like you, I should eat it. I said, "But I still don't like it. It tastes yukee. I was still scared because my jaw hurt from holding his penis in my mouth." I said, "It hurts Daddy, I cannot do no more."

The next day Daddy told me, "Leslie, why don't I teach you how to do it, then you will like it. Here, I'll show you. You open your mouth and suck six times moving my penis in and out."

" I tried but I could only do it three times because my mouth was hurting so much. The next day Daddy said it was okay to do it only five times."

Daddy said, "Don't be afraid. I don't have any sperm left. Look, I'll show you where Daddy has been cut three years ago. See, it is right here so you cannot have Daddy's baby."

The problems with the children became unbearable. I wanted them to be happy. If they didn't want me, that was quite *all right. I started more and more to think about giving them up for adoption, but to whom?*

I phoned Barry trying to get in contact with you. His attitude was clearly evasive: I have my problems, you have yours. I even called your mother only to hear insults and accusations. When I told her that her son had molested her granddaughter, all she had to say was: "Do you believe a six-year-old child?" All I know is that my ex-husband is a master in mind manipulation, a fact he often boasted about during our marriage and which he had been trained in during his career as an undercover agent for the government. He knows the law and how to get around it, and I would not be surprised at all if he got away with not even a slap on the hand.

Now I am in a situation which I have great difficulty in making anybody, except Tom, my husband, understand. Being illiterate at 30 years of age makes me a handicapped person, totally unfit to do anything in modern society. Communicating with my own children becomes increasingly difficult, and this will only degrade further as they grow up. Even with all the love I can display, I feel I am still fighting a losing battle. I am not prepared to lose two battles, the one to try desperately against all odds to make them loving, gentle and mature individuals; the second one being my own life which I do not want to sacrifice for a lost cause. I have asked Child Protective Services to help me with putting them up for adoption.

I have to tell you one more thing. For years, Barry has been interested in me. At first I thought it was sincere affection. During his back operation, I nursed him, as you know, and opened up and related much of my miserable marriage life. He insinuated that he would divorce you and then expected me to divorce Ray so there would be no obstacle. When I told him I could never envisage a relationship with him because of you who, as you know have been the person closest to me all those years, he backed off. For years, I heard him tell you how much he loved you and could not live without you, and I knew all the time what he really thought.

Tom and I think of you very often. To us you are not a Chambreaux or Ray's sister. We both felt hurt when you thought you had to hide from us after getting out of the hospital. We will not write you any more letters. You may wish to remain behind your wall in an attempt to escape the hurt, but there is no escape, only truth itself.

This package of material was too sophisticated for Trinh to have written it, but I was still devastated. Tom must have on her behalf.

I brought this material to my next therapy session, and asked Maria to read it. Afterwards, she sat next to me with her arm around me as I cried my eyes out. The pain I felt was choking the life out of me. When I was stable enough, I drove home and cried myself to sleep.

Chapter 14

Hospitalized Again

I continued to put up a good front at work even though I had just been re-traumatized. A large number of my peers were unfriendly and some were outright hostile. I was the *outsider* chosen, probably over some of them, to bring strategic direction to the team. Their resentment only pushed me to focus harder on my work, but inside I was falling apart.

Trinh's letter had upset me in many ways. My overall reactions were that her package was clearly insensitive concerning my needs. I resented that Trinh did not warn me upfront about the graphic material, particularly since she knew I had just gotten out of the hospital. I was especially galled at her suggesting that I had my head in the sand.

I never heard from Trinh again. I have never seen or been in contact with Ray since 1983, and I have never been able to reconnect with Leslie or Eric. Shortly afterward, I called Barry and told him what Trinh had said about his advances toward her. He denied it.

I was getting in touch more and more with the fact that I had no family, spouse or children. I knew, though, that I had a lot of friends.

I was beginning to understand some of the things Maria had been teaching me about being more in control, but in different ways. It was very interesting. The more I was able to let go, the more in control I felt.

I understood she was communicating to me it was all right to express anger, pain, sadness and despair. I didn't even realize I had those feelings. To get in touch with the disgust, terror, and pain was hard as I had buried that many years ago. I realized there was an inner shield I kept between Maria and me. I believed that if I could not cope once that shield was dropped, I would give up the struggle.

In late July I screamed until I woke myself up at midnight. I felt nauseated, very dizzy and short of breath. I was beginning to wonder how long I would be able to keep up my pretentious sham of confidence. The next night while trying to go to sleep, I kept thinking about slitting my wrists. What kept me going one more day was remembering what Maria had said that day: "It's all right to lean. You've run a long race and are exhausted."

On July 31, 1984, Barry wrote me a long letter expressing his love and wanting us to reconcile. He said he felt I was trying to just dump him like excess baggage. I couldn't take it anymore.

On August 3rd while in my therapy session with Maria, I felt very dizzy, passed out, and fell on the floor.

"Diane, are you in a grocery store? Are you in a restaurant? Diane, are you in a grocery store?" When I opened my eyes, I realized I was lying down in a small enclosed room with large windows. The nurse to my right squeezed my hand. "She's back," she said.

Seeing the doctors and assistants through the windows, moving between curtained cubicles and a central workstation, I hazily realized I was in a hospital emergency room. A large status board hanging on the far-right wall caught my attention. Scribbled across it I read: CHAMPE   DEPRESSION.

The IV pinched my hand as I started moving my body. Everything seemed to be in slow motion, which matched the muted voices scurrying from patient to patient.

How could it be 9:30 at night? I remember talking about painful memories with Maria, feeling faint and falling out of the chair onto the floor, but that was three hours ago. And why am I in the emergency room?

"How do you feel?" asked a kind voice in a white uniform standing next to me.

"I feel pretty weak."

"Your friend is waiting to take you home when you feel stronger." Maria had called her.

Elizabeth had been through a lot with me and now, six years later, was sitting in the waiting room. She was providing the support I would grow to depend upon even more over the years ahead. As I lay there, I could feel the anger within me.

Here I am, I reflected, *after working my ass off for 19 years to get to the position I'm in at work, and I'm still paying the price for what my fucking parents did to me. And I haven't even seen or talked to them in 12 years!*

"Diane, do you think you can sit up?"

I felt a little light-headed but managed to bend forward. Within the hour, Elizabeth and I were in her car, driving from Georgetown University Hospital onto the Whitehurst Freeway.

"What happened?"

"I fainted, woke up for a minute and said I was cold, so Maria covered me with a blanket. After that I blacked out again and awoke for a moment as they loaded me into an ambulance. I didn't wake up again until 9:30."

"I'll take you home so that you can rest," Elizabeth said.

The next day, as I drove to see Maria, I felt shaky but knew I was going to a source of comfort. We talked for about an hour and with her admonition to, "Take it slow," I went home.

The following day I rested and went back to work on Monday as if nothing had happened. I didn't want to jeopardize my job. I managed to get through the week until Friday afternoon.

I told Angie what had happened the previous weekend, but instead of being supportive, she asked in a stern voice, "Why aren't you staying on your diet?"

I looked at her and asked, "I don't know, Angie. Why do you think I'm having a problem?" Her stupid question was her way of ignoring my psychological distress.

"Oh, Diane, cut the bullshit."

It seemed incredulous to me that someone would be that insensitive. I was also very angry. After walking back to my desk, I composed myself and got ready for a long drive to corporate headquarters because my boss said I needed a new Company pass. As I drove out of the parking lot, I passed Angie and became angry again. More and more it was becoming difficult for me to split off my rage.

On the way home from headquarters, my heart was pounding so hard I thought I was having a heart attack. *What's going on with me?* I wondered. Once again I felt dizzy. All I could think of was, *I've got to get to Maria.* Luckily she was meeting with someone at her colleague's townhouse. Twice I had to pull off the road because I didn't think I could make it.

As I drove up, I knew Maria was probably with another client, but at this point I was gasping for air. After pulling up to the townhouse, I managed to pull myself out of the car and stumbled to the front door, doubled over while hanging onto a wrought-iron fence. I knocked, paw-like, one after another until she opened the door. Seeing me bent over, she helped me inside and guided me to the couch before I fell onto the floor.

"I'm either having a heart attack or the same thing I had last weekend."

Maria immediately went to the office door, explained to the patient there was an emergency situation and dialed 911. I remember paramedics giving me oxygen, taking me outside on a stretcher and then all went blank. When I opened my eyes, some-one was removing my clothes.

"She was just here this week," I heard and blacked out again.

As I came to, I realized I was in the same room as the previous week. This time, Maria was standing next to me with her pocketbook and mine slung over her left shoulder while she held my hand. Tears streamed down my face.

"What are the tears from?" she asked softly. I wiped them away instantly but couldn't talk.

I watched as Maria talked with one person after another. Afterwards, she explained she had reviewed my background with them. She had also called Andrew.

Both he and Maria agreed hospitalization was needed since my reaction to stress was falling into unconsciousness twice within one week.

"You need to be hospitalized." Maria held my hand, and I could see from her expression it really was best.

"I can't believe this is happening to me. I have fought all my life to deal with what happened and now this. I can tell you this, I'm only going somewhere where I will receive proper treatment."

"Andrew is in the process of having you admitted to the Psychiatric Institute (PI) on MacArthur Boulevard. Do you think Elizabeth can take you?"

"Yes," I professed, feeling dejected and angry. I hated the fact that I would be hospitalized again because of the effects of my abuse.

"He will meet you there at midnight. I have to go now but will be there tomorrow. Are you okay for me to leave now?"

"I'm very frightened, but I know this is what's best."

As she gently released my hand, she walked slowly toward the medical staff to have a final word. As I lay on the hospital bed, my eyes followed her when she turned to leave. It seemed like forever, but she held direct eye contact with me until she left the room.

"You can get dressed now."

"I need to call a friend to pick me up."

Fumbling with the hospital gown, I pulled the silk dress over my head that I had recently bought at Bloomingdale's, something Patricia had coaxed me into buying because I wasn't used to such extravagance.

Once Elizabeth and I were in her car I said, "Well, Elizabeth, once again you're here in the middle of the night."

"No problem. We'll take you home first to get your clothes, and I'll drive you over there."

"Can you ask my neighbors to watch my kitty cats?"

"Sure. I'll do that tomorrow."

As we drove in the dark, I felt so frustrated and angry. *Why do I have to do this? I thought I was free from good ol' Mom and Dad. I'll just have to keep moving forward as I've always done.*

When Elizabeth and I arrived at PI, all was still and very quiet. She helped me with my bags into the admitting office where Andrew was waiting. Hugging her, I resigned myself to making the best of this and bade her good bye.

Andrew and I looked at the woman seated across from us. As I blankly answered questions about why I was being admitted, I thought about my parents. I didn't know what was going to happen next, but nothing could be worse than the concentration camp I grew up in.

Chapter 15

New Insights into My True Self

As I was trying to adjust to my new surroundings at PI, I thought about the Sam and Carolyn Freak Show I grew up in. I realized I managed to function and survive because I was able to split off and compartmentalize my painful experiences. After so many years, that defensive survival technique became natural to me.

As Maria and I kept going deeper into the hidden compartments of my mind where I had stored the pain, my feelings were coming out faster than I had anticipated, and it was extremely difficult for me to control what was happening.

Having a supportive environment with Maria, Andrew, and my friends, I told myself, *provided me the opportunity to look at the issues and to try and confront them more directly.*

Another voice said to me: *Nice try, Diane. Putting on a good show.*

Maria wanted to know what the "real" Diane was like. The "real" Diane was hungry for love, acceptance, peace of mind, rest and understanding; was very angry, frustrated, confused, and tired. The "real" Diane was also scared to death of being rejected, put-down, or abandoned. The "real" Diane felt very alone and had little hope. Of course, at the time, I didn't know who the "real" Diane was. Only much later through my therapy did I gain this insight.

The more I opened my eyes, the lonelier I became.

Calling Al was humiliating. I had to tell him I was hospitalized again in a psychiatric hospital. He was very nice and said he would like to speak to Maria. I consented.

I had a dream that night that Barry was pulling me back into his ugly world. We made love as adults. He then turned into a baby with large bloody teeth and began devouring me. I pulled out a gun and shot him. When I woke up, I felt nauseated.

After reading a letter from Barry the next day, I stuffed food down my throat which told me there was a lot churning in the emotional side of my brain that I had not yet acknowledged.

I realized I felt guilty, as if my mother had been the victim. In my child's mind, I could have stopped the abuse and did not. I wanted to hurt her, so Carolyn had every right to turn against me. Emotionally I was justifying her behavior instead of mine.

I thought, *how can Maria accept me, knowing what I had done?*

I had expected Maria to reject and abandon me just like Carolyn had.

I was livid about the wounds my parents had saddled me with. Thanks to them I now had my own private hell on earth. Once again, I was in a hospital—twice in the same year.

The middle of October, I wrote what I had learned and concentrated on while in PI:

- I only substantiated negative feelings about myself which was a distorted way of thinking.

- I felt enormous guilt for the role I played in my incest experience.

- I learned there were many ways to constructively express negative feelings.

- I had to consciously pay attention to the amount of stress I experienced each day.

- There was nothing wrong with acknowledging my strengths and talents.

- I wrestled with self-sustaining versus dependency issues.

I ended up spending six weeks in PI. It helped tremendously because I developed new coping skills, had time to myself to regroup, and had stabilized after all my recent traumas. Elizabeth picked me up and drove me home. It took another few weeks for me to reorient myself back to normal society. I was looking forward to going back to work and getting on with my life.

The response I got from my boss and co-workers was unbelievable. Only one person, my secretary, acknowledged I had even been gone for eight weeks. She put a "Welcome Back" sign on my office door and hugged me. Al had told me the day before we were going to have a staff meeting.

When I went into the conference room, no one approached me or asked how I was doing. When Al came in, he started the meeting immediately. Afterwards, everyone just got up and left. I felt just like when growing up. Everyone acted like nothing had happened. I decided I would jump right in and do my best while continuing to struggle with my demons. My career meant everything to me, and no one was going to take that away from me.

Barry, who kept acting the part of the spurned husband, even though he had asked for the divorce, would not let up. He was the one who had acted as if he didn't need me while at the same time scaring me to death with his irrational behavior. And now he kept pleading with me to take him back. I started thinking this must be similar to what battered women go through.

A friend asked me to go to the movies with her to see *Country*. Near the end of the movie (which dealt with coping with what seemed like a hopeless situation), the actor was in a barn with a gun. The actress said, "Let's go into the house and talk." He said, "Don't worry about me. I'll be all right. Go ahead inside; I'll be there in a minute." A minute or two after she left, we heard the gun go off.

I immediately left the theater. My friend came out a few minutes later and found me standing with my back to the wall. She said I had no color in my face. I was not capable of driving home, so we went to get something to drink. I talked about how it had reminded me of my father with his gun. It had hit too close to home. I started crying and tore both of our napkins to shreds. I drew a picture of my parents and then destroyed their images with my pen.

In my next session with Maria, I compared a 12-year-old's reality to an adult's reality. If I were 12, I'd feel guilty for participating in an intimate relationship with my father which meant crossing boundaries inappropriately. As an adult, I knew that my father had seduced me. He had taken advantage of my innocence, but he was the only source of caring and affection I had. My father had tried to reinforce to me that there were no boundaries, even though I fought desperately against his behavior.

As a 12-year-old, I might believe I was the cause of an unspeakable crime for my mother to totally reject me and to never take care of or nurture me. I'd feel like I had done something wrong by reaching out for her care.

I know as an adult that my mother had a lot of her own individual, emotional problems. She had made a choice of who she would sacrifice—my father or me. She had an impenetrable boundary. I did everything I could possibly do to penetrate it but was unsuccessful.

This helped put a few more puzzle pieces together.

One Saturday morning, Brenda and I met at Tysons Corner Mall. While we were there, I mentioned to her I had written Barry a short letter saying once again I couldn't see him. I needed to prepare for the holidays. She told me to stop worrying that Barry might be upset with me. She said at a recent District party Barry had tried to act the top stud. While dancing with one of his peers, he kissed her right there on the dance floor in front of everyone. Later on, the receptionist he was seeing came to the party. For the rest of the evening he was with her.

While driving home, I was finally able to look at the fact that Barry was just as phony, heartless, and controlling as his father. It hit me like a ton of bricks.

As I turned into the entrance to my housing development, I spotted a black, oval-shaped Buick just like the one we traveled in when I was growing up. It propelled me back in time. My heart began racing. I immediately sped up. As soon as I opened the front door, I ran up the stairs, sat down at my kitchen table and began writing.

November 25, 1984   8:00 PM

Tap into my child's brain. What do I see?

I am going to have a good time, and no one will understand or discover my true motive. Always look innocent.

This life of intrigue is fascinating. No one will catch me because we are moving from town-to-town. I can produce practically anything anyone wants to see, especially my mother.

I live in a secret world all my own and no one can touch me.

My father is handsome. I can get anything I want if I am patient and deceptive enough.

Let's play sexual games. We lay next to each other and feel each other.

Don't worry. They won't catch us.

My mother is stupid and fat and I hate her. I can do anything she does but better.

I produce my own warmth. I am very smart. They won't catch me.

HA-HA, You are looking for me, but I am up in this tree watching you. I move very quietly and am in control.

HO-HO-HO I'm a cowboy traveling on the trail. I have enough clothes and food to survive. Watch out! There is someone by that tree up ahead. Step back very carefully and slowly. Slide down slowly to ground level and they'll never see me.

OK BITCH. I'll get ready for school to entertain you and myself. I am bored to death.

Let's try something new. Each new town is a new adventure. Ray and Joanne can just shut up and leave me alone.

She thinks I am watching them, but I could care less what they do.

As long as there is a commotion going on, no one watches me, but I'm watching them.

Stay away from me you ugly bitch. Daddy is handsome and funny. I love to be around him. You make me sick.

I feel like vomiting. Even though I am constantly on the alert, I wish I could get some rest. Don't hurt me. I won't do it again. [Yes, I will, HA HA].

I HATE YOUR GUTS. BOTH OF YOU.

What are you doing to me? Why do I have to keep it a secret? If I am so special why doesn't someone treat me that way?

What are you doing? GET OFF OF ME.

Can't you see, you bitch? Can't you see what is going on?

Of course, she can't, because I am the master of disguise. I love the outdoors because I can pretend I'm leading another life (cowboy, Tarzan, whatever).

All of you are crazy, but I know what is going on.

Doesn't anybody love me? Why won't you hold me and care for me? I played those games so I wouldn't go crazy. Don't ignore me. Look, I can produce anything you want to see. I can create any type of character you want. If I find the right combination and personality, then will you love me?

I DON'T WANT TO GO IN THOSE CLOSETS AGAIN. BUT I HAVE TO OR HE'LL FIND ME.

This is horrible. I am scared to death. He is too strong for me to handle physically, but I can beat both of them mentally. I can produce anything they want to see, but no one can touch the real me. NO ONE.

I was exhausted after writing these free-flowing thoughts. Even though I didn't understand the meaning of this strange outburst and handwriting, I felt relieved. I was confident Maria would be able to help me decipher it in my next session.

When I showed this to Maria, she said she believed this was my true self speaking out. I found that both scary and fascinating.

Over the Christmas holidays, I reflected on the past year and the tremendously stressful situations I had endured. I resolved to keep working hard in therapy and to get back on my feet at the Company.

My work, as usual, gave me some respite. Right off the bat I was in back-to-back meetings. On January 2, 1985, I took the train to Philadelphia for some advanced training. On January 8-9 I held meetings to discuss what I had learned. It felt good to be working hard again, but my inner turmoil was awful.

My reaction to those recent feelings was to literally stuff myself with food and physically wear myself out by working late. I was starting to see that I could not bring myself to put my anger and resentment in its proper place (toward Carolyn).

I said to myself, *I deserve to be mistreated. I deserve to feel guilty for even thinking about expressing my angry feelings.*

When I looked back over the previous few days and saw how much I had overeaten, it scared me because I was beginning to get a gut feeling of how explosive my anger was.

From January 17-25 I was pretty busy at work. I took the train to New Jersey for two days of training, conducted a day-long meeting for our team, and went on a Company ski trip for five days in Quebec. Racing down the hills on my skis was exhilarating. I had a lot of fun.

After I got back from the ski trip, I kept very busy. I attended a training seminar in New Jersey, conducted day-long meetings with major clients, and spent a week documenting the significant trends and issues facing our industry. At the same time, I kept working daily on my trauma issues.

I identified my methods of coping as compartmentalizing and denying or discounting my feelings. I understood that whenever I felt insecure, afraid, angry, overwhelmed, guilty, or jealous my programming said: "You are a victim and are helpless. You deserve to be punished. You have no right to express yourself."

My programmed behavior was to go into the closet [figuratively], shut the door, overeat, and mentally chastise myself unmercifully. Writing always helped, though, to get my deeply held secrets out in the open.

I was going to try a different approach. Whenever those emotions surfaced, I needed to: recognize and acknowledge their existence, not analyze the situation, but as quickly as possible externalize my feelings constructively and move on. That way I was not structuring my emotions around my daily life; I was not dropping deeper into my depression; and I was reinforcing constructive behavior.

I told myself, *I am no longer a victim. I can come out of the closet.*

I found it interesting that when growing up, the more I could tolerate and *contain* my feelings, the more in control I felt. Now it was the exact opposite. The more I could tolerate *expressing* my feelings, the freer I became.

I was beginning to understand this was going to be a long, slow process. I was discovering myself for the first time. It was very painful but reassuring. I knew I was finally on the right path.

Chapter 16

The Little Girl

After being hospitalized twice the year before and now somewhat stabilized, I concentrated on my work, but my therapy issues were daunting.

My goal was to pull out of the sick system I had grown up in and the unhealthy one I had lived in while married. It would take tremendous stamina, courage, and a willingness to risk it all to attain my goal. The primary and most difficult obstacle was to overcome my programming. Only by challenging it repeatedly would I be successful.

I asked myself, *why are all of my destructive thoughts directed at me?* The answer was that because of the brutal conditioning by my parents, I didn't know how to direct it appropriately outward because of the fear of being punished.

As I thought about this, I had a sudden urge to write in my journal.

February 21, 1985   7:30 AM

Uh oh. She caught me.

Please don't tell anyone. I didn't mean to do anything.

Yes, you did you bastard. You ruined everything.

Shut up. Do you hear me?

What do you want me to do?

How am I supposed to live?

I hate his guts.

And you bitch, take your fat ass out of here. He likes me so shove off.

I need someone to take care of me. No one is here.

If I hide under the covers and don't move, maybe he'll go away. He's not going away.

I never get to rest. We are always on the move.

Get in the car, Ray and Joanne, we have to move to another town. At least with everyone together in the car, I will be safe. I'll just stay over here and hug this corner of the car. I'll be very quiet and won't move.

I'm tired of bologna sandwiches. That's all we eat when traveling.

Stay on your side of the car bitch. He's mine. I'm watching everything you do. And I know you're watching everything I do. But I'm smart and you are dumb.

I don't want to have anything to do with you.

I'm going to shut down now because I need some rest.

My guts were turning inside out. I hated the world and my life. I felt like getting the old bricks and mortar out to start building my mental walls back up. Another part of me, though, told me to remain vulnerable and to keep moving forward.

In order to survive, the price I paid was to look at my parents, straight in the face, and seal off all my emotions. Now I was trying to look at Maria, straight in the face, and express all my feelings. The price I was paying this time was reliving the guilt and expressing the pain.

During the week of March 4th through the 8th, I was in a lot of meetings with top management. As usual, I was able to compartmentalize my agony and focus on getting the job done. To meet my high expectations, it had to be an outstanding job too.

On the weekend I could let my true feelings out.

March 9, 1985   7:30 PM

I feel myself going into a trance.

I feel lightheaded and nauseated.

What is going on in my head?

I want to scream. The feelings are mysterious and frightening.

Maria, I need you.

I feel my brain needs to throw up.

Where am I?

It's okay. When I'm riding my bicycle I am hiding.

Even though they see me they don't notice me. I can slip away and hide anytime I want to.

GET AWAY FROM ME. WHERE IS MY MOTHER? I DON'T KNOW WHAT TO DO.

As soon as it is daylight and everyone is up, I will be left alone.

I used to like being around him, but now I'm afraid of him. She acts like she likes me, but I know different.

She doesn't fool me at all.

Why is this happening to me?

I know that Ray and Joanne sense something is wrong but none of us will talk about it.

As soon as I walk in the front door I immediately check out who is in the house and where they are.

What he's doing feels good, but I'm scared to death to move.

Good. He's leaving.

Oh no. He's back.

GET AWAY FROM ME.

She never cares for me.

I need her to care for me.

I can never rest.

Go ahead and hide, Diane. Try to get some rest. No one loves you. Try to comfort yourself. No one loves you.

Amazingly, when I walked through the doors at work, I shifted into the "responsible" person who needed to attend to important work. I didn't understand at the time that this is what I must have done the whole time I grew up. I had no idea there were other parts of me to handle my feelings and roles, and couldn't understand why, at times, my handwriting looked so different. I functioned at a very high-level by compartmentalizing my torment and only releasing it at home or with Maria. I was aware my inner life was becoming much more bizarre.

The cadence of my life now consisted of marching back and forth between two worlds: work and therapy. I had less and less contact with friends because I had a hard time coping. When my mind wasn't on work assignments, it was flooded with either memories of my past or trying to figure out what was going on in my head in the present. As I delved deeper in therapy, more puzzle pieces were coming together.

It came to me that I was blackmailed by Sam because I had innocently shared my emotional needs with him. My father used extortion to meet his needs by his exercise of power. I didn't willingly participate in anything. Either I "put out" or I would be abandoned. I felt deceitful because I felt as though I had gratified myself at the expense of my mother. Was that a crime for which I should be eternally punished? I said to myself, *self-punishment comes from a feeling I did something wrong for which I should feel guilty*. I was innocent. I didn't deserve what they did to me.

The beginning of April, I flew to Chicago to line up strategic objectives for our region. Work was my lifesaver, my link to reality. As soon as I got back home, though, my old fears resurfaced.

My mother's brother, Uncle Bob, called Barry to tell him about a death in the family. Barry called Maria to tell me Munder had died.

Maria was very kind in breaking the news to me. I had not expected her death. I sat on Maria's couch in shock. Afterwards, I went home and cried about this significant loss.

In my next session with Maria, she did something very different. Instead of asking like she always had, "What are you thinking?" she looked at me and asked, "Who are you?" I looked at her and without any prodding said, *"I'm the little girl."* That night the little girl openly expressed herself.

June 30, 1985   10:30 PM

I am a little girl. I am afraid and frightened and confused because I am trying so hard to act how grown-ups want me to act, and not how I really feel.

I am doing my best to do what my mother [Maria] expects of me.

I just want to hide and cry all of the time.

Someone help me, please. I am way over my head and Maria is leaving me.

I am not a grown-up. I am a child. I've tried to do the best I can but it is too confusing. I don't know where to turn anymore.

I want people to understand that I am a little girl.

A little girl? This was no fantasy. She was a real part of me. I had finally reached the point in therapy where my stress was so great, my old stoic ways of coping were no longer effective. I felt safe enough to allow a child part to openly express herself verbally. That was a major breakthrough. It was a difficult time, however, because Maria was going on vacation. We had agreed I would see Andrew while she was away for continuity of therapy. She then tried pushing me to express how angry I must be feeling about her leaving. That night I wrote:

Maria, you have missed the whole point.

The issue is not me telling you that I'm angry at you leaving me.

The issue is that I am coming out of the closet. Your pushing me to express direct anger at you is forcing me back into the closet.

Don't do that to me.

It took tremendous willpower and trust on my part to let you see me. I dared to actually speak to you (not just write it) and tell you that something was causing me pain. You weren't listening.

Toward the end of the session I just started agreeing with what you were saying. Then I told you I had left to go to "Never-Never Land" because I gave up.

The whole time I went through all of that horror, I never, ever cried out for help. This is what I'm trying to get out and you are talking about an entirely different issue.

I am trying to stand up (finally) to the "Don't you dare speak!" message of my parents, and you keep asking me about how angry I must be at your leaving.

I feel the pressure inside of me is to conform and produce what you want to see.

That's when I said, "You'll get what you want; I'm not strong enough yet to speak for myself."

I have been pushing myself unmercifully to

get to the point where I was today. I was saying to myself, "No grown-up is stopping me now. I am going to tell Maria how I really feel."

When you responded by wanting me to pull out of that and talk about my anger at you leaving, I felt I had done something wrong, and I should not have shown you that. To me it was a clear sign to go back underground and produce what you wanted to see.

I finally just shut down.

After I read this, I had a better idea about what had happened in session.

I had drawn a painfully graphic picture in Maria's office showing my hand on my father's penis. Maria (Carolyn) was going away and leaving me in the care of Andrew (Sam). When Maria kept asking what was wrong, the Little Girl kept saying, "I'm not supposed to say anything" and "I can't get away from him." When the Little Girl interpreted that Maria (Carolyn) didn't see what was going to happen, it set up the old fear I had had as a little girl. That part of me even said, "You know exactly what is going on."

Maria didn't understand what had transpired since I liked Andrew and never had a problem with him. That is when the Little Girl went back into her closet in my head.

Using different penmanship continued to confuse me. Enormous emotion would overcome me at times. I would always immediately sit down and start writing, many times feeling as if I were in a trance. I just assumed it would become clearer to me at a later date as I kept working hard in therapy.

Chapter 17

Validation, Rage and Pain

The survivor in me kept pushing to function so that I could hang onto my job. I had lost my family and husband, but my career at the Company meant everything to me. I was able to confide in my secretary, but no one else. Having to work at optimum speed and performance levels, while being treated for trauma with no support at home, was absolutely excruciating.

On August 7, 1985, my father's older sister, Annie, tried reaching me. Someone put her in contact with one of my friends, Eleanor, from my old division. I asked her to take the call. Eleanor telephoned me afterwards and related the conversation she had had with Annie.

E: "Diane asked me to call you to find out why you are trying to get in touch with her."

A: "I want to talk to Diane because it is a family emergency. Every time I have tried to talk to her parents, they would not talk about her and said it was a private family matter. When I tried to contact her about her grandparents' deaths (Pappa and Munder), Barry said he would make the decision whether or not he would let Diane know. That is why I am trying to contact her. I did not know how to reach her. I have always loved her since she was a little girl."

E: "Where were you when she needed you?"

A: "I didn't see much of her because they traveled so much. What is the problem?"

E: "Let me enlighten you about your brother. He sexually molested her from the time she came into this world until she got married and left home. Diane tried to tell everyone the best she could, but no one would help her. She even told her grandfather." (I corrected Eleanor. It was my grandmother (Mamma), but that was okay because Annie's responses furthered my suspicions of incest between Mamma and Sam since it was one of her uncles who had tried putting his hands into my pants as a little girl.)

A: "I had no idea. I know that Diane must not have told my father because he would have done something. He would have talked to Sam. I know my father, and he would have done that."

E: "The tradition of incest is still being carried on today by Diane's brother."

A: "Yes, the court dismissed it and found him not guilty."

E: "I have seen Leslie's testimony. It was very explicit. I also know that Diane sent for her sister-in-law and the kids to try and help them, so I know it is true. We both know at times the court will let people off because of loopholes in the law. Diane has said it has gone on for generations. I asked her whether or not her whole family was crazy?"

A: "No, we are a very moral and close family. It only went on in her immediate family. We always knew there was something wrong because almost from the time Diane could talk, she said she didn't like her Daddy. It was always a problem. We didn't know what to do. We had no idea what to say."

E: "Why didn't you ask Diane?"

A: "We just didn't know what to do."

E: "Diane endured the incest all those years because no one would help her."

A: "I thought that was what it was, but I didn't want to believe that about my brother. Are you sure?"

E: "She's been hospitalized twice; she takes pills to go to sleep but still has nightmares and flashbacks; I've talked to her doctor. She's told me how she had to sleep in closets to get away from her father. By the way, what was her mother like?"

A: "I never knew her well. She was a very cold person and would never let people get close to her. I've always loved Diane and would like very much to talk to her."

E: "I find it really odd if there was so much love between you, Diane would have mentioned you. It is difficult to believe why Diane has never said anything about you to me."

A: "I just don't know. She knows I love her."

E: "No, Diane would have mentioned you."

A: "It is just so hard. My brother did have a drinking problem as well as his wife."

E: "Are you condoning his actions?"

A: "No, there is no excuse. Just let Diane know I'm willing to come down there to see her. I've still got pictures of her on my wall."

I had no idea why Annie was calling me. I had not seen her since the summer I visited my cousin Angela in 1961. To hear everything validated by a member of my family was overwhelming.

In my next session with Maria, the Little Girl was talking to her about how she felt. Someone started turning the office doorknob which was always locked. When I looked up and saw the knob turning slightly, my anxiety immediately sky-rocketed, and my eyes opened wide with terror. Maria told me afterwards my pupils had dilated. She spent the rest of the session calming me down and helping me to stay present within my current surroundings. Maria reassured me I was safe, and that someone had just gone to the wrong office by mistake. But for me, that turning doorknob held a much more sinister meaning.

By the fall of 1985 when Maria and I tapped into my deep trauma memories, my whole body literally felt like it was in shock. My physical tendency was to sit with my mouth open. My tongue felt swollen and enlarged. When in a trance, I couldn't see clearly. I felt I was in another dimension with everything moving in slow-motion. My whole body felt stunned, and, as usual, I was nauseated. The more I got in touch with my traumatic feelings, the more despair I felt.

My emotional life now was full of rage and pain. I began to understand that the magnitude of my abuse was such that the repeated shock treatments and beatings my mind suffered when growing up were so incessant, I could have almost been pushed over the brink into insanity.

Late one night I began writing:

Everybody is coming after me. I'm trying to hide, first in the trees, then near the water.

I've passed out. Now my whole body is spinning around and around.

Mama. Can you hear me?

Yes. I'm right here.

Mama. Are you there?

Yes. Everything is all right.

I'm still spinning around. There is water all around me.

Mama. Are you there?

Yes. I am right here.

I am beginning to slow down spinning.

Don't leave me. Hold me so that I don't drown.

I'm right here.

HELP.

All of the mass confusion I was experiencing was because I was expressing my feelings from the past for the first time, not knowing where these feelings were coming from and why, and then not knowing what to do with them.

The process was exhausting and frightening, not only because it was new to me, but because I was learning to express myself by dealing with traumatic issues. No wonder I wanted to give up.

By the end of the year, I had begun to acknowledge and take ownership of my needs, wants and feelings. I was no longer going to be a victim of other people's behavior or be destroyed by their ruthless desire to control and manipulate me.

Since my anger was at such a flash point, I came up with a good solution. I created an "anger room" in my downstairs bathroom at home. Whenever I felt my rage bubbling up, I went to my bathroom, closed the door and screamed my head off. I took rolled up magazines, beat the toilet, then ripped them into shreds. I always felt better afterwards, and this was a safe way to let my anger out without hurting anyone.

One day I ferociously scrawled across the bathroom wall: SAM CHAMBREAUX—I COULD KILL YOU FOR WHAT YOU DID TO ME and CAROLYN CHAMBREAUX—YOU LET HIM FUCK ME.

Afterwards, I ripped the wallpaper off.

That felt great.

I was in a long, painful, uphill struggle. I wanted very much to pull out of that old system. The more I could get a handle on the source of my pain and express it, the closer I would be to working through my trauma.

As we started 1986 both Maria and I had high hopes. We knew there was still a lot of work to do, but I was finally stabilizing in my job.

Things went well for the first three months, however, my psychic pain started building again. I was seeing Maria three times a week and was practically crawling out the door after each session.

I had identified for the first time what the screaming in my head meant. It was the child-Diane expressing the horror non-verbally. The terror I experienced growing up was so horrible, I was just now able to listen to her and empathize with myself.

Al had been lining up a strategic study to be done in conjunction with a major accounting firm in Washington, D.C. The results of the study would heavily impact the work we were doing as a region. He gave me the good news. I would be the primary interface working with them. Al had no idea the level of trauma I was working through. I actually got a pay raise and a $1,400 bonus check for the work I had done the previous year. Incredible.

When I got home, nighttime brought the horrors back. Alone, with no work and no one to distract me, the voices in my head would emerge. It was becoming more difficult to get a full night's sleep, and many times I would wake up feeling like I was in my parents' home. I would be terrified, had to calm myself, and was exhausted the next morning.

I was eating non-stop. I had no control. The rage was so powerful within me, I wanted to kill someone.

On July 21st I gave my strategic plan overview to the Area Manager. I felt really good about what I had accomplished. It felt wonderful to experience satisfaction and competence. I earned those feelings. I needed them.

With my newfound confidence, being in touch with my true feelings, and making important connections about my trauma, I put together critical insights about my relationship with Sam and Carolyn.

I said to myself, *for two people, husband and wife, mother and father:*

To turn against and devastate their own child to vent their anger, frustrations, and jealousy;

To subject their daughter to being raped and tortured while showing no mercy;

To humiliate and strip her of her dignity; and

To abuse their child until she was in shock just to make sure that "outsiders" wouldn't know what was happening to her, was tantamount to emotional manslaughter! They did not break me. I am putting the blame squarely where it belongs—on them.

This statement was a major turning point in my therapy. It meant I was finally able to judge their actions for myself. I was rejecting the decades of conditioning by my parents, I was livid, and I was taking full ownership for how I felt and thought.

Chapter 18

A Tragic Mistake

I was moving into a new stage in my therapy. Everything hit me all at once, and I screamed from the bottom of my soul. It was that crushed and battered child screaming to be let free from her torment.

I felt like I was at a turning point in my life. I envisioned a steel shell of a body with a child ready to break it at its seams. This robot, housing the lifeblood of a struggling human spirit, was about to be destroyed.

During the last week in September, I participated in a joint presentation with the accounting firm to our entire team. It reflected all the work I had done that year and provided an opportunity to showcase my abilities. I got rave reviews.

That good feeling didn't last long. A week later I spent 35 minutes ripping up magazines in Maria's office. I understood that to function and emotionally survive when growing up, I had to hide my anger from myself. Maria helped me to see just how much I had contained all those years.

My rage went to the bottom of my soul. I was in the process of looking at the savage, unmerciful brutality, but this time allowing myself to feel my emotions and express them.

In October I had lunch with Patricia, and a lot of anger surfaced. I told her I had to get out of the restaurant. I had been telling her about all my progress, and then something triggered my rage. My pupils immediately dilated, and I spaced out.

She paid the check and then walked me across the street to the back of a local restaurant. She asked if I could smell the awful odors coming from the dumpster.

"No."

"You can't smell that?"

"No."

"Stay right here." She walked to a corner vendor who was selling soft drinks and came back with a plastic bag filled with ice. She said, "This should do the trick." After pulling the neck of my blouse out in back, she dumped the ice down my back. I was instantly back in the present.

The next day while working at the accounting firm, I ate tons of food. That night I had a nightmare that Carolyn was beating me, and all I could do was scream for help. I frantically tried to mouth Maria's name, and finally I started screaming for her. That woke me up.

The next day I ate more junk food, watched TV shows and went to bed. It didn't take long before I started screaming and beating the bed.

I was bouncing off the walls. I had definitely moved into a new stage. I felt totally overwhelmed and out of control. When I thought about the suffering I had endured, I wanted to strangle my parents.

The battered, bruised, deprived and terrorized child in me had been locked in a closet for 27 years for a crime she had never committed. Not only had she carried the rage from all the degradation and abuse when she lived with my parents, but also the fury and excruciating pain from being forced to stay in the closet[figuratively], gagged and left for dead with the intention that she would be forgotten and all memory of her abuse would be erased.

We had reached my terrorized child.

I told Maria my whole body felt like it needed to explode. Over the previous three weeks, everything had been building. I screamed on my way home.

At home I beat my toilet seat with a magazine screaming, "I don't want to live like this anymore. I've had to deal with this all my life. I'm tired of dealing it. I hate what they did to me. He got off on me, fucked me, and she did nothing."

Late that night I wrote:

I am in a state of profound dissociation. I hurt from the bottom of my soul. I want to be free.

Maria had explained to me that dissociation was a psychological defense mechanism to separate from distressing thoughts and emotions. This gave me a better understanding of what had been happening all this time. Whenever I went into those trances, my mind was actually splitting off and defending itself because the material was too stressful and/or threatening for my psyche to handle. It helped me to understand and to feel like I wasn't going crazy after all.

During the summer, Barry and I finally set a date and met at the courthouse to finalize our divorce. I barely said two words to him. It was over. This provided another area of closure for me.

The stage I was now in was different from the others. The nausea was not there. In the past when my feelings were stirred up, I could actually feel some type of inner movement. There was no inner distinction now. My whole body and soul were tied together, and I was scared.

On November 15, 1986, Joanne wrote to me.

I have tried every way under the sun to contact you for years and have been unable to. I want you to know I have been to hell and back. I have no family connections anymore with anyone even though I do live in Snakeville. I haven't in some time. I worry about you. I understand you and your pain more now than ever and am deeply sorry I was so mentally ill to not be able to earlier. I at least hope you have me in your heart and can for-give my past ignorance.

Love forever,

Your sister

I decided I would let her know how I felt about her contacting me.

Dear Joanne,

Words cannot express how wonderful I feel. I am over-whelmed with joy. I have read your letter about ten times and cried for two days. I have missed you so much. Joanne, you don't know how many years I have waited to hear what you said in that letter. I can tell just by the way you expressed yourself that you have taken that giant step to remove yourself from that sick family we inherited.

It takes a lot of courage and strength. I am so happy you are taking control of your life. I want to start rebuilding our rela-tionship very much. To know that after all these years there is hope we can not only be friends, but can also reconnect as family is overwhelming to me.

Very soon I will call you. I love you, Joanne.

Your sister,

Diane

I scribbled my thoughts in yet another style of hand-writing.

How can an abused person feel lovable? You can't, because being abused and tortured for a long period of time makes a person integrate the abuser's view of real-ity. It takes a lot of time and work to turn that around.

I received another letter from Joanne.

I am so excited. As soon as I saw the white envelope that said, "I love you very much" on the back of it, George [her new husband] and I both began to cry. We are very happy.

Hearing from you has made me feel complete. I need you very much. I need your friendship, your love and I need to give you mine.

I love you very much.

I called Joanne a few days later. She said that Sam had started a business, but the only thing Sam and Carolyn had done for the last five years was to work and direct their anger at her. Carolyn held a job at the hospital all day, while he ran his company at night. This arrangement helped him to continue having sex on the side. Joanne said she had caught Sam in bed with young girls.

Joanne shared an amazing conversation she had had with Sam. He confided that when he was five-years-old, he, too, had been molested, so he understood how she felt. She also said Sam blamed me for Ray going to jail. His dismissive comment was, "Another innocent victim."

She said she got on a Trailways bus with the boys a few weeks later and went to California to visit Ray. While she was there, she had to visit parts of her childhood with him. I didn't ask what that meant.

After hearing Joanne's stories, I was very upset. That night I jumped out of bed, went to my living room, and was in a state of delirious rage. I screamed, cried, hit my couch, rolled on the floor, beat the floor and couch with my fists, and begged on a gut level all of this could come out.

The next morning I went to the grocery store, bought dough-nuts, candy, and some regular food but ate all of the sugary stuff as soon as I got home.

Joanne called again to fill me in on more of Sam and Carolyn's activities and her sad plight. She had been financially dependent upon my parents with her two children for so long that she was literally trapped there. She said George was drunk one week, so that is why she went to visit Ray in California. Ray admitted to her he had molested Leslie, and then raped her. Joanne called George to come and get her, but to not attack Ray because he would go to jail and she would be back with my parents.

I decided to pay for Joanne and George to come to my home and visit. At the time, I had no idea I was reenacting my old tape which was to take care of everyone. I felt so sorry for her, I was very lonely, and I wanted to be connected to family.

On December 23, 1986, I gave my final presentation on the strategic plan to top management and got a very good response. Joanne arrived the next day for the Christmas holidays.

After only two and a half days, I was overwhelmed. Joanne said that Annie's [my father's sister who had tried to reach me by talking to Eleanor the year before] son was flown to California with my parents' help. Annie had acted like she was so interested in my welfare, and yet her son was Ray's defense attorney! Once again, the overarching priority was to protect my parents from incrimination and the Chambreaux name.

I was finally on my feet at work, my divorce was final, and I was internalizing and recognizing how important it was to express and take care of myself. Joanne's very sad plight, my poor judgment and desire to rescue her overrode my decision-making process. This course of action proved to be a total disaster.

Part 4

My True Self Becomes Uncaged
1987—1989

Chapter 19

Launching a Vendetta

We had a wonderful time at Christmas. I planned an extraordinary trip for New Year's. Joanne and I first flew to New York, then waited for George to fly in from Mississippi. We met him at LaGuardia, ate lunch, went to the top of the Empire State Building, ate dinner at the Russian Tea Room, saw a Broadway play with Hal Linden and O.C. Davis, took a limousine back to the hotel and went to my room.

Joanne called home to check on the boys and was told my parents had been calling everywhere (including going to work locations and bothering the people who worked for Joanne). She called Sam and Carolyn and got into a huge shouting match. George flew home the next day, and Joanne flew to Virginia with me.

After a few days of rest, Joanne talked about how she had lived a nightmare for eight years. Her sad story was too much for me, so I decided to help her get a fresh start by having them move in with me until they could get on their feet.

Joanne and I got to talking about Carolyn. Joanne said she asked her at one point, "Even though you knew what Daddy was doing to us, why didn't you leave him?"

Her response: "Because I had a roof over my head, money in my pocketbook, and food on the table."

I felt the rage within me eating away.

That night the giant wheels in my brain were turning again. I had thoughts of hopelessness and a desire to end it all.

In my despair, I finally realized that my crying was that little baby that was never held, that little girl that was never loved, and that child that was horribly molested and abused.

After Joanne flew home, George called me and said she had suffered a psychological breakdown because of the sharp contrast between staying in my home and living in Snakeville. Joanne wrote that she was pulling out of it and looking forward to living with me.

They packed their bags after she got out of the hospital, and immediately left Snakeville. After only two weeks of them living with me, however, I was already starting to decompensate. Maria had worked with me for a long time to center within myself and to start the psychological separation from my past. My fantasy of rescuing Joanne and getting back at my parents was so strong, though, I had put myself into a very risky situation. I now felt stuck, and the situation would only get worse.

Even though things were very tense in my life, I told myself I would be able to continue the great progress I had been making at the Company. Al could see my improvement, and I really wanted 1987 to be a turnaround year for me. But with what I had learned about my family, my feelings were crashing over me like rough waves. They seemed out of control. I felt like I was drowning in despair.

My evaluation at work for 1986 stated:

> *Ms. Champé provided the market and strategic planning interface associated with representing our corporation's products to our key client. Her analysis was an integral part of securing a major sale.*

In spite of all the traumatic material I had worked through the year before, I had accomplished my assignments and was given a pay raise along with a $3,000 bonus.

Without my knowledge, Joanne and George began a major letter-writing campaign. She wrote the Mississippi Attorney General's Office for information about the rights of incest victims. Uncle John wrote Joanne complaining about a letter George had written to Mamma.

Joanne and George also asked a Mississippi attorney to address their many complaints with Sam and Carolyn. When I got home after a business trip, they showed me a package they had received from Sam's attorney. It contained several letters and legal documents exchanged among Joanne, George, Sam and Carolyn—all of whom were threatening one another.

I had thought I was giving Joanne and George an opportunity to get away from my parents and start a new life. I wanted to be supportive, but they took it upon themselves to begin a full-blown retaliation against Sam and Carolyn from my home. All that Maria and I had been working on concerning my own trauma and the practice of "taking it slow" was thrown out the window. I tried telling them to slow down, but they were hell-bent on using my home as their new base of operations.

The immersion in their lives 24-7, and how enmeshed they still were with my parents, was taking a serious toll on my ability to cope. I slowly began to fall apart again.

I attended strategic planning meetings in New Jersey the first part of March, and when I got back, Al showed me a memo he had received from Product Line Management with high praise for my work. My friends and I were amazed at how I was able to continue functioning so well and at such a high level with all the turmoil in my life. I explained I had become an expert at doing that the whole time I grew up, so it seemed like second nature to me.

Joanne got angry one day at Sam and Carolyn and said to me, "You either support me or you don't, but one way or another, I'll be doing something about it in the next few months." I explained I didn't appreciate being given an ultimatum, and I felt insulted. Joanne was still angry and started yelling at me. When I came home from work, she apologized with an explanation that she was scared. In my session with Maria, I was able to see that I had been the one who had been dumped on.

On March 26th George wrote a letter to the Department of the Navy reporting both Sam's and Ray's incestuous behavior, again, without consulting me first. They received a response on April 3rd stating that our case had been turned over for investigation.

Joanne and her family had lived with me for only three months, and my life was being turned completely upside down. Instead of just concentrating on building a new life, they plowed ahead in going after Sam, Carolyn and Ray.

My individual therapy was now centered on dealing with current crises instead of continuing the progress I had been making in healing from my own abuse.

In addition, I was having a great deal of difficulty concentrating at work with all the stress at home. I resented their actions very much because none of this was discussed with me beforehand. I had made a terrible mistake. They had taken over my home, and I was out of control.

As I began the fourth month of Joanne and her family living with me, it became clear we needed another car. I bought them a used-car plus put $900 in their personal checking account instead of them having to ask me for every nickel.

On April 12th I used a phone extension to listen in on a call from Joanne and George to Mamma and took notes.

G: "You sure did show how chickenshit you really are."

M "They are grown women, and if they can't handle their problems, that's their problem."

J: "I'm ashamed to have you as my grandmother. Diane and I are ready to burn your fucking ass and your whole fucking family is going down in the dirt."

M: "Sam Chambreaux don't owe you a dime."

G: "Oh yeah? He stole my stuff, and I want Sam to give back two little girls' hearts."

M: "That happened 25 years ago, and the statute of limitations ran out. Diane and Joanne are the ones who are going to lose. The Chambreauxs can't be hurt."

G: "Emily, are you saying that it was okay what happened to those two girls?"

M: "I wasn't there. If you call again, I'll call the police for harassment."

When they hung up the phone, I just sat there in amazement at her smug answers. What kind of grandmother would or could feel that way about her granddaughters?

The next day Keith Hendricks, a Navy investigator, called about George and Joanne's letter. He said there may be nothing the Navy could do about Sam, but they were definitely interested in Ray. George mentioned that Keith had seen my name on Ray's military records, that I had been involved with the court conviction concerning Leslie. He also said when he looked at the documentation, all of a sudden it said, "No further details."

Keith was suspicious that there was possibly a bribe involved. Joanne told me Carolyn had flown out to California with $25,000. All three of us wanted to keep it confidential. We didn't want Sam knowing we were talking to the Department of the Navy.

My rage had been stimulated again. Every time I thought about Ray, he made me sick to my stomach. And, to find out that he had been doing this to Joanne the whole time she grew up, I hated him even more.

All along (with the exception of the first month when George and Joanne were getting checks from the jobs they had worked in Snakeville and her child support checks), I had totally supported them financially. I was almost to the point of wanting to completely withdraw from the world. That meant everything from locking myself in my bedroom to killing myself.

George, Joanne, and I knew the extent of my help. They told me repeatedly they were keeping a record of everything spent and would reimburse me. But they did not actively seek employment.

A few days later Joanne and George were in a loud shouting argument. She told me she was very depressed about what she had experienced with Ray, and George couldn't understand why she wanted to stay in denial. George was trying to use his AA techniques which were not appropriate. I acted as intermediary and finally was able to help him see the difference between AA and therapy (justifying why long-term therapy was not a form of denial), and that Joanne needed a lot of support.

Joanne said she talked to Keith Hendricks who told her Ray got a five year suspended sentence and one year in jail. Ray should have been kicked out of the Navy. Keith said the police detective who was involved in the case was mad as hell at Ray's sentence.

I was going insane.

I was sinking lower and lower into my depression. I was also very angry at myself because before they moved in with me, I had been making great progress in therapy. Now I was taking care of them at my expense, which would prove to have tragic consequences.

My unbridled rage had also been stimulated. I didn't want to be hospitalized again, and I dreaded going home from work. They talked about the Chambreauxs every day, as well as the Navy department, Ray, and the lawsuit.

I extended myself one more time by allowing them to use my car to drive to Snakeville to tie up loose ends about their home and business.

I was finding it increasingly difficult to function. I kept having sensations I would faint.

My goal was for them to be self-sufficient. I was paying off the $2,500 car loan, they were using my Exxon credit card, and they were on my car insurance. As I told Maria, I felt if they had a place to live and a car, they could get started on their own.

On May 1st when George and Joanne got back from Snakeville, I talked to them about moving out, but it didn't go over very well. George said, "Sam Chambreaux will rule you from the grave. We had them on their knees begging us to leave them alone while we were out there."

I told them to stop talking.

Joanne said, "You've been in therapy for five and a half years and are still acting like this. Every time we say something you get stimulated. You get stimulated even if we don't say anything. Until you can get down in there and cry, vomit, and scream or do whatever you have to do, you can stay in your quiet house with your two cats and do nothing."

George said, "We'll live as totally separate lives as we can while we are still here."

I was very angry. She was out of Snakeville. They had an opportunity to start a new life. They were the ones that had pushed and pushed and pushed about Ray, a lawsuit, the Department of the Navy, etc., and somehow all of that was glossed over. Because of their overzealousness and pushing me, I somehow didn't have the "guts" to face the situation. I gave them their dream on a silver platter, and somehow their success or failure, once again, was based on their reactions to me. I wasn't buying into that.

I was not responsible for their life responses. Maria said the way out was for me to let go of the responsibility. I trusted her.

A few days later I felt like I was going to explode.

Joanne started screaming at me at the top of her lungs about all she had suffered in life and was implying that I had done nothing for her. After all, she had been beaten, had been on welfare, and had almost gotten herself killed on this last trip to Snakeville, and (as she said), "You're having a rough time? I've had to sell pussy to put food on my table."

She stomped upstairs. As I tried to talk to her about my concerns, she looked down at me and said in a very loud and hateful tone of voice, "I'm not listening to anymore of your Sam

Chambreaux crap!" Her sons were in the next room, so they heard everything.

For five years Maria and I had worked together to help me feel safe enough to face my demons, but in a controlled manner. After Joanne and George moved in, I reverted back to how I behaved when growing up, that was to make sure the household ran as smoothly as possible, to ignore my needs, and to be the problem solver.

My work at the Company was suffering because this daily turmoil at home prevented me from working at my best. I was afraid of the repercussions.

The inner wall in my mind which allowed me to keep functioning was breaking down.

Chapter 20

Boundaries

My work performance began to deteriorate even more. I couldn't handle all the stress at home, but I couldn't confide in my manager what I was going through.

The next day I felt suicidal after meeting with Maria. When I walked in the door at home, they knew I'd had a rough time and said what I needed was to get out, so we went to a restaurant. I tried to explain that Maria and I went very deeply into my abuse memories.

Joanne said, "Diane, you have everyone fooled into thinking you can't handle things, but you're strong."

I said, "All right. I'm going to put my cards on the table. I feel we need to plan on you getting a place of your own and getting jobs while you are building the business you want." They had talked about being self-employed with a home cleaning business.

"When do you see us moving out?"

"About six to eight weeks. That's not cast in stone, but it is a time to plan for."

"Diane, you can't work a 40-hour week and build a business on the side," George said.

I asked, "Do you think I've treated you dirty or wrong?"

"Yes, you've put us in a real bind," Joanne replied. "There is no way we can be self-sufficient in six to eight weeks. We have to uproot the boys again. I wish we had never come here. In Snakeville I had to put up with Sam, but financially I was getting somewhere. I am responsible for my own mistakes, but I should have never come here."

"I thought you were desperate to get out of Snakeville."

"Emotionally I was, but financially I was getting somewhere. I am much better emotionally now, but we have no money, so we still have a lot of problems."

We got up and left.

As we were driving home, George asked, "You are going to let us have this car, aren't you?"

No answer.

Joanne said, "We might as well start up the lawsuit again; we can be sure of getting money then."

George said, "Yeah, we know they'll settle out-of-court."

I didn't say anything else on the way home.

I knew they felt torn apart and betrayed, but I didn't see what I had done wrong. I felt suicidal.

The next day I called home and talked to George. He said not to worry about anything because he had talked to someone at AA whose building contract was about to expire. The man was going to help George get the contract. He said, "By the end of the summer, we'll have our own place and will be on our feet."

I said, "Good."

I was finally beginning to understand what Maria had been talking about when she mentioned the word "boundaries."

In the beginning I had all my negative feelings sealed off. I always wanted to do everything for everybody and under no circumstances would I make anyone feel uncomfortable around me.

The second stage involved my awareness that I can and do experience negative feelings, but they were so totally threatening, I did everything I could to ignore them, seal them off, and ridicule myself for feeling them.

During the third stage my blind rage broke through, and I felt totally out of control. During that period I was hospitalized twice within one year. On top of that, my marriage dissolved, I experienced deaths of friends and family, and I was dealing with my brother's incestuous behavior and conviction as a child molester.

The fourth stage involved my exploration and acceptance of those feelings. During that time I began to understand, "I have a right to my own feelings and how I choose to deal with them." That stage was so powerful because it vividly brought back the extent of my abuse. Not only did I re-live everything that had happened, but I also allowed myself to feel the excruciating pain associated with it.

The fifth stage focused on understanding ways to channel all of those overwhelming negative feelings constructively. Trying to learn new behaviors is a horrendous job. It takes a total commitment and is an all-consuming and draining process. Along the bumpy way, there were incidents which triggered painful memories as well as current happenings that required a lot of support just to manage them. Overall, this was a huge, complex balancing act.

The sixth stage, where I now found myself, was pulling all of that insight together and establishing healthy boundaries with people. It involved allowing myself to be my own person and letting go of the chains from the past.

With the knowledge that Joanne and George were finally going to be self-sufficient and move out, I felt like a changed person. I believed I had control over my world again. Enormous emotional weight was lifted off of me. I was my old self again.

After my discussion with Joanne and George about moving out, there was still an undercurrent of tension. Joanne said, "We're trying to save up the $850 we'll need for the monthly rent to move into an apartment."

I said, "That sounds pretty high, isn't it? Can't Peter (the owner of the apartments who gave them their contract) find you something less expensive?"

She said, "Not in Silver Spring, Maryland" (near their work).

Originally my accountant called Peter as a way of helping them get started in the business which paid $2,000 net per month. In the meantime, they had been handing out flyers all over town for their home cleaning business they wanted to start.

I was in excruciating pain the following week after a therapy session. As I sat outside of Maria's office trying to calm down before driving home, I kept asking myself, *I wonder if it would bother her if I killed myself?*

When Maria told me I did not have to subject myself to Joanne's abuse (her yelling at me), it finally hit me the amount of shit I had been putting up with.

They were acting like somehow I was abandoning them, that I was kicking them out for no good reason. What in the hell did they want?

I had been too giving, too generous. They were somehow trying to put a guilt trip on me for pushing them out on their own. I didn't owe them anything.

I wasn't obligated to do anything, and yet it came across like I had let them down somehow. It was just incredulous to me that they had even expected more from me. The facts are: I got them out of Snakeville, paid all of their expenses, got them a car, and gave them time to stabilize.

If I accepted their view of reality, I would feel guilty for somehow not having done enough. My past behavior with Ray and Trinh, Barry, and now with Joanne and George had been for me to see people in need, and then I took it upon myself to make their life as easy as I could. Somehow I saw that as my responsibility.

I could understand their anxiety and fear, but I couldn't help that. I wanted to live my life for ME.

If I wanted to continue to help them, that would be my decision. And that was another major perspective which fueled my rage. They were doing their emotional kicking and screaming and trying to force me into the same role as when I grew up.

The whole thing was idiotic.

I was not going to be badgered into taking care of their lives anymore. And this time, if Joanne started screaming, I was going to tell her to shut up or don't talk to me at all. That was another badgering technique.

By June 1st I wanted them out of my house. I also wanted to slit my throat.

I told them about a new crisis involving my job. I was being demoted a half level. For the first time in my life, my job had suffered because of my personal problems.

The first thing George said to me after I told him about my downgrade was, "Are you implying this happened because of me and Joanne and these two boys?"

"No."

"What is this due to?"

"I haven't been performing as well as I should."

"How long?"

"These last six months."

Then he said, "Just as soon as we can, we'll be out of here. Diane, you need to face your problems. I don't know what you and Maria have cooked up, but you need to quit worrying about everybody else and worry about Diane. You rolled out the red carpet, and you need to be told a few things."

I said, "The last thing I need right now is more stress. I'm going to bed."

"Well, when you can handle more, let me know."

My whole life was falling apart. I had worked so hard for so long to at least keep performing at work while the pieces of my emotional life crumbled around me. But with all the stress I was going through with Joanne and George, I had reached my limit, and things just kept getting worse. My despair felt like a bottom-less crevice.

Chapter 21

Abandonment and Breakdown

My life was spinning out of control again.

By the end of June, I was in deep despair. I sat at my desk and thought about what happened each time I went into a trance. My body would feel like it was in shock, my physical sensations were numbed, and I was not fully aware of my surroundings.

Operating at an adult level and encountering so much hostility at home, I had a better understanding of what I had had to cope with as a child. To function as a little girl, my brain had developed an automatic mechanism (dissociation) that would shut off my feelings of rage without me even thinking about it.

By the beginning of July, the screaming in my head had started again. I realized I had been mimicking Carolyn by showing that no matter how deep and intense my rage, I never showed it and kept it under control by overeating. I was also mimicking Sam by using my intelligence to gain power and control through the workplace. It was hard to accept that I had incorporated those behaviors into my own.

By the middle of August (seven and a half months of them living with me), I was pretty disgusted with George and Joanne. For one thing, George vented his anger a lot at Jason and Allen.

Most of the time it was verbal, but he also spanked them periodically with a belt. Joanne did too. My personal feeling was that it was unjustified. They were 12 and 14-years-old and were good boys. Consistently, they didn't clean their room or do other chores they were supposed to do. What teenager did?

Jason had been outside playing with a friend. When he came home, he went upstairs and was talking to me about something.

George came upstairs, looked at Jason and said, "Get your ass downstairs right now."

A little bit later I heard him being hit with a belt. The next night, I heard George yelling at Jason in the basement and up at Allen who was in the kitchen.

Jason next yelled at George, "Don't hit me with that stick, George, it hurts."

George said, "I'll hit you wherever I feel like it. You just won't do what you're told."

Jason yelled, "Don't hit me in the face with that stick, George, it hurts."

I didn't hear anything else after all of that died down. Needless to say, I had a hard time getting to sleep, so at 12:00 AM I took a sleeping pill.

The next morning before going to work, I told George he had to find another way of disciplining the boys while they lived with me. He didn't like that.

When I got home from work that night, I was totally disgusted after George told me he had gotten angry while on the job and had lost a major source of their income. I felt like kicking them all out in the street and saying, "Good luck," but it was not that simple. My life was so horribly painful. Something had to change, and soon.

Even though I had been demoted a half level, I still had a lot of responsibility within the Company. The end of August I went to New York to attend a conference while staying at the Waldorf Astoria. I couldn't sleep even after taking a sleeping pill. I felt like I was bouncing off the walls.

A few weeks later I had to attend a two day meeting in Hunt Valley, Maryland. The morning of the second day I called home to check how everyone was doing. George answered the phone.

"Hi, George, can I speak to Joanne?"

"She's gone."

"What do you mean she's gone?"

"She packed the car, took the boys and drove back to Snakeville."

My mind exploded. I had just cashed in shares of stock worth $1,300 so they could pay the first and last month's rent on an apartment and start living on their own. She had taken the money and ran home to Sam and Carolyn.

A few months back, I had bought a used van for them to use in their business. George said he was in the process of packing what wouldn't fit in the car. I just hung up the phone.

For the second time in my life, I fell to my knees in disbelief. I felt like the room was swirling around me. My equilibrium was so off balance, I literally could not stand up.

After crawling to the bed and pulling myself up off the floor, I called Maria. She helped me stabilize, advised me to drive home slowly when I felt better, and asked me to call her that night.

It took several hours before I could stand up. I called the office, said I was very sick and was going home. When I finally got home, George was packing the van with more of their belongings. I said I would loan him $1,200 to get home, but I expected to be repaid.

He just stared at me. When I asked him what he was thinking, he said, "How much I want to kiss you." I told him to finish up and get the hell out of my house.

After he left, I noticed that they had not only taken most of their things, they had also stolen several of my things as well, including my Hoover vacuum cleaner, a new $450 rowing machine I hadn't even removed from the box, luggage, and other belongings.

I couldn't function. I called the Company's EAP (Employee Assistant Program) psychologist, Dr. Albertson, and told her what had happened. She had already had several interactions with Maria over the past few months and agreed I needed to take it slow.

By the beginning of October, my state of mind was worsening. I woke up, but it was difficult staying in bed. I had to go to the living room and look out at the street to feel safe.

To heal, I told myself, *I must forgive myself for feeling that searching for tenderness and caring from my parents somehow encouraged their abuse. Quite the contrary, both of them used my neediness as an opportunity to vent their own hostilities toward each other. I was the unfortunate spider in their web.*

I had carried around guilt all those years because I was not able to protect my sister from that fate, no matter what I did. Now I understood I had placed totally unrealistic expectations upon myself because I was no more in control of helping her than I was of protecting myself. Joanne was an adult now and could choose for herself the road she wanted to travel. I was no longer going to carry the responsibility for her life on my shoulders.

Even though I had attended training meetings for my new job, the skills required were totally different from any of my previous assignments. Instead of keeping me in a marketing position, which would have capitalized on all my past experience and training, they placed me in a job which required a skilled computer analyst. I had never even turned on a computer. Even though I voiced my disapproval about this placement, my protest fell on deaf ears.

The tremendous stress and additional trauma I endured with Joanne meant my defenses were torn apart. While in session with Maria on October 9th, I said I was experiencing something different. My brain felt like it was splitting up into particles. I had no control over it. That night I wrote:

Something terrible is happening to me and I do not know what it is. Neither does Maria.

My brain is coming unglued.

Maria, I need you.

You don't see what is happening to me.

I am different. I don't belong. All of you are in the human race. I am in hell.

My brain is splitting up.

I am isolated again. I'm afraid.

This is different from other times, and Maria can't see it.

I had a discussion with my new boss, Andy, the end of October. I told him I needed to take some time off on short-term disability and was concerned how this would reflect on my work. He didn't respond to that. I explained that both my doctors and the Company doctor agreed I was doing the right thing. Andy said he would check with Dr. Albertson.

My rage was building at the continuing price I was having to pay due my parents' abuse. All my physical symptoms were due to the level of stress I was working under. Everything needed to be geared toward relieving that stress as much as possible and focusing on getting myself back on track.

I didn't feel safe at work. I felt threatened because I had let the *secret* out by showing them I was overwhelmed by my trauma.

Andy called me back and confirmed I was going on short-term disability.

By the middle of November, I was finally able to settle down. It had taken two and a half weeks of doing nothing to start feeling calm again. I was finally centering everything within myself. I wanted to react to things the way I wanted to instead of searching for what other people needed or desired. I was beginning to accept that that was okay.

It felt funny but good to experience my life by reacting spontaneously with my emotions. Knowing it was safe to do so, and that I had a right to do that, was exhilarating.

Before I went back to work, I found out I had a new manager. Andy had been replaced by Connie Brown. She called Maria in a very stern, businesslike manner insisting I needed to return to work. When I called Connie, I tried to let her know I had been dealing with significant trauma work which was helping me. Her response was, "You need to be here." End of story.

I wanted to get back to the work I loved and hoped my new boss would be empathetic. I had no way of knowing how horrible working for her would become. I forged ahead with determination to do the best I could. What else could I do?

Chapter 22

Insights into Psychological Weapons

I went back to work the middle of January 1988. From January 29th through February 4th I was in planning meetings in Philadelphia. I was building relationships with my new peers and meeting deadlines, but I couldn't seem to manage the amount of traumatic material that kept coming forward.

By the middle of February, I could feel my brain shutting down. The gift shop downstairs sold Milk Duds. At times I ate three boxes of them just to calm down. I decided to leave early one Friday afternoon, go home, and go to bed.

On Monday morning Connie said, "We have a business to run here, and we need to count on you 100 percent. When you are not here, someone else has to pick up the slack."

"What happened Friday afternoon?" I asked.

"Nothing, but we need you here." She went on to tell me, "You need to get over this and quit dwelling on it. I can't worry about things that may send you back to Vietnam." (I had tried to explain to her that my diagnosis of Posttraumatic Stress Disorder (PTSD) was similar to Post Vietnam War Syndrome.)

She said, "I can't be empathetic with you, and I'm becoming less sympathetic. You're no different than someone coming back from heart surgery."

"But I am. It's a mental injury."

"Well, maybe you'll have to go on disability. We need you 100 percent."

"I have worked very hard since I came back. What you're saying means you don't understand the issues or how hard I've worked. Normally a person going through what I've gone through would take 10 to 20 years to work through it, but I've taken six. I think you and I should sit down and talk with Dr. Albertson."

She refused. Grudgingly, I continued attending training courses over the following weeks, one at the Omni Hotel in Maryland and another in Northern Virginia.

At 1:20 AM I wrote:

I am so nauseated I can hardly stand it. No one believes me. I have endured beyond anyone's imagination. I have suffered for so long and have kept it all inside.

My mother doesn't love me.

They hate me because I am not playing their game.

I am extremely nauseated.

Mental torture shows no scars.

I'M VERY SICK.

Over the next few weeks, I studied and reviewed our regional market-sizing and strategic opportunities. On March 17th I gave a presentation to top management and felt I was getting back into the swing of things.

That night I was so nauseated I could hardly stand it. The container in my brain was filled to the brim with bile from the 21 years I had been tortured. I wished I could throw it all up at one time, but I couldn't.

Because the mental, emotional and sexual abuse was so traumatic during my childhood, my brain at 8, 10, 12, and 14-years-old repeatedly went into shock.

On April 7th I gave a presentation about the Addressable Market to the Vice President. At least I was holding things together in the work environment even without any support from my manager. Afterwards, Marsha, a friend of mine, and I decided to take a fun trip to Boston just to get away.

With my newfound understanding of my right to healthy relationships, I was becoming aware of my negative reactions to Marsha's behavior. Most of our trip to Boston was fine, however, something was gnawing at me the whole time. Late Sunday afternoon it became clear to me that Marsha's constant negative comments reminded me of what I had lived with at home.

She knocked everything and everybody, such as: "Look at those two lovebirds. They're disgusting." And, "Did you hear what that person was saying? She's ridiculous." On and on and on.

My parents made fun of or put people down all the time. I felt like I had been propelled back in time. I was beginning to find it very difficult to accept that behavior anymore from her or anyone else.

I discussed my reactions with Maria and understood that to keep from being mentally destroyed I had to develop some way of coping to survive. Learning ways to hide was easier with my father because it basically boiled down to a physical battle. It was a matter of looking out for the warning signals when he was home.

My mother, ah, that was the true test. A baby, a child, cannot survive being nurtured by a cold stone. I don't give a shit how sad, lonely, afraid or depressed she was; her behavior was criminal. We moved so much, they got away with their abuse. The bottom line was it was a true power game. She was going to hang onto Sam, at any cost, and that included rejecting me.

Maria helped me to understand there were very sound reasons for my behavior, and by acting the way I did, I survived.

By the beginning of May, I could see I had come full circle. My very first therapy notes expressed my fears of being destroyed. It was even clearer to me now that the bottom line of all my behaviors was the need to protect myself from being mentally destroyed.

All my compulsive, irrational fears stemmed from that, thus the reason to feel the need to hide, shut down, overeat, and hold in my rage.

By my mother abandoning me emotionally and rejecting me, I had to put the blame on myself as a child to survive.

I finally felt connected enough with my child parts to start working on those issues from my teenage years (14 – 18) which were the most traumatic.

The horrible dilemma I found myself in when growing up was that just as I was trying to develop my own identity, my torture at home grew worse. My rage at Carolyn was the most vicious of all. Protecting the person you hate the most is a real test of your mental abilities.

Maria and I were beginning to go into my "secret chamber." I had never allowed anyone in there. This was not a new phase in my therapy; it was the two of us going into a totally new area of my brain.

I was beginning to connect with Maria even deeper, where the void was, where my mother and I had never connected, because the child-Diane was sedated at birth.

The middle of July, I had a strong reaction when Maria said that Barry, Sam and Ray had no conscience. I had trouble focusing. I felt in shock. I couldn't close my mouth, and I felt like I was in a stupor.

Two weeks later it again registered with me at a very deep level that all my reactive and defensive behaviors had evolved because of my number one fear, that of being mentally destroyed. I realized that each time I reached a point of feeling nauseated, my thoughts were thrust back into a time when I was living with Sam and Carolyn, and I had split off to survive. I asked myself, *what were my parents' weapons to destroy me?*

- Keeping me isolated.

- Not allowing me to show or express my feelings.

- Humiliating me as a means of power (nothing was too crude for them).

- Only touching me in an abusive manner (both of them in their own way).

- Abandoning and neglecting me, even as far as basic life needs, such as comforting me when I was sick, etc.

- Mentally torturing me, always expecting me to jump through nearly impossible hoops; and then criticizing whatever effort I made.

- Physically and sexually molesting me and escalating the violence as I got older because I was more difficult to control.

- Dismissing me if I dared to voice a negative emotion.

- Threatening me if I tried to break free to be my own person.

My parents *tore at the very glue that made my mind whole* in several ways by:

- Constantly distorting my sense of reality.

- Assaulting my senses, my emotions.

- Binding me with confusion in such a way as to retard my natural growth.

- Torturing my soul by humiliating me.

- Threatening any chance I had for a sound mind.

- And making no attempt to provide me with any sense of security or trust.

I had come to the conclusion that the supreme effort and depth of my therapy was to get me to the point where I would have enough confidence in myself to know that I wouldn't be destroyed. Once I could grasp that understanding, I would be able to comprehend the magnitude of my torture.

I realized the balancing act I had performed throughout my therapy, of experiencing all of the pain but continuing to function, had been a miracle.

This work had also been quite expensive. After seven years in therapy going three times a week and having been hospitalized twice, my medical bills totaled $67,800 of which I had had to pay around $25,000 out-of-pocket. Those expenses would go even higher over the coming years.

The increasingly intense pain of my teenage years was a reflection of my growing awareness of the enormous loss I had suffered. I understood that as a teenager I had had to accept the fact that I was being abused, but also that the primary people connected with me psychologically wanted no bond with me at all other than to satisfy their selfish needs. I had to "connect to myself" to remain sane.

The enormity of the pain had to be buried. By bonding with Maria, I could now re-experience the pain with the knowledge that my spirit was connected to another human being.

If I didn't feel connected to Maria, the trauma and pain had to be self-contained, otherwise I wouldn't have survived mentally. By being connected to her, I would have the flexibility of experiencing the trauma without the fear of losing my mind.

We were making progress.

Chapter 23

Multiple Personalities

My friends were continually amazed. Even with all the work I was doing in therapy, I presented on September 26th our five-year, $1.5 billion strategic plan to top management in New Jersey. It went very well. I gave the same presentation to the Regional Vice President on September 30th in Philadelphia. His reaction was just as receptive.

One night in October, I experienced feelings associated with my abuse, not in a dream or a trance, but consciously around 1:30 in the morning. The option to scream was not there, just as when I grew up. I was experiencing it in "real time." This meant that on an unconscious level, I was gaining strength in experiencing those terrifying emotions straight on.

I was working through those horrible teenage years. I had to keep that in focus because it explained all the fluctuations I had been experiencing between my high anxiety, associated with past memories, and my present-day acknowledgement that I was safe. This was going to be a rough ride, and I dreaded it.

The week before Christmas I had another horrible nightmare in which my parents were trying to kill me, but I was too cunning for them. I had two children with me that I had to protect.

When I woke up, I had the taste and sensation of vomit in my nostrils, however, I knew I was safe and in my own home. Sam could no longer hurt me, that sick and horrible person who abused me during the night under the cover of darkness. Such a coward.

I began to see I needed to live in the present but accept the suffering from the past. I saw why it was important to take care of and pamper myself, especially since I was suffering so much at that time.

I had been worrying about going back to work and feeling trapped again. I feared dealing with Connie's anger. When she was not pleased with some of my work, I saw Carolyn's face screaming at me.

I came to another sickening realization. The look of propriety by Sam, Carolyn, and the other Chambreauxs (that whatever they were doing was perfectly all right; how dare anyone question them) was their secret magic trick to fool the children. If they could fool adults, how could mere children figure it out?

I had survived another year. As I started to tackle the deepest wounds of my teenage years, I was buttressed by my reliable and comforting psychological connection to Maria. I was determined to continue all my good work throughout 1989.

Over the next four months, I attended several high-level meetings and seminars: Sales Management, Line of Business, and Market Planning in New York City, Atlanta, and Philadelphia. These were all helpful in my preparation for another presentation I was to conduct for the Regional Vice President. My confidence on a professional level continued to improve, especially after I received a $3,160 performance award for my work in 1988.

In March 1989 I began looking at another aspect of how my mind had split. I thought about the fact that as horrible as my circumstances were, that was all I had. Sam and Carolyn had locked me up in an "emotional closet." After awhile, my intellect took over and put my sense of sanity into my "secret chamber."

I reminded myself that every time I felt pain, despair, sorrow, anger, loneliness and emptiness; that was the child-Diane trying to make contact with me so that someday the adult-Diane would free her.

In the past, I had chastised her, punished her, stuffed her with food, berated her, split her off, but worst of all, silenced her. I wanted to set her free.

I saw my enormous struggle, though, as that of loving myself versus hating myself. I understood that instead of focusing on my rage, I needed to focus on loving myself enough to get my rage out. There was a big difference between the two.

A few weeks later when I got to work, I found a note from Connie on my desk saying she wasn't pleased with one of my recent assignments.

At that point I began accepting my situation instead of beating myself over the head about it. My situation was different from everyone else's. Not being able to truthfully discuss my diagnoses, I was misunderstood. It was going to be my choice to pursue my total recovery at the expense of my career if need be.

I was no longer ashamed. It was like any other major illness, and it was unrealistic to be expected to perform full-steam ahead in light of my circumstances. I was finally giving myself credit for what I had accomplished. I had no idea, though, that I would be confronted with another enormous shock in dealing with my trauma.

In my next therapy session, Maria very slowly and gently made an announcement. She explained I had multiple personalities. At first I was absolutely shocked. Then the reality dawned on me. This explained everything, how I didn't remember my actions at times, my different handwritings, talking to Maria in a range of different voices, and a lot of what I had been expressing in my writing.

Maria carefully described the function and presentation of dissociation in more detail to me. Everyone dissociates to a degree. There is a continuum. On one end there is the simple daydreaming while driving a car or being totally engrossed in reading a book to the point where you are oblivious of your surroundings. Then you "snap back" becoming aware of your surroundings and are once again "present" with your environment.

On the other end of the continuum, there are a complete split of memories, identities, and behavioral patterns which are unconsciously known to the person. I had been displaying those characteristics for a long time.

Now that we had a specific diagnosis, I felt a sense of relief. I understood why I could never be totally in control. It was because when one or more of my personality states were functioning, I had no way of overriding the system.

From what I could see, I had six personalities/alters:

1. One alter controlled everything, and when she got tired and overwhelmed, she would shut everything down;

2. Two child parts. Both were very active and strong;

3. A part who had unbridled, savage and brutal rage, who was filled with self-hate and punished the adult-Diane instead of externalizing it;

4. Another part who was free, who wanted to have fun and enjoy life; and

5. One alter who could put things in perspective.

I could see that by accepting that reality (Multiple Personality Disorder), I could finally take control of my life. Like Maria said, it was a process of negotiation.

As I moved forward in my therapy, I could appreciate more what was happening. All my personalities were in a tremendous tug-of-war. I felt that when I could master who spoke each day, I would be in a lot more control.

On September 3rd my very angry alter came out.

My name is Mommie Dearest. The full impact of my parents' abuse hit me. I was so traumatized, my mind had split in order to not go completely insane.

I just finished tearing up a magazine and slamming it against the floor. My immediate reaction was to eat something.

I know these are emotions from my past, but they are very real to me. I'm proud of myself. I got it out immediately and did not eat food.

The next day a part of me I named 10-Year-Old wrote:

Run wild, run wild. None of this is real. Everything outside the car is interesting. I don't want to sleep in the front seat with him and her in the backseat.

I am on a dangerous mission. I detect their every move. I'm standing real close to the building. They can't see me. Good.

They are scary monsters.

I am being forced to live a double life by my torturers. No one listens to me. No one believes me.

While traveling by car, I am safe as long as he's driving.

Now the personality I named One Deep Inside, the part that shut down when overwhelmed, wished to say something.

The child-Diane is desperate. She feels so vulnerable. This is a continuous nightmare for her because she has had to experience this almost from the day she was born. She's never known true peace. I need support in calming her down and making her feel loved. She has been traumatized for a long time and sees no end in sight. Her whole experience as a child has been one of suffering, fear, and pain. I need assistance in helping her.

Maria and I were now in my "secret chamber." I was so happy I finally trusted her enough that we could do the most important part of our work. It was scary, but I felt very relieved we had reached that point.

I named an alter Teenager. She had written in the past, but now identified herself as 14-years-old:

I used to be a young girl who loved life but was caged like an animal. They didn't kill me though. I wanted to be free but they wanted to kill me.

I'm 14-years-old. I am always afraid. I don't like living in Jacksonville. Nobody protects me. People at school don't know the hell I live in.

I felt very heavy. I was in a partial trance. The Little Girl, whose writing I now recognized from earlier writings, I named 6-Year-Old:

Maria, don't hurt me or leave me. I am only a little girl and don't know how to escape. I'm not old enough. I know One Deep Inside is letting me write all of this. I feel good about it. She's not putting me in a closet.

I told myself, *it is time to come back to the present now. I feel better.*

By the middle of October, my head was in knots. I was tired of going through all of the turmoil. I said to myself, *acceptance is the key. The more I stop fighting it, the easier it will be for me.*

From that point on, my personalities/alters all wanted to express themselves. They had been split-off for decades. They felt safe enough now to come out. It would take all my willpower, though, to manage my life and struggle through this next phase. My rage about what I had to deal with was almost tangible but, on many levels, totally unbelievable.

With my psychological life in tremendous turmoil, I began to withdraw from many of my friends and was no longer active in recreational activities like skiing, dancing, or anything else I loved. It was all I could do to go to work, therapy, and get home safely at night. It was so upsetting for me not to be able to tell people what I was dealing with. I was sick and tired of not being able to explain my behavior.

I identified another alter I named Survivor. She was the one who got upset every time Maria had to go on vacation or attend a conference. Survivor held all my abuse memories and literally saved me by storing those feelings in my unconscious mind.

All the different parts of me who reacted spontaneously to Maria and wanted to talk exhibited the normal feelings of everyday life. The problem was a piece of each of them was tied to Survivor, like Crazy Glue (appropriately named). As those parts tried to act naturally, part of Survivor got pulled on, and painful memories surfaced.

Anytime Maria left, Survivor got greatly alarmed which caused a chain reaction and all of my real pain was stimulated. Now, once again, it was up to Survivor and One Deep Inside to take care of me.

By December I was getting more in touch with my rage. The memories of Norfolk during my teenage years were continuing to surface. It just kept sinking in that my mind was damaged because I was put through hell by my fucking parents. Here were two people who did whatever they felt like doing, and I was still suffering for it. All of the trauma, depression, and personality disorders were there because of two fucking people. I felt he should be hung up by his balls, and she should be locked up for the rest of her life.

I had to cope every day with a society that stigmatized people with mental illnesses. I felt in shock a lot of the time. I was functioning on autopilot but dissociated whenever something painful was triggered. I was getting very depressed.

(Teenager): My father walked around all the time in his jockey underwear. I hated that. Such brazen power. He was saying: "I can do anything I damn well please" while thinking I bought into his sense of reality.

By the middle of December Connie was always angry at me. She said, "Well, I've just about had it with you, Diane. Andrea (another manager) wanted a number where you could be reached in Maryland, and I had to admit, I didn't even know you were in

Maryland. You should have left a reach number. I don't feel like I need to treat you like you're in kindergarten. We are talking about basic administrative things here."

I said I was sorry, and I would try very hard not let it happen again.

"If it happens again, don't even come in. You're out of here."

I started crying. Someone else needed to talk to her, so she left. As she walked out the door, she said, "Compose yourself before you go back to your desk."

I was livid.

When the Christmas holidays rolled around, I was glad I had a few weeks to regroup. Not being occupied by work, though, only made it worse. I wanted to scream. I was in excruciating pain but didn't know why. I asked inside who wanted to talk.

(Survivor): **I do. They pushed me almost over the edge that Christmas in Norfolk when I had to be carried into the hospital. I couldn't even walk. They both hated me so much they wanted to kill me. I represented all the good in the family and they wanted to destroy me.**

I struggled through another Christmas, but on December 30th as I stepped up on my front porch, I slipped on some ice, grabbed the door handle (which jerked my arm backwards as I fell), and fractured my shoulder in five places. I would be out of work for three weeks. I dreaded calling Connie and telling her of my misfortune.

I said to myself, *no one would ever believe the life I've led. No matter how hard I try, something happens. It is just unbelievable I haven't already killed myself.*

Part 5

**The Final Blow
1990—1992**

Chapter 24

Coping With WWIII

Falling and fracturing my shoulder added another layer of stress to my life. I was out of work for a month. Connie surprisingly visited me at my home with news that our group missed me and wished me a speedy recovery. That was different. Hopefully the tide was turning and this would be a better year.

Maria was going out-of-town again which always created high anxiety for my child parts.

(6-Year-Old): Don't leave me. I'm only a little girl. I'm afraid. You always leave me. I don't know what to do. I don't like anybody. I'm going to hide from everyone. Nobody will be able to find me. I am special. I need to hide.

My defenses were continuing to drop to show what was underneath. The horror filled Little Girl kept coming out.

On March 1st Connie gave me a "Partially Meets Requirements" evaluation for the previous year. Her perception of my performance was skewed. She had refused my request earlier in the year to jointly meet with the EAP psychologist and continued badgering me instead of working with me. I had attended training sessions, conferences and strategic planning meetings and had given two presentations to top management on the state of the market. My presentations were well-received. What I continued having difficulty with were the crunching of financial statements. Having to learn how to use a computer, while being expected to merge and analyze corporate financial documents at the same time, would have been very difficult for anyone. She focused entirely on my weaknesses, not my strengths.

I had learned of my multiple personality diagnosis, and my alters were very near the surface. Under those circumstances, I felt I did extremely well, but without Connie's support or understanding, it made my job even harder.

There was hope however. She said she could see how I was progressing, and she just knew 1990 would be my year.

"We have been trying to put a square peg in a round hole."

"Yes, I am not a number-cruncher," I replied.

She said Al was requesting my help in conducting the market analysis for a new organization he was forming. He was in the process of asking for the funding he would need for me to do the job. Al was now reporting directly to the Executive Vice President. I was very happy.

The middle of March several of my personalities were upset with me.

(Mommie Dearest): I can really tear you apart. Ho Ho Ho. You can't get to me, though, and thus I have power over you. You are slimy. I hate you. Don't open my mouth. You are filthy. You play with yourself and then put it on me.

(Teenager): I don't know what it is like to be held and loved by my parents. I walk around in a prison.

(10-Year-Old): I can scope everybody out in one minute. They think I'm dumb but I'm not. They don't know what I'm thinking. I don't like you. Don't hit me. I'm all mixed up. I don't know what to do. Help me. I like to count the cows as we drive by. Also I read all the billboards. I only sleep when the car is moving. When it stops, I am wide awake. My mother hates me. My father is awful.

It felt strange writing those things, but those were my thoughts.

I am an adult survivor of child sexual abuse, I said to myself. I wish I could have hung that on my office door. My peers didn't have to live with that torment every single day.

I decided to take a chance on Sunday and stood up in front of everyone at church. I made my pronouncement about being a survivor with no stammering. The rest of the day I was doubled up with pain until 11:30 that night. All week I had been overeating.

I kept thinking about all the fun I used to have when all of this was split off. I kept saying to myself, *why can't that happen now?* It was because trauma memories and emotions were ever-present. My head was throbbing. Against my better judgment, I was trying to get to know Mommie Dearest. But who would want to activate a monster?

(Mommie Dearest): My mission is to destroy you. What a sad life. Never underestimate me. If you do, you lose. Sam and Carolyn taught me a lot. They are two sick people, but they trained me well. If I'm not happy, you certainly are not going to be. I am miserable, so I'm going to make your life miserable. Maria knows about me now, and that is dangerous.

I wanted very much to stop hurting.

In my next session with Maria, I learned that Mommie Dearest harbored all the unexpressed rage just as Survivor remembered all the abuse. Mommie Dearest was miserable and tried to make me (the Adult) upset, too, by getting the child parts riled up all the time. Maria asked me to let Mommie Dearest talk on the weekend but to channel it by writing or drawing, not directing it inward.

I was also going to pay close attention to what Mommie Dearest had to say. If I felt myself shutting down, it would be her trying to get my attention or Survivor remembering some abuse.

With WWIII going on in my head, it was hard to function. My brain was now my prison, just like the car was years ago.

By May, 1990 I was very upset. Connie yelled at me all the time, and I was working with my multiple alters. My torso was ensconced in pain. I spent 45 minutes throwing up in the bathroom. I had said before, part of *getting well* was me having to accept that I had multiple personalities just like someone else was diabetic. The problem was that diabetics didn't carry the shame or stigma that people with multiple personalities did, and sufferers could be more public about getting support. In the past, I had to defend myself against my parents' behavior toward me. Now I was doing the same thing but the attacks were coming from within my brain, something very hard to escape or work around.

While sitting outside of Maria's office, I talked to a fellow "multiple" from a former support group. It helped somewhat. She talked about how she could detach from herself and watch each personality. Also, she looked at it as a way of downloading different roles and tasks. For example, she said, "Jennifer does all my lectures, another personality does such and such, and I just step back and watch them perform."

By mid-year, my physical pains were becoming much more severe. Even though I kept trying to keep quiet at work about how sick I was, the pain was excruciating. I had to silently take care of myself.

As usual, support at church wasn't forthcoming. I told one woman my pain and vomiting was so bad the weekend before, I had to go to the emergency room. She said, "That's all in the past."

I felt like screaming at her. The minister asked, "Would you like to be cured of that? It will only take fifteen seconds with prayer."

It was all I could do not to scream my head off at him, too, and not tell him to go fuck himself. I was drinking one Diet Coke after another and eating chocolate. That meant my whole system was stirred up a lot.

The next day, all the top managers had been in a high-level meeting for two days. Connie informed me the consultants leading the meeting said the "Strategic Directions" booklet everyone was using was excellent. I smiled internally knowing that I had written that booklet.

I began to understand that I associated *feeling* the trauma with *being* abused. That was what I had to separate in my mind. That was because as my feelings associated with my trauma (anger, pain, resentment, jealousy, etc.) came up, when I was a little girl and then grew into a teenager, I was being abused (or made to feel I was at fault); so feeling those feelings always meant abuse. Feeling those traumatized feelings today did not mean that I should hurt myself. It meant I needed support as I worked through them and expressed them constructively.

My vomiting was accelerating. Around 5:00 AM Saturday morning on July 7th I drove myself to the emergency room. I had a temperature of 101, was still vomiting and in a lot of pain. I was admitted to the hospital for the entire weekend.

My internist told me if I had another attack to go straight to the hospital. On July 16th I was in severe pain and vomiting again, so I drove myself to Georgetown University Hospital. I had emergency surgery during which they made a 9" abdominal incision and removed my gall bladder. I was in the hospital for two weeks.

After I was released from the hospital, I stayed with Elizabeth for a week and then went home. I had called Connie to let her know what had happened, and she was furious with me for missing work. I tried to explain that I didn't elect to have major surgery, but she completely ignored the facts and took it personally. She didn't call or visit me the entire six weeks I was out. My surgeon said I could return to work on a half-day basis on August 27th and full-time on September 4th. In the meantime, I focused on recovering from my physical wounds and tried to stabilize mentally.

In my inbox when I went back to work was a Company bulletin from Human Resources. It stated:

The Americans with Disabilities Act (ADA) was signed into law on July 26, 1990 by the President of the United States. Every Company employee who makes personnel decisions must understand that discrimination on the basis of disability or because a person requires a reasonable accommodation will not be permitted. This has always been our Company's position.

Around the same time this bulletin came out, a Virginia lawyer, Rena Anderson, wrote an article in the *Washington Post* about the state extending the statute of limitations on lawsuits pertaining to child abuse. When I read this, I decided to investigate to see if this new law could help me. In doing so, I entered another painful, stressful time in my life.

After only being back at work for a few weeks, I was already filled with rage. On my way home, I let go of the wheel of my car as I was leaving the toll booth. I did a 180° turn but was blessed that no cars were coming.

When I got home, I felt like I was going berserk. I listened as Mommie Dearest told me how angry she was at herself for beating up on the rest of us on the inside. The good news was that she was beginning to turn her perceptions around.

The following Sunday the minister said to me, "I'm sure if you took that hour you are with your doctor and spent it praying to God for 60 days, you would be cured." I felt like I was cracking up.

That week Connie said, "Maybe you might want to talk to your marketing friends in our other division."

"What are you saying? Are you saying I don't have a job?"

"No, I'm not saying that. I know you are not in the right job, but there is no marketing job here for you."

"I'll do the best I can."

I felt myself breaking down again. It was all I can do to sit at my desk. I hated working there, and my mind was nearing a state of oblivion.

Since Connie didn't appreciate my marketing or strategic planning abilities, and was basing my performance on a job for which I was poorly trained, I decided I would talk to Daryl, a Marketing Manager, to see if I could firm up a new job assignment. He had the only marketing group on our team. If I were able to transfer to his group, I would feel more secure and stronger. I didn't need this shit, but once again, no matter how traumatic my experiences were, I managed to hold on.

As Christmas approached, I went into my yearly doldrums. For the first time, 12-Year-Old identified herself. She revealed that she was the first alter who had started journaling.

> I am sick to my stomach. Someone is trying to get me.

> I don't want her to hurt me anymore. She [Carolyn] is very sneaky. She acts like she doesn't do anything wrong. But she does. She's just as bad as he is.

More specific images were coming up about my mother, but I couldn't make them out clearly. I experienced them as repulsive and felt like I was in shock.

Out of the blue, I received a Christmas card from Carolyn. I was filled with rage because I wanted her to leave me alone. This had been another horribly stressful year for me. My job performance was rated *Partially Met* again, and my parents were trying to get in touch with me. I didn't know how much more I could stand.

Chapter 25

Confronting Discrimination and Denial

As I started another new year, I realized I had been trying to erase or forget my past, but that would never happen. I thought since I had totally separated from my family I would be in a position where I wouldn't be affected by them anymore. I was wrong. I would be linked to them for the rest of my life.

I was very interested in an upper-level management notice I had recently received. The Company's <u>Affirmative Action Program for Individuals with Disabilities Bulletin</u> said:

> No individual will be unlawfully discriminated against because of a physical or mental disability. Our Company's policy is to prohibit unlawful discrimination or harassment against an employee because of a physical or mental disability, and make reasonable accommodations to the physical and mental limitations of otherwise qualified employees or applicants with disabilities. All employees and applicants for employment are informed of their right to voluntarily self-identify if they believe themselves to be disabled. All employees are informed no individual will be intimidated, threatened, coerced, or discriminated against by the Company for filing a complaint.

Reading this gave me some comfort that at least the legal department was informing top management of its responsibilities to people with mental disabilities.

By the end of January 1991, my alters were coming out strong.

(Teenager): I hate being molested. He does it all the time. She looks at me like I'm disgusting and I'm not. I'm a nice person. I'm afraid. I'm afraid because they both hurt me. I don't know how to get away from them.

After I wrote that, I understood why I resisted so strongly when people tried to control me. I said to myself, *they made me do things I didn't want to do.* That explained it all.

I didn't know how I got home from work the next day. My mouth was hanging open the whole time and the lower back part of my head had a lot of pressure. Once home, I sat down with my journal.

(6-Year-Old): Maria won't hurt me. I am very little. She helps me. She believes me.

(10-Year-Old): I am very sad. My life is hell.

On Valentine's Day I received another card from Carolyn. I thought to myself, *these people are insane. They must want something. It pisses me off.*

There was a time when I would have run to her side and would have probably wanted to protect her like I did with Joanne. I got a dry run with Joanne, though, and as bad as it was, I was glad I now knew what to expect. My defenses were not down as they had been with Joanne. I had grown a lot since then.

After contacting Rena Anderson about the new law in Virginia that provided a one-year window for survivors to sue their perpetrator(s) no matter how old the case, she agreed to represent me in a lawsuit against Sam. I was to be one of her trial cases that year. I immediately mailed a card to my parents.

Even with that bit of encouraging news, my driving was becoming more dangerous. When going home, I thought about driving into the pylons on the Cabin John Bridge. I was going out of my fucking mind. Part of the problem was I was switching between personalities almost instantaneously which gave me no room to think. I was becoming very worried.

On February 27, 1991, Connie wrote a memo stating:

Since January 1, 1984, Ms. Champé has demonstrated she has good skills in conducting market research. She has been able to obtain strategic marketing plans from our customer that no one else has been able to obtain. Her ability to "dig in" and locate market research information has allowed her to successfully prepare position papers for use by our Team. A new trial position within our organization is being established with a focus on market intelligence functions. If Ms. Champé's performance is appraised Partially Met or Unsatisfactory, though, at the end of 1991, disciplinary action will be taken and could include demotion or termination.

Along with my work situation, I was sick and tired of having to work through the denial of the people at church. They felt by "surrendering to Christ and earnestly praying all would be taken care of." I was sick of being put in the position of having to defend why I was in therapy. At a very deep level, however, I recognized I was taking control of my life. I felt hopeful. Once again, that glimmer of optimism was short-lived.

I received a card dated March 13th from Sam and Carolyn.

We were so happy to receive your card. I am just sending a short note as I want you to know we love you and miss you. Would like to hear from you telling us how you are doing and how you are getting along.

Love,

Daddy and Mama

The following Sunday I didn't go to Sunday school but got there about five minutes before church services started.

The minister said, "We've missed you."

"I've been through hell and have been dealing with a lot."

"You're keeping your eyes on the Lord, aren't you? You can listen to someone else (Maria) and be drawn away, but the Lord will be there."

I felt like hitting him and walking out, but I just went to my seat. During his sermon he said, "If you didn't come for God's blessing, you ought not to be here. Don't let the enemy win or disrupt this service. You know who you are."

I wanted to throw up.

In the past he had said to me, "Whenever those other personalities come out or memories come up, give the devil a black eye and plead the blood of Jesus." That was their answer for everything. They didn't want to understand. They didn't listen.

I was tired of not being heard. The pressure to conform to their way of worship was enormous. Their mentality was really bringing up how the Church had made such an imprint on me when growing up.

Pappa was the minister, and we were all watched closely. The idea was if you didn't conform, "you wouldn't receive Christ's blessings and would be led by the devil."

Pretty strong stuff for a child. I decided I was not going back to that church. I saw that it was still the same as it was 40 years ago. It was almost like a cult. It was still the same old shit, and I couldn't stomach it anymore.

I also received a letter from Rena dated March 27th.

The letter you sent me from your father dated July 4, 1961 is superb evidence in this case. The attitude he exhibits towards you is certainly the type of domineering and controlling personality which is so often characteristic of an abuser. The case is proceeding very well.

On April 17th I sent Sam and Carolyn a card stating:

"It has been a long time since we've had contact, and I have to take it very slow."

It was nauseating for me to write my parents, but I was trying to lull them into a false sense of security. I wanted them to give me information for a lawsuit.

On April 20th an unnamed alter who had written before wrote:

> I asked myself why I felt self-destructive when growing up. I was treated as if I were the one causing the pain of their marriage. I never felt I belonged. Thus, I felt I deserved the pain. All this time, there has been this deep, internal struggle for the truth. That search for truth has driven the whole process.

I named this part Perspective Person.

The younger parts of me felt like I was doing something wrong by fooling Sam and Carolyn, pretending I cared about them to get something in writing so I could sue them. They didn't want to do anything wrong for which they would be punished. I needed to explain to my child parts I wasn't doing anything that would put them in danger. Rather, their fear was related to how Sam and Carolyn had made them feel in the past. I further explained that when people hurt other people, especially those who are helpless, and then make them keep quiet under the threat of more violence, they are people who deserve whatever the criminal justice system can impose upon them.

My mind was exploding. I needed to take it slow.

Chapter 26

Harassment

My efforts at gaining support from Connie were not working. She and I reviewed my major project, but she said it needed to be more concise. I explained I was preparing an Executive Overview for each section in the document.

She said, "How are you doing?"

"Fine."

"Are you still on your diet?"

I said I was no longer on Slim Fast but was eating correctly and smaller meals.

"Are you exercising?"

"Yes, in fact I am walking at lunchtime for about a mile two times a week."

"You should do that every day."

"Yes, I know that."

"Is your house still up for sale?" I had decided to leave old memories behind and buy a new home.

"Yes."

"I would wait to buy a new one around here. You could end up somewhere else."

I said I could not move to another city. She said I may not have a choice. I was not going to move to another city. It would create a hardship for my therapy.

She mentioned a supervisor's name in another city and said I might want to consider working in customer service.

Connie said people have perceptions about people based on outward appearances. "I see the days you come in when you haven't washed your hair or aren't wearing makeup. Some people do sloppy jobs but look great whereas others can do a terrific job, but looking at outward appearances, project a negative image."

I told her I understood.

What I said to myself was, *she wants me to do a good job and physically look polished so she can justify passing me off. If I have to take that job, I will be totally humiliated. Me? Go back to being a service rep? I don't think so.*

The more I thought about what Connie said, the madder I got. There was nothing wrong with my work, and now she was focusing on my physical appearance. I was not going to work in another city.

I made an appointment with Dr. Albertson and was close to talking to an attorney.

I called Patricia. She said instead of focusing on what I was losing at work such as my job level, prestige, etc., to focus on how my personal priorities had changed during this part of my life. "Think about your desires to help child abuse survivors by writing, your artwork and speaking out. What you are doing is a lot more courageous than anything you would ever do for the Company. The Company is a job."

I believed I was being railroaded and felt suicidal. Connie just wouldn't let up. She was driving me insane. I could hear a voice saying, *time to split off.* Connie was in for the kill. This was harassment.

When I reviewed my work with Connie on the Small Business Market Analysis project, a staffer, Jennifer, from another office joined us. Jennifer started firing questions at me one after another as she kept looking past me at Connie. After I shared what I had prepared, Jennifer shoved the binder on the table and said, "No one's going to read that."

I met with the EEO Manager the next day and thought it went well. We talked for over an hour and a half, and I explained in detail how I had been treated. I made the point that it was a health problem whether Connie wanted to believe it or not, and that Connie refused to contact or work with Dr. Albertson.

After I stepped through all my notes with him, I said I wanted the hostility and harassment to stop, to be treated fairly, to have Connie sit down with Dr. Albertson and me, and for her to help me find a job in this area. He said she certainly was not saying the things a supervisor should be saying, and "your requests are entirely reasonable."

Things were looking up. The EEO Manager had confirmed my suspicions that Connie's behavior was way out of line, Dr. Albertson was in my corner, and I was communicating with Sam and Carolyn with the hope of getting them to say something incriminating in writing. I was starting to feel a little more in control, and as always, relied heavily on Maria and my friends to get me through my daily struggles.

I had had enough.

I made an appointment to meet with Jack, the Regional Vice President. On June 17th in a steady, clear voice I told him about the major difficulties I had been having working for Ms. Brown. Then I handed him my bombshell, an EEO Filing. He was surprised but said he would review its contents and get back to me. After shaking hands, I slowly walked back to my desk.

His concern was whether or not I could competently perform my job as there were scarce resources. I said if he put me into a market research/sales job or strategic planning position, and there were discussions with Dr. Albertson on how to best accommodate my handicap, then I would perform my job very well.

Part of me was saying internally, *at least, it is all out on the table. There was nothing wrong with saying I was diagnosed with PTSD and depression. What had happened to me wasn't my fault, but I was trying to work through it.*

A new letter arrived from Sam.

June 20, 1991

Diane,

We are very hopeful we can keep in touch with you. There are some things that are the absolute truth. We have never stopped loving you. We have never been unconcerned about your well-being. If we are overly cautious or solicitous, forgive us. It's only because we miss you so much.

Daddy

While I was struggling on a very personal private front, the matter of child sexual abuse and repressed memories was gathering massive attention in the media. Unfortunately, the coverage wasn't very appealing. In fact, trying to recover was difficult enough without "experts" spreading lies about Multiple Personality Disorder.

On September 25th in the *Washington Post*, there was a "Letter to the Editor" written by Charles Whitfield, an expert in the field of sexual abuse. His letter was in response to an article written by Joel Achenbach that had been published earlier in the week. Dr. Whitfield wrote:

Joel Achenbach's "Why Things Are" column on Multiple Personality Disorder (MPD) quotes two people—Richard Ofshe and Paul McHugh—who speak against the reality of MPD as a diagnosis [Style Plus, Sept. 22]. The fact is neither [Ofshe or McHugh] has published any research on MPD, and both are charter board members of the False Memory Syndrome Foundation, which sponsors the denial of both accused and convicted child molesters.

What they don't talk about is that what is actually a nonentity is "false memory syndrome" (FMS), which they so passionately advocate and defend. There are no published case histories in any peer-reviewed clinical or scientific journals. FMS is their creation.

False allegations of child sexual abuse are few. False denials are the norm. Abusers, whom McHugh and Ofshe support, have always bullied their victims into silence. FMS is just another weapon, as are their attacks on MPD.

Dr. Whitfield's strong rebuke about professionals denying this disorder confirmed the very real multiple personalities that were competing, cooperating, agreeing and fighting within my mind.

In my journal I talked about how my multiple personalities existed because of my inability to tolerate their feelings in a conscious state. They spoke to Maria directly from an altered state that each one represented. My goal was the integration of all of them.

My overeating and compulsions were the ways I used to reject experiencing my uncomfortable feelings in the present. I was functioning the best I could, though, while juggling therapy and work.

Connie was forced to set up a meeting with me and Dr. Albertson. My impression of the meeting was that she was there to find out where I was coming from as it related to what I had written in my EEO Filing and to defend herself. I thought she still didn't have the foggiest idea how to work with me.

In the meeting Dr. Albertson explained that when I saw Connie looking angrily at me, I would just withdraw. Connie said, "So Diane just brings it all on herself when she sees me busy. Can't she just say okay, let's not feel this way?"

I said, "No, because it is not something I can control. I know what I must do to take care of myself once that happens, but no, I can't control it."

Dr. Albertson made it very clear to Connie that even though I processed information slower, I was an overachiever and compensated by working late at the office and long hours on the weekends. She told her I had left messages many times and told her to call me at the office during those off times.

Dr. Albertson explained I was getting the best care I possibly could because my psychologist was the best in the area and a national expert.

The whole discussion was about defending her actions or trying to discredit me. If I had been in her shoes, I would have made it clear I was sorry my behavior had been so harmful. I would have asked more about PTSD and how my behavior could be changed. But she didn't.

On July 24th about five and a half weeks after my initial meeting with Jack, I requested another meeting with him. I stated: "Since our meeting on June 17th, very little has changed; it has actually gotten worse, so much so that a major effort on my part is necessary to complete my assigned projects. In my EEO Filing, I had asked for the harassment and hostility to stop, the adverse memos to stop, Ms. Brown to meet with me and Dr. Albertson to determine how best to supervise me, and Ms. Brown to work with me proactively in finding me a job in this area."

"Ms. Brown has curtailed the number of times we have interacted, however, the few times we have met, our discussions have focused on what I wrote in my EEO filing, and Ms. Brown has not changed her managerial style. It has gotten to the point where interacting with her is psychologically harmful to me and counterproductive."

"She is not open to a discussion of the real reasons behind my performance (how her managerial style is counterproductive to an incest survivor diagnosed with PTSD) just as she is currently demonstrating that."

Jack ended the meeting by saying, "I think a lot of Connie, and you need to perform on the job."

On Monday July 22nd, Connie left a message for me to see her. After I sat down, she pulled out her documentation of my work. I said to her twice, "I cannot deal with that now." I also told her that I could not interact with her anymore that week if she wanted me to finish my projects on time.

As she put her papers away, she said, "This is a done deal anyway" (whatever that meant).

I had high hopes that Jack, as the Regional Vice President, would be more decisive and stop the harassment. That wasn't going to be the case.

Chapter 27

Total Injustice

I continued my correspondence with my parents to keep the hope of my lawsuit alive. I sent them a card on July 25th stating: *It has been so long. I don't know where to start. Why don't you let me know things in general about how you're doing?* Shortly afterward, I received a letter from Sam dated August 4th.

> *As your mother said, I have had a lot of surgery in the past few years. I had to quit my regular job after open-heart surgery, so now both of us are retired. Since that surgery, I have had five aneurisms repaired and two other operations on my major arteries. I think I am now a bionic man.*
>
> *Just to hear from you and to know that you are well is good for us. The void of the past years hurts and I hope it never comes to that again. You are our firstborn and we love you. If you have anything specific that you would like to hear from us, let us know. We will do our best to answer.*

Carolyn wrote a letter as well. It was light and superficial. She talked about what they were doing in their home, where she used to work, and how much she wanted to hear from me. As expected, there was no substance at all. She went on to say how she loved her dogs and how much they were spoiled. I wanted to throw up. I wasn't treated that good.

I wanted to tell them I had been having brain surgery over the last nine and a half years. These were the same two people who had physically, emotionally and sexually abused me the first 21 years of my life. I wanted them both to be criminally charged for what they had done to me, and I wanted every dime they had.

My reply to Carolyn included these statements: *Even though it was at my request, it's been 20 years since we've had contact, and it hasn't been easy. How were you able to cope with that? I like writing because it gives us an avenue to understand each other better.* I also inquired about Ray and Joanne.

In a separate letter to Sam I said, *By writing, I'm hoping we can rebuild our relationship. You wrote in your February 1980 letter that you wanted to ask forgiveness. I think I can work on that now, so tell me what you can, and we can go from there.*

Carolyn responded on October 2nd saying, *Your daddy had a stroke on Sunday which left his mouth and left side numb, but he is okay from that now. He has to take it easy.*

On October 4th I wrote another memo to Jack hoping for a reply about my EEO Filing. I was getting very impatient and stated:

> *I have reviewed Ms. Brown's documentation concerning my performance this year. What is absent, however, is any mention of my primary contention, namely how her managerial style detracted from my productivity.*

> *As an adult survivor of child sexual abuse diagnosed with acute PTSD, it is practically impossible for me many times to even concentrate. Ms. Brown's style of management was hostile, defensive, contradictory, and impatient. She was irritated by my presence.*

> *Ms. Brown's caustic attitude and behavior toward me did not change until the first week in August, so there should be no surprise that my performance suffered this year. She obviously has been coached because her demeanor has changed considerably. She is no longer hostile or harassing in her remarks or behavior.*

I really didn't give a fuck what Jack thought. That was why there were laws on the books, to stop this kind of discrimination. The only thing he understood was "EEO." I was tired of trying to be logical with these people.

On October 10th I requested a meeting with Jack for an update since I hadn't received any response to my memo. During that meeting, I made it clear that I needed resolution about my job situation. His replies were non-committal. He kept saying, "We haven't made a decision yet."

Unsatisfied I nudged, "I am making an assumption I will be working for another manager. The relationship between Connie and me is not good. There have been too many things she has said to me that were uncaring and hostile that made it very difficult to work for her."

"Well, the Company's position is that you are not producing."

"I cannot function in a hostile environment." I was desperately trying to remain calm.

"You can talk about these issues, but the bottom line is you need to perform on the job."

"I agree with you 100 percent. But I cannot function in a hostile environment. I need for us to work through the medical department. Let me give you an example. After trying to explain to Connie one more time what I'm dealing with, she walked out her office door with people walking by, raised her hands over her head and said, "Incest! Child Molestation! AAAGGHHH!"

After a brief moment of silence Jack said, "The bottom line is you need to be productive on a Company job, and we don't know how to solve that."

"Give me a supervisor whose managerial style is open and compassionate and who'll work with the medical department."

"I need to talk to Connie. I'll get back to you."

Throughout the week, I found myself playing the conversation over and over in my head. I was trying to figure out how to convince Jack that I really did want to perform well for the Company. I was not some derelict employee. I was a topnotch executive having some extremely difficult personal problems. I wasn't asking for less work. I needed my manager to get off my back. The following week, I resolved to write another memo to Jack.

In light of my EEO complaint, I had hoped Ms. Brown would behave towards me in a more professional manner. She did, but only for a short period of time (and seemingly after some obvious management coaching). I want to restate that I am capable of being a productive employee. Ms. Brown's adversarial managerial style does me harm by exacerbating some of my Posttraumatic Stress symptoms which directly interfere with my functioning.

I feel I can no longer tolerate the psychological damage she continues to perpetuate by the way she interacts with me. Her "documentation" obscures her behavior with me, and I strongly challenge its accuracy. Accordingly, I ask you to reassign me to another supervisor as I will no longer interact with Ms. Brown.

A few days later, I received a letter from Carolyn saying,

Joanne has remarried [husband #5]. She has a good man and we like him a lot. Ray has remarried. He changed his name and lives out west. He lived here awhile after he retired out of the Navy. He doesn't write or call. I don't know what his problem is, but it is nothing we have done. You asked how I coped with years of no contact. It wasn't easy. The past is past. We can't go back. All I have is today.

I didn't know how much more of this I could take. They still acted like nothing at all had happened in the past, and it all should be swept under the rug.

I wasn't doing very well. I wished Munder was around. She always knew what to say or do to make me feel better. I talked to Sally (Munder's sister), and she told me Trinh had remarried and was living in Japan. She also said my parents were raising the two kids.

I couldn't believe what I was hearing. She said Ray wouldn't let them out of the country as they were American citizens. She confirmed that Ray was living in Snakeville, according to her daughter as of two years ago. Living with my parents was bad enough, but if Leslie and Eric were with Ray, that was criminal.

I was in shock.

All of my personalities were really shook up.

(Teenager): I am livid. No young children should be around any of them. That is why Ray has been quiet because he has his kids back. I cannot believe what Trinh did. She is worse than my mother. She not only abandoned Leslie and Eric, she left the country entirely. Boy, are their heads screwed up now. I am in deep shock and pain.

(One Deep Inside): **Teenager and all the children are terrified. Six-Year-Old is not quite sure what is going on but sees how upset everyone else is. My goal for now is to comfort my child parts. Survivor gives me a lot of help as we went through all of our abuse together.**

I took the weekend to regroup because I had to face my troubles at work. On Monday morning, I called Bill Jackson, the EEO Manager, and asked what a typical period of time was for an EEO Filing because it had been four months.

"Well, there is no average time."

"What is the next step I need to take?"

"What do you mean the next step?"

"What is the next step?"

"You are dealing with the Regional Vice President. I don't know who his boss is."

They had not initiated any discussions about my complaint. I had to initiate everything myself, including following up with Bill in EEO, who I thought was my advocate.

It appeared to me the Company had no intention of complying or responding to my complaint. The Regional Vice President had Connie documenting everything. She was not assigning me any work. I was getting the impression that they were planning to fire me for non-performance.

I had been through so much in my life; I was not going to let these uncaring people get the best of me. Free Person, a new alter, helped me. She was full of life. She made sure I had down-time with my friends. She liked to laugh and have fun. She saw the good things in life. Somehow her spirit must have been a catalyst to keep me in the fight.

I shouldn't have had to go through this needless aggravation. I had legitimate diagnoses, and they were still ignoring the medical department's recommendations. If they wouldn't work with me, I would sue them. I knew I had to keep fighting for my job. They would not win.

Even my friends kept telling me I was doing the right things. But, some days, I wanted to run and hide. It was difficult enough just to keep managing my symptoms and alters and interacting with my family without having to deal with the extra stressors of work.

On November 1st I was moved to a new manager, Daryl Strickland, where I could use my strategic planning and marketing skills. He was very cordial and welcomed me into his group.

Things were really looking up. I finally had a manager who appeared to be sensitive and understanding. I was also back in a marketing position, one in which I knew I would excel. I was still anxious about my long-term stability with the Company. After all, my diagnoses came along with me to the new position. I knew the Company would continue to watch me like a hawk. And I still had the issues surrounding Sam and Carolyn.

About four months prior to my move to working for Daryl, I had contacted the Equal Employment Opportunity Commission in Washington, D.C., wanting to know their thoughts on how I was being mistreated. I finally received a reply. They indicated I had a pretty strong case against my employer. I also followed their suggestion to file a complaint with the Department of Labor (DOL). I decided that in my complaint to DOL I would illustrate how I had coincidentally been transferred to a new supervisor after I had contacted Bill, the Company's EEO Coordinator. I notified Bill that it had been <u>143 days</u> since I had filed my EEO complaint with no resolution in sight. I wanted to speak to Jack's boss. That is when I was moved to another manager. My letter to the DOL also outlined a conversation I had had with the Regional Vice President several months ago.

I had said to Jack, "You cannot divorce the medical. In the very first or second paragraph of my EEO Filing, I said I felt like I am being discriminated against because of my handicap." I asked him what the Company medical department told him.

"I have never talked to the medical department," he replied.

Astonishingly I asked, "You never talked to medical?"

"No."

"Why not?"

"I feel I have honored your request."

"Everyone wants to shove it under the rug, and I don't know why. You're going to put me in another job, assign me to another supervisor, and as problems arise (due to my medical handicap), you're going to tell me, 'You still can't perform.' You cannot divorce the medical from my work performance. I have legitimate diagnoses that aren't being addressed."

"Well, I'm telling you what I expect."

"I'm not closing my EEO Filing until my medical problems are addressed."

"You can do what you want with your EEO Filing," he replied.

My complaint to DOL also included a copy of my EEO Filing with the Company. At this point, I was ready to pursue legal action. I felt entitled to compensation for the pain and suffering I had had to deal with because of the Company's managerial negligence and insensitivity. I was ready to take the next step and asked for DOL's assistance.

In the meantime, I worked hard at my new assignment. I felt good about working for Daryl, but I still didn't trust the Company. Having communicated with the Department of Labor gave me some sense of confidence I had other people looking at the situation. I focused on doing the best job I could in the six month trial I was allotted.

Around Thanksgiving, I received a letter from Sam.

November 25, 1991

Dear Diane,

You have a good job with a blue-chip company. I have always thought you would succeed in anything you started out to do. That trait was obvious when you were still in your teens. I hope you will continue to enjoy your assignment.

We have a spiritual program that we live by. My parents were religious fanatics and forced their conceptions of God down our throats. For the past 18 years, I have changed my idea about God and now I am at peace with Him.

About 11 years ago, I asked your forgiveness for the harm I had caused you. All I ask is do what you can, and I will continue to do what I can to make amends by living the concepts of my program. There is one thing I can state absolutely, you are not to blame. I bear the responsibility.

Love,

Daddy

In Carolyn's letter, as usual, she wrote about Sam's medical problems. She also added,

I didn't mean for my letter to sound like I didn't want to talk about the past. I meant I didn't want to live in the past. I live a spiritual program and have learned we don't forget the past, but we don't dwell on it either. I try to do the best I can today. We don't drink or party and haven't in almost 18 years.

The middle of December, Daryl wrote that I had accomplished a lot. He made an appointment to meet with Maria and me to see how he could support me on the job. What a change.

With the work situation slowly improving, I was ready to move forward. I needed to end all contact with my parents. Communication with them was literally making me sick. It was time to provoke admissions of their behavior.

> *Daddy,*
>
> *When you said, "You are not to blame. I bear the responsibility," were you referring to the fact that you drank too much? were suicidal? What I remember is that in Jacksonville in 1961, you were in command of an oceangoing tug and that our standard of living finally started to improve.*
>
> *In 1962-63 we lived in Charleston, S.C., where you were the security officer for the base and we lived in a big house. Things got pretty stable until we moved to Norfolk.*
>
> *From 1963-1966 while living in Norfolk, I was so confused. I thought you were doing so well in your career. You were in command of an LST. What happened? I remember a lot of parties and drinking.*
>
> *Both of you talked about forgiveness. That is something I would like to do, but I need more discussion about what happened and why. I need to understand why I was treated the way I was because I certainly didn't deserve it.*
>
> *Diane*

By the second week in 1992 I was on a roll. I didn't have a manager looking over my shoulder making snide remarks every week. More importantly, I was working for someone who thoroughly understood marketing and could recognize the contribution I was making. It was a time for moving forward in my life. I finally felt some level of security and confidence.

It had almost been a month since I had written my parents, and I was concerned I wouldn't be able to get incriminating evidence in writing from them. Any direct questions about their past behavior were taboo. That was a big guarded secret. They asked for forgiveness, again being superficial. They didn't dare scratch the surface.

On January 28th Daryl wrote:

> *Since our last review on December 17, 1991, Diane has accomplished as required the work identified in our agreed upon activity timeline. During the last month I have seen a marked change in Diane's attitude and confidence level. As she has gotten more into her "element" in working with customers, she has become enthused, and, as a result, increasingly effective in doing her job.*

Not only had I received two positive reviews from my new boss, but a client I had been working with for four months officially requested my assistance in implementing our product into their pilot program. The last sentence of their memorandum concluded "We appreciate all the support you can provide us in accomplishing this and look forward to working with you to make this a reality."

I was so proud of myself. I was back doing what I knew best, strategic planning and marketing, and within just four months, starting from scratch, I had secured a commitment from our client to trial our new products.

Daryl's performance review of my work on February 28, 1992, contained this excerpt:

> *After four months of working in the area of Marketing, Diane has made significant progress in satisfactorily meeting all the milestones established. I have continued to see her effectiveness and confidence increase with each accomplishment. Her knowledge and experience in marketing is evident in her approach to the customer and this project.*

March 1st I received a $3,614 performance award! Maybe my problems at work really were becoming a thing of the past. I started to feel hopeful again.

I received a letter from Jack dated March 5, 1992, stating:

I regret to inform you that you have been identified as an employee who is at risk of involuntary separation from the Company. Unless you are notified otherwise or unless you are reassigned to another position within our Company, your last day of employment will be May 4, 1992.

I immediately contacted attorneys and delivered a package containing the EEO Filing and all my documentation.

Once again, no matter how hard I worked, I ended up getting screwed. Like Connie had said, this was a done deal long before I was granted an accommodation for my disability. My entire world was now starting to totally fall apart.

On March 26th I signed a Retainer Agreement with an attorney, Mr. Kilmont, to represent me in a lawsuit against the Company. In the meantime my alters were torn apart.

(10-Year-Old): I didn't do anything wrong and I am not a bad girl. I am smart.

(Teenager): I haven't slept well over the last two weeks. It is all beginning to be real again. I don't want to be hurt anymore. Reporter, a new personality, is remembering things that are painful.

In the process of finding another job, I asked my co-workers to write letters I could submit with my application to other departments. All the letters were favorable.

One of the letters stated:

In my capacity as a Senior Product Planner, I have worked with Diane Champé from approximately November 1991 through March 1992. During that time, she has impressed me with her ability to focus on (and make sense of) the task at hand, no matter how complex or unfamiliar to her. The insights she gained were creatively developed into an action plan that could be a model for any business looking to enter new markets or generate revenue in current ones.

A letter from a Senior Corporate Product Training Specialist avowed:

I have had the opportunity and the pleasure of working with Diane Champé since last year. She demonstrated to me she is a high-energy, positive, and forward-thinking professional, with special strengths in Market Research, Sales, and Strategic Planning. I would gladly work side-by-side with her on any project because I know it would be a success.

And my current manager, Daryl, acknowledged:

Diane Champé has worked in my organization for the last six months. During that time, she has demonstrated knowledge in the marketing area as well as skills in researching, planning and implementing projects. Based on her performance over the last six months, my opinion is that Diane could handle any marketing/sales position at a minimum performance level of Fully Meets. My rating of Diane to date in 1992 is a Firm Fully Meets Requirements.

In the midst of trying to salvage my job, I kept trying to get information out of my parents. Clearly this was going to be a greater challenge than I was prepared for. On April 7th I wrote,

Daddy, you said you and Mama are walking on eggshells and worrying you'll say something that is too direct or upsetting enough to me to break off our communication. It's the other way around. I want to know more and for you to respond directly to my questions. That would not cause me to stop writing.

We need to have more correspondence about the past and present and about family members so I can start to get reconnected. I can tell you this very clearly: I want a relationship but you need to help me with information if we are going to have one. The only reason I will stop writing you is if you won't answer my questions, help me understand what happened, and ask me about my life. We have a lot of time to make up for. I hope you can help me and decide to be more open.

If I didn't find another job and the Company fired me, they were going to have a tremendous fight on their hands. I said to my friends, "They are messing with the wrong cookie."

On April 14th my attorney wrote a letter to the President of my division stating:

> This law firm represents Ms. E. Diane Champé, who is a management employee. Ms. Champé has been notified she will be terminated on May 4, 1992 as a result of the downsizing that is taking place in her office.
>
> This letter is to inform you it is our strong conviction Ms. Champé has been scheduled for termination as the result of unlawful handicap discrimination.
>
> Ms. Champé has the longest tenure with the Company of all the employees in her job category. Her most recent performance review, from a supervisor who is affording Ms. Champé the accommodation she requested, confirms that she fully meets the requirements of her job.

The Company's Attorney responded April 20th stating:

> It is indeed unfortunate, but business conditions sometimes require the reduction of the employee work force and the resulting termination of otherwise perfectly satisfactory employees. If any change in her status should be warranted, she will be advised by her management.

On May 4, 1992, a very cold, dark and rainy day, I was told to pack up my belongings, turn in my Company pass and leave. When I walked out the door, I was in shock. I couldn't believe this was happening to me. I walked out the door with no severance pay and no benefits. I had worked for the Company since I was 17-years-old. I was a devoted, loyal employee for 28 years, and now I had nothing.

I said to myself, *now the gloves come off.* There was no way they were going to get away with this. I felt I had been screwed for the very last time. I wrote in my journal:

> *May 10, 1992*
>
> *I wish I were dead. I don't feel I have a life anymore. I feel like I've lost my way somehow and can't get it back. I've had to fight for my rights all my life. And for what?*
>
> *I don't know what to do anymore.*

Part 6

Hitting Rock Bottom
1993—1995

Chapter 28

Hopes Crushed

I didn't know what I was going to do with the rest of my life. One avenue I was going to continue to pursue was the prosecution of Sam and Carolyn. They were acting and saying the same kinds of things they did when I grew up. They pleaded to keep contact, but only on their terms. Their words of love were a joke to me. They were pathetic but also criminal.

As an adult and not having seen them for 20 years, their old tricks were still the same. No wonder I was so terribly confused as a child. How in the hell was I able to keep functioning in that den of deceit and anger?

I received a birthday card from Carolyn.

It was April of this year before we heard from you. You wrote making demands, giving ultimatums, certain limits and conditional love. We feel that is selfish and unfair.

You walked away from us 20 years ago. In all those years you could have called, written, and our door has always been open. There are three of us with Joanne and there could be four. We have been through a lot with Joanne but we now have a good relationship. It didn't take going back through years of explanations or re-living the past. We made amends to each other and accepted each other the way we are. A person cannot change anything but themselves. The three of us are happy and live a good life.

We love you and always have. We hope someday soon we can be a family again. If you decide not to write again, that's your decision.

On June 7, 1992, the *Washington Post* in an article titled, "Virginia Ruling Limits Childhood Sex Abuse Victims' Right to Sue," it stated that the Supreme Court in Virginia would not allow this legislation as it would "<u>violate the due process rights of the alleged abusers</u>."

Once again my hopes were crushed. First Ray got a slap on the wrist, now Sam and Carolyn got away with decades of abuse and neglect. Without this legislation, my civil lawsuit went out the window as well.

My only choice was to move forward and make a better life for myself. For now I was working in a commissioned sales job for a local financial company. I refused to work for a corporation again. Those past eight years at the Company were horrendous. I just couldn't go through that again.

My alters also shared their anger and despair.

(12-Year-Old): I am a young girl who would like to be loved by my Mommy and Daddy. But neither of you will do that. You just want to do what you want but you hurt me.

My body was changing. It was new to me but you made me feel ugly and dirty. You wouldn't let me ask any questions Mama, and Daddy, you sneaked into my bedroom at night and put your mouth and hands between my legs and lips.

You scared me to death. You didn't have any clothes on!

All of my teachers like me, Mama. You always look at me like I'm a bad girl. You hurt my feelings because I just want to love you. You never hold me.

(10-Year-Old): Mama and Daddy, I don't love you. I don't ever want to see you anymore. Mama, your last letter is how you always treated me. I am a good girl. I am not a bad girl. I never liked being alone. You always left me. I wish I had a Mommy and Daddy who love me, but you want to use me. Good-bye.

(Teenager): What you did to me is unforgivable. I hope both of you rot in hell.

When we lived in Norfolk, I had to hide and sleep on the bathroom floor or in the closet so that you, Sam, couldn't find me. And the nights I didn't, you were usually there to put your filthy mouth or hands on me.

Carolyn, you talk about me giving ultimatums. You're damn right. At my age you can never hurt me again, and I will tell you openly what's wrong, not play your silly game that you and Sam always played, by acting like whatever happened to me wasn't bad enough to create rage and doesn't need to be discussed.

You're wrong. I don't play your fucking game anymore.

(Free Person): Carolyn and Sam, you fucking bitch and sanctimonious bastard; you are monsters from hell. You wounded me very deeply, but I'm free. You don't know me at all. As malicious as your behavior was, I escaped. My spirit and morals are all there. Both of you sold your souls to the devil, and you will pay.

All parts of me were enormously upset. I focused on what I needed to do financially because I no longer had a substantial paycheck. I was back in survival mode.

With my rage so intense, Reporter was highly stimulated and came out full blast.

(Reporter): Diane is under so much stress it has awakened me. She was able to handle things up until my mother's letter. When Carolyn finally came out and truly showed herself, I felt the awful reality of my past.

All of this has tapped into the deepest piece of trauma that Diane hasn't been able to pull up yet. That means she is close to collapsing. She's been trying to do too much.

Trauma memories have been activated. The flashpoints of my anger are explosive. It is all I can do to restrain myself.

On September 2, 1992, I filed a Discrimination Complaint with my County's Human Rights Commission.

My depression was worsening and Maria was getting worried. I could barely function. I kept waking up all night long. I was overeating to the extent that I was making myself sick.

By the middle of October, I told Maria I was feeling suicidal, I couldn't go on anymore. There was only so much pain and loss a person could handle, so on October 18th I was admitted to the Psychiatric Institute (PI) again in Washington, D.C.

On my first day at PI, I went to a lot of different therapy groups, had blood work done, met the staff, listened to other people's stories, and adjusted to being hospitalized again. By 4:45 PM my head was ready to explode.

When staff asked about my parents, I said they were a *tag team*. I described myself as the baton, an instrument that kept my parents connected in a bizarre way. The biggest difference between me and the rest of my family was that they seemed mentally locked together. My parents and siblings worked from the same frame of reference, which was to bully other people and act out their aggression on others. They had no qualms about how their behavior affected people, and sex was the answer to all their problems. I never felt nor acted as they did, so I was the outsider. But in their minds, I was the scapegoat. It was always my fault.

That night I had a nightmare, just a short picture. I saw my face go totally blank and into shock. I turned to the people around me and yelled, "Help me, now!" and then I woke up.

The following day the staff social worker asked me about my life as a teenager. I said I was always jealous of other girls in my classes. They could wear makeup, go to football games, and have boyfriends. I, however, lived in a *circus of horrors* where my father was the ringleader, my mother the silent mime, my brother the sword-swallower, my sister the clown act, and me—I was the lion-tamer.

The purpose of my hospitalization was to provide a safe place to express my fears and rage in whatever fashion I needed. This would allow me to stabilize so I could try to find a way to support myself while the lawsuit was pending. I couldn't believe I was 45-years-old and still suffering from my past.

During my third day I had a very hard time in Psychodrama. It was supposed to help me get in touch with my feelings. I wished I could cry. I wished I could let that terrified teenage girl express herself. She was a crazed, walking zombie who searched desperately for help from someone when growing up.

I cried alone in my room that night just like I did when I was a little girl.

My psychologist wanted to know what it would take for me to express those feelings verbally. The bottom line was I was afraid of uncovering the truth in someone else's presence.

Teenager was petrified. When she was younger and wanted to express herself, she was silenced by violence.

The next day I had stomach pains and was nauseated. After lunch, I dissociated. A memory was coming up, so I drew what I was visualizing the best I could in Art Therapy. Reporter described my reactions.

(Reporter): I feel like I'm in shock. The picture I drew, showing how much I had disintegrated after he [Sam] tried to kill me, really upset me. It was difficult to look at. It showed the level of torture I had to endure. My parents are criminals and are walking around. They should be in jail.

The nurse and I decided a good way to help me get the support I needed, when I needed it, was to carry around a card which said, "You can help me most by gently asking me to explain what I'm feeling."

During my second week in PI, Survivor wanted to talk.

(Survivor): Where is the darker side? Sam and Carolyn, both of you really keep that hidden, don't you? I had no choice but to live with your flights of fantasy. You experimented on me and found you liked it. It had nothing to do with me personally. Sam, you just craved power and sex so bad you took it wherever you could find it.

Each time you shoved your penis into my mouth, you were telling me you had the right to ejaculate your filth down my throat. Each time you touched me or licked my genitals, you were telling me you liked how I felt and tasted, and it was all right to have sex with your father. What you really are is a coward. The way to take care of your marital problems was to violate something that couldn't fight back, me.

You're damn right it was your fault and responsibility. You don't get to destroy people's lives and then walk away. What is your explanation about why you were so stimulated to ejaculate on a 10, 12, 14 and 16-year-old girl?

Your line now is you are sorry. What you are blindly projecting is that you regret what you did. What a ridiculous excuse. You can't admit you just wanted to experience life on your own terms. That's what you are really saying, isn't it?

Mama, you asked me to forgive you. Did you not see what he did to me all those years? Particularly in Norfolk?

You slowly sliced pieces of my brain away over 21 years. Those wounds didn't heal. Some of them got highly infected. Some are dangling by a thread. Some are excruciatingly painful to touch.

How does saying you're sorry heal my mind?

Dissociation was my survival up to a point. I almost went insane.

This was very difficult and excruciatingly painful work, but I wanted to heal, to get on with my life. I told myself to trust Maria and the hospital staff and do the best I could.

Chapter 29

Repressed Memory

Toward the end of my second week in PI, Maria and I started talking about Christmas 1964. I asked her to accompany me to one of the padded rooms and have Christmas music playing. I wanted to bring my deepest trauma up with her if I could.

After a few minutes of calming myself, I thought about that Christmas and what had happened. I remembered I had been lying on our couch in the living room. It was around sundown. The Christmas tree was lit up in the corner, snow was falling, and Christmas carols were playing softly on the stereo. My eyes were closed. It was one of those rare occasions when I felt comfortable and relaxed.

My father sneaked into the living room and before I knew it, he was on top of me wearing only his underwear. What proved to be much more traumatic was that this time he had a gun. I had on my nightgown and bathrobe but no underwear. I didn't realize I had been carrying around shame because of that (lying there with no underwear on).

Maria asked, "Do you really believe that would have made a difference about how your father behaved?" The answer, of course, was "No."

He pulled his penis out of his underwear and was trying to rape me. I struggled but he picked up the gun and pushed it into my mouth causing my mouth to bleed. In my desperation, I tried to look backwards over my head, looking for my mother.

I saw her in the hallway watching what was happening. After our eyes met, she got her coat and pocketbook and left the house! I went into a trance and just laid there until he was finished. When he was through, he got up and went to his bedroom; I got up, went upstairs and cleaned myself up. I was completely humiliated. I felt dehumanized. The next morning nothing was said except, "What would you like for breakfast?" as if nothing had happened.

This explained a lot about why I felt so panicky every Christmas, and why Maria's departures engulfed me with enormous pain.

Anyone who raped a stranger in this manner would have been sentenced to prison. But my parents were my perpetrators and got off scot-free. This was the ultimate betrayal by my parents. It totally confirmed the fact he would stop at nothing to get the sex he wanted, and my mother would do nothing to protect me.

Even though I had always remembered my abuse, this climatic memory had been repressed all those years. I was glad I was finally able to get it out.

It is interesting to note that as Maria and I first started talking about this incident, I was sitting up. At the end of our session, I was laying face down on the floor with my face covered. I didn't realize I had carried around that much shame.

Maria was very kind and gentle with me. That went a long way toward reinforcing my efforts to continue getting my feelings out.

The next day one of the group leaders talked about the Child Sexual Abuse Accommodation Syndrome. As he stepped through the concept, I followed it very closely. Then I said to myself, *Diane, don't just intellectualize it, try to get in touch with your feelings.* Very shortly after saying that, the picture of me being raped came up as he said, "You learned to accommodate and got caught up in the entrapment."

When he said that, I was overwhelmed with feelings. I said, "I'm sorry, I can't take anymore of this," and left. Later on another patient told me she had never seen that look on my face before. I looked like I was in total pain.

I got to the nurse's station, saw the tech (a mental health staff person), and all I could get out was "Help." I sat down, and a nurse took my pulse and blood pressure. I vaguely remember hearing their voices. Everything was cloudy, hazy and seemed far away. She and the tech walked me to my room. I don't know how I made it because I was really out of it. They helped me to lie down, and the tech talked with me.

I told him I didn't feel safe being alone. He responded positively by reinforcing my right to ask for what I needed. He got a cold washcloth with crushed ice in it and gently patted my face. His response made me feel good. After a few minutes, I said it was okay for him to leave.

That night Maria called and reassured me I had done nothing wrong, that I was safe. I felt better after hearing that. Teenager needed that reassurance too. She was still waiting for the violence to come.

Now I understood why I had decompensated so much in 1964, and Sam had to carry me into the Little Creek Naval Base Dispensary. The ongoing humiliation I had endured while living in Norfolk had worked to seal in my shame.

I had done a very good piece of work while in the hospital. I packed all my belongings and went home on November 16th. After saying my good-byes to the staff and other patients, I went downstairs and out the front door to try and pick up my life where I had left off.

On December 4th I wrote Sam, Carolyn and Joanne my last letters. After all I had been through at their expense when growing up, losing my job, and the legislation now out the window, I didn't give a shit anymore about their feelings. They were going to hear from me what I really thought.

Dear Sam and Carolyn,

Over the past two years, I have tried as nicely as I could to get you to explain why you treated me the way you did when I was growing up. You will never know the pain and consequences I've endured because of the sexual, psychological and physical abuse you both inflicted upon me which included the use of force (a .45 pistol) in commission of a felony (statutory rape and oral sodomy) and attempted murder by strangulation.

You've chosen to put up a ridiculously pathetic front by saying you only "live for today." The truth is both of you have lived a lie for 45 years. It's one thing living your life as the victim. It's entirely different living it as the guilty party, and both of you have to live with yourselves for the destruction you caused.

And, Carolyn, don't insult my intelligence by getting angry at me for cutting off our relationship 20 years ago, as if you don't know why. Both of you earned my rejection. Just as when growing up, both of you have continued to demonstrate that my needs are irrelevant, and you can ignore them as you plod through your pathetic existence. But, because you have decided not to be honest, and you have chosen to ignore my attempt to understand the past, I will never communicate with either of you for the rest of your lives. Both of you could drop dead today, and I would never shed a tear. You don't deserve it.

You may feel like you've gotten away with what you did, but your tragic loss is you never got to know me. I'm a wonderful and successful person in spite of the suffering you caused.

So continue to live your lives your own dreary way because I want nothing more to do with you.

Diane

Dear Joanne,

At no time over the last five years have you felt it necessary to apologize or try to make amends for leaving as you did, stealing many of my possessions, the money from the stocks I sold for a down payment on an apartment, and the car and truck loans I took out for you so you and George could get around and start a new life. I ended up having to pay the loans off without even being able to sell the cars to get my money back.

The money I expended I did gladly to help you here, not to sustain your life in Snakeville. You also stuck me with a $250 phone bill for calling Sam and Carolyn 43 times while I was away from home, so your leave-taking was not a spur-of-the-moment decision as you would have wanted me to believe.

You behaved totally irresponsibly and proved to be very immature in your juvenile stunt. There were no thanks either for paying to have your crappy furniture and other belongings driven back by George. I should have had all of it sent to the dump, but I don't treat people the way you do.

You've decided to kiss and make-up with the perpetrators, so as far as I'm concerned, you've crossed over to the other side.

I gave you the chance of a lifetime, but you blew it. But you know what? It will never happen again. I won't give you the satisfaction of knowing what happened to me when you ran back to Sam and Carolyn because you don't deserve to know, and you could care less anyway.

Because you made the choices you did in psychologically abusing me while you were here, I want nothing more to do with you. Both you and Ray project your rage onto other people, use them and then discard them. So you can continue to live in your fantasyland like Sam and Carolyn do, but you know deep-down what you did; just like they do.

Have a rotten rest of your life.

Diane

It was time for me to move on. After writing those letters, I was more centered within myself and felt good about mirroring back to my parents and Joanne my feelings about their abusive behavior.

I focused on continuing to work hard in my therapy, finding a new job, and assisting any way I could with my lawsuit. It was going to continue to be a long hard pull.

Chapter 30

Managing Unconscious Material

At the start of 1993, I realized this would be another difficult year with new surprises. I verified with Beth (a friend still working at the Company) that neither Jack nor Connie had ever entered my EEO Filing into the official Company records. I went through the roof. This piece of information helped to solidify our case.

Starting in February, I tried putting each personality into the safe place (in my head) before going to work, but I wasn't always successful. Performing that function was going to have to become a ritual until it became automatic. It was ironic, I worked all those years to get them to come out, and now I had to work on putting them back in.

The psychological work I was doing was unbelievably hard. Knowing when to feel my intense emotions, put them away, let this personality talk, let that one go to sleep, re-experience the trauma, disregard my short-term misfortune, do fun things, look at my pain directly—all of that was exhausting. As the *Cathy* cartoon would say, "AAAAAGGGGHHHHH."

I had now accepted my multiple personality diagnosis. Different parts of my unconscious were becoming known to me, but my task was to manage and understand each part's specific needs. It was a very big juggling act I needed to master.

The next morning while driving to work, Perspective Person said,

My baseline fear when growing up in that abusive environment was that I would be mentally destroyed.

That has been the same issue I have been struggling with in therapy. Everything Maria and I have been working on, as we were reframing my thought processes, has been a systematic method of breaking up my old set of mental building blocks and rearranging them.

I thought about what Perspective Person said. Whenever I felt the sense of a conveyor belt of strong emotions starting in my brain, particularly when one or more of my personalities became very active, my behaviors tended to focus on old learned patterns (such as isolating and overeating) to stop the strong sensations I was experiencing. Again, my unconscious fear was that I was losing my mind.

I stabilized for about a week and reported to my part-time job. As I sat at my desk, the image I got was of a maze with walls made of mud bricks. Water started flowing and cracks developed in the structure. It was taking a lot of effort to repair the walls and keep functioning.

My financial situation kept getting worse. I cashed in stock to pay bills. The money I got would last until April 1st.

As difficult and stressful as the process was of listening to what each alter had to say, I was making progress. Only by understanding their needs and fears would I be able to carry on the internal negotiations necessary to function. At this point, that was my major goal.

I received an update from my attorney letting me know that they had filed my case the 23rd of March. He also mailed out the official summonses and complaints to the Company. They would receive the documents within a couple of days and would have 20 days in which to file their formal responses.

Knowing that we were finally going through with the lawsuit gave me some solace. I could relax a little.

My good feelings only lasted a month. My personalities were hurting so much, I went to bed early. The next morning I allowed them to talk.

(12-Year-Old): I know the things that happened to me in the past won't happen again, but I feel the pain I wasn't able to feel back then. It is overwhelming.

(Mommie Dearest): It's very important to me that Connie and Jack are punished in some way for what they did to us, and I don't just mean the aggravation and inconvenience this lawsuit will put them through. I am one of millions who go through this every day. I am fortunate to have Maria help me and the documentation alone will be hard for them to dispute.

(Survivor): I'm very angry about what happened at the church [a new one I had started attending]. It was disappointing being treated that way in an institution where love and support should be provided, but I was put-down again. I didn't go back last Sunday.

(Perspective Person): Diane is overloaded with this lawsuit. She feels like "she should be able to handle this by now." She's worried Jack and Connie will get away with what they did. She really can't see the progress she's made because she feels it will never end. Her behavior is radically different than it was ten years ago.

WWIII was going on in my head again. Part of it was my depression which showed its head with regularity. The part of me that loved being around people, that was adventurous and fun-loving, was screaming to come out and really enjoy herself. The pain I had endured, however, after opening myself up was too much.

(Teenager): What a hell I live in. I want to experience things. I want to have fun, but I know every time that happens, I pay for it. Either my mother gets hateful or my father gets turned on. So I retreat to my private world where I can be as creative as I want to be.

(Survivor): Diane is re-experiencing the dilemma she constantly faced the first 21 years of her life—whether to be herself and risk their [Sam and Carolyn's] reactions, or to let them get their way to keep her environment as stable as it can be. I'm tired of living this way.

At last, all of my personalities were openly communicating. I could switch back and forth to see what everyone was thinking. It also helped Maria understand what the different parts of me were dealing with and how to better help me.

With my depression deepening, another new alter appeared.

(Despair Person): I've talked many times through Diane and other personalities, but I've been hiding behind Survivor. I've carried about 90% of Diane's despair from Day One. When I feel as bad as I did on Tuesday, there's very little Diane can do. When growing up, I couldn't show any sadness or despair because my mother would get angry at me or put me down. As I got older, I wouldn't give her the satisfaction of seeing me cry, so I built up a very strong wall.

I was very happy Despair Person had decided to reveal herself to Maria and me. It meant she felt safe enough to come out, but it added one more alter for me to manage.

The beginning of June, just like when my other alters first came forward, I had sharp pains in my head from my right eye and forehead to the back of my head. Another new alter, who I named Spirit Person, made herself known. She carried memories of the whole brutal experience. All my personalities welcomed her to the fold.

When I looked at my current situation, I realized I had slowly dropped out of life. I used to be much more active, but with all the pain and trauma I had experienced, I had just withdrawn because my constant struggle had been to keep my mind stabilized.

I couldn't take it anymore. I laid down when I got home and totally focused on what was happening. I figured out that too much trauma had been coming forward into my conscious mind. And, I had to change how I managed it.

My personalities had come forward out of the fog and mist. All of them were injured in some way. Some made the journey in better shape than others, but all were in need of love, kindness and joy.

I had to better manage the forward movement of traumatic material but in a totally different way. I wasn't going to ignore my personalities, but instead, look out for their well-being. I wanted to focus on doing things that made each of them feel good about themselves. If something was triggered, I could write it down, and then choose whether or not I wanted to go any deeper with Maria or hold off for a little longer. In the meantime, I would listen to pretty music, go for walks, ride my bike, have friends over, etc. I needed to build the foundation first before going further.

I was 46-years-old and my life was slipping by. I wasn't enjoying it, not in the least. But I felt I was finally getting some internal control. That gave me hope.

> (Despair Person): **My attorney said she got a letter from the Company stating Connie and Jack's theory that I was using my medical problems as an excuse. What did I have to do? Kill myself?**

After all the work Maria and I had done, it finally hit me that all my personalities were "me." That sounded strange, but I just now understood it. I knew my emotions were very intense but wondered why I didn't express them. Now, I realized I did express my feelings but through my other personalities. They were all part of me, but because it was not safe to show those feelings when growing up, I had to dissociate to manage them.

As the adult-Diane, my perception of myself was I didn't feel or show rage, disappointment, sadness, fear, etc. They [my personalities] did. But "they" were all "me," and the abuse was no longer happening.

In late September, I called Jackie, another attorney assisting with my case, and told her I had had enough of this shit. The Company was dragging this thing out. I told Jackie, "Call their attorneys and tell them that in two weeks we will take depositions from Regional V.P. Jack Preston, Connie Brown, the head of EEO, the head of Personnel, and Dr. Albertson. That will get them off their butt." Jackie said she would.

Another new alter appeared.

(Depressed Person): I'm losing it. I need help. Even though I feel like my depression is lifting somewhat, today I feel pretty down. The money situation is really working on me, and the holidays are coming up.

I said to myself, *I have severe mental illnesses that flair up with acute, painful symptoms. When that happens, I need to tell my friends, ask for support, and take care of myself because it will subside, and I'll feel normal again.*

It had been about 18 months since I had lost my job. I had gone through another hospitalization and was on my third part-time job. My personalities were very active, and just like when working at the Company, I couldn't tell anyone about my disability. It was all I could do just to function.

My deposition strategy worked. The end of December 1993 the Company informed Jackie they wanted to go through mediation to bring my lawsuit to some resolution. I was right. It would have cost them an arm and a leg to prepare and go through five depositions. Now they wanted to settle out-of-court. Those fucking bastards. I hoped they all would rot in hell.

On February 17, 1994, I attended mediation proceedings with my attorneys, the Company's attorney, Connie and Jack. They agreed to settle out-of-court! I was ecstatic. I could finally get my life back, be financially secure, and have some measure of justice.

On May 21, 1994, I wrote a memo to my attorneys reminding them we went to mediation on February 17th which was three months ago. I told them if they didn't get a concrete counteroffer by the middle of the following week (Wednesday May 25th), I wanted them to resend the letter for depositions. That way, they would receive it on Friday, May 27th just before Memorial Day weekend. Again, I emphasized the urgency of needing a resolution because of my financial situation. The deposition threat was the only thing they understood.

On June 3rd I faxed a copy of my bills for psychiatric care and prescriptions to my attorneys. I let them know I was asking my second tier of friends for more money. I begged for a status report.

My next letter to my attorneys on June 10th enclosed copies of checks I had received from my friends to help pay for my living expenses. I also asked Maria to write a letter to my attorneys providing an update on my psychological frame of mind. Maria wrote to Jackie on June 15th.

> *I am writing to express my concern about the amount of time that has elapsed in resolving the mediation between Ms. Diane Champé and the Company.*
>
> *Her therapy has been interrupted by this process and particularly its long delay and lack of concrete resolution. As a result, Ms. Champé is not able to focus her energy on resolving her posttraumatic symptoms and continues to be seriously depressed and anxious.*

The end of June I received a letter from the Company stating they were moving forward, but any prolonged therapy had not been due to their treatment toward me.

On August 25th the Company made a significant offer. I told Jackie to accept it. She told me I had been the star from Day One and to let that in. It had been a hard struggle. I started working for Connie on January 1, 1988. That had been almost seven years of turmoil.

Finally, on September 19, 1994, we signed the settlement agreement.

Even though it was signed, my internal parts were very agitated. I had not gotten to the point yet of managing them. I just wanted it all to end so I could have some peace of mind.

Chapter 31

Decompensation

Maria and I worked very hard over the next four months so that I could stabilize as well as allow each alter to express themselves. Some alters were feeling comfortable being friends with others, which meant I was experiencing a partial integration. We still had a long way to go.

As Christmastime approached, I was dissociating a lot, but was trying very hard to stay in the present. One morning I felt like the room was spinning around, not a good sign. I was tired of suffering every year, but I had twenty-one years of traumatic memories to work through.

One of the customers I met the end of February 1995 while working my part-time job was an attorney. She took a personal liking to me and asked me to lunch. As I talked about my organizational abilities, she explained her firm was in desperate need of those skills and wanted to hire me part-time.

I accepted her offer. The pay was really good, and I would be back on my feet in a professional job.

By the end of April, my depression started acting up again. I was at a crucial part of my life where I was deciding if life was worth the effort anymore. The struggle had become too difficult. All I did every day was try to function, stabilize, eat to kill the pain, and sleep.

I was tired of having to fight for everything in my life. My mind had been totally ripped apart, and I was trying to put it back together again. I hated having to force myself to function every day. My gut feeling was to go for the brass ring. But my greatest fear was I wouldn't succeed. I asked myself, *if that were to happen, what would I lose?* I believed I would lose my will to live.

While driving into work, I felt like my brain was falling apart and I would cease functioning. By the first of May, I was deteriorating even more.

I needed to be in the hospital. I felt like screaming. I knew I would be in a safe place where I could get my feelings out before I hurt myself or someone else. Maria agreed. I was admitted into PI for the third time.

During this recovery period, I wanted to face as directly as possible my feelings of loss, hopelessness, loneliness, and despair. There was a lot of anger underneath that needed to be addressed.

I developed a major insight after a stressful session. The reason I had not been able to let the good in about the lawsuit was because I had internalized the Company as my family. I fought them until I got back what was rightfully mine, but now I was grieving my loss.

During one of our support groups, I learned grounding and self-awareness techniques. As part of that assignment, I was asked to write what I knew about my alters.

6-Year-Old: Knows there are a lot of unsettling memories being stimulated; has fears of being around a male authority figure who will make her do unwanted sexual acts; is not old enough to understand the significance of what was done to her, just knows she didn't like it; and does not want to be around a cold, uncaring female, authority figure.

10-Year-Old: Is always nervous and afraid of being abandoned; didn't think anyone loved her but now pretty much believes Maria, Elizabeth, and others do; feels life in general is not safe, but really enjoys going to the "safe place" with One Deep Inside who she knows will protect her; likes to play games and be outdoors; and is beginning to accept the fact that my parents are sick people.

12-Year-Old: Is very quiet and fearful; was traumatized by the escalation of my father's sexual advances; was embarrassed by my mother's harsh attitudes and comments; desperately wants others to know what happened to her and to make sure it doesn't happen again.

Teenager: Dissociates a lot and is always nervous; was constantly on guard to get away from my father; was raped by him; sees my mother as harsh and cold; is afraid of being raped again; trusts Maria more than anybody; can't understand why that happened to her; and is very angry and confused.

Survivor: Remembers all the abuse and has carried most of the pain; in addition, has carried the pain from all of my personal crises over the last 10 years; needs to be comforted, supported in her feelings of grief, and reassured that the people I have chosen as family in my present life will never treat me the same way my biological family and ex-husband did.

Despair Person: Has carried most of the depression; with each succeeding painful loss, she has come to believe this will continue to happen for the rest of her life; needs to be acknowledged for the tremendous load she's carried, and to have validated that the losses have been enormous. She also needs to understand the people in my present life do value me and love me.

Perspective Person: Is totally unemotional; is able to remember everyone's viewpoint, has the ability to present a balanced picture when assessing a problem or making a decision; and is invaluable in advising all the personalities as the need arises.

One Deep Inside: Is my Rock of Gibraltar; is always there to comfort any part of me, particularly the child parts. Her primary role is to provide internal support to those who need her and needs to be acknowledged for her work.

Spiritual Person: Possesses my greatest strength and wisdom. At times such as these, she has ensured that Maria and my friends know that I'm collapsing and can no longer function. Her role is to guide me and provide the insights I'll need in completing my work during this hospitalization.

Even though I couldn't recognize it at that time, I had made tremendous progress. I knew myself better than I ever had. I understood many of my personality's needs and wants, and I was ready to face the demons that fostered my depression. It was going to be a rough ride, but I was willing to do whatever it took to get well.

After about a week in the hospital, I was able to gain another significant insight into my family's conditioning. Sam, Carolyn, Ray and Joanne had kept me in a psychological box very forcefully in their own way. If I tried to express myself, I was met with anger, abandonment, neglect, ridicule and/or abuse. I needed to break out of that box. When I did my anger work, I needed to focus on:

How each family member had kept me in the box to meet their personal needs,

How that made me feel as a person, and

What I needed to do to get out of the box.

I spent a lot of time in group therapy working on these issues.

The rest of my time in PI was spent on winding down, practicing my self-soothing skills I had learned, and to continue focusing on not staying in the mental box I was forced into as a child.

I had done another major piece of work. I was beginning to emerge as my own person and to develop my own identity separate from my family. My discharge from the hospital was on May 19th.

About two weeks after I got home, I received a letter from my insurance company.

We are writing in regards to your claim for Disability benefits. We have reviewed the information submitted by Maria Anderson, Ph.D. It is noted you do still suffer from sporadic bouts of depression, spontaneous flashbacks and intrusions that, at times, do debilitate you. However, your continued psychother-

apy and maintained levels of Amytriptiline (a drug for depression) indicate these bouts of depression do not severely limit you.

Your ability to work 30 hours per week seems to substantiate the limited bouts of depression. Your current occupation may not be as stressful as your job with the Company, yet you have proven you are able to handle steady employment.

Due to the reasoning outlined in this letter, we must terminate your claim effective May 17, 1994.

When I got this letter saying I didn't qualify for my disability benefits, I went ballistic.

I hated the Company. The Company had won. I told myself, *I lost by signing that fucking settlement agreement when I had them by the balls.*

I felt suicidal again. All that work for nothing.

I would have killed myself right then had I not had a contract with Maria.

I thought I had been screwed for the last time. I was not only enraged about what was happening to me, I was livid because this is what adult survivors of child abuse have to go through all over America with their employers and insurance companies. It is unconscionable, and the general public doesn't have a fucking clue about this inhumane behavior.

On June 7th I wrote a memo to my attorney.

Yesterday I received the enclosed letter from my insurance company saying I no longer qualify for disability benefits.

I have been unemployed since April 28th. I was hospitalized at the Psychiatric Institute because I was suicidal again due to the ongoing trauma I'm dealing with. I was in the hospital from May 4th to May 19th and have been trying to regroup since then.

Contact the person who sent this letter and advise him of my recent hospitalization and the fact that I'm still unemployed.

This is very discouraging because I was finally getting on my feet again. Also remind him I do not just have minor bouts of depression. I suffer from major depression and Posttraumatic Stress Disorder.

Maria was also frustrated. She wrote a letter to the insurance company.

I write this letter to correct some obvious misperceptions associated with my previous correspondence with you.

Ms. Champé is suffering from major depression, posttraumatic stress disorder and multiple personality disorder, along with associated anxiety symptoms and physical concerns.

She has recently attempted employment at a firm for the maximum of 30 hours per week but the job proved much too stressful. It only lasted several weeks, exacerbated her major symptoms, led to a marked increase in her depressive symptoms and resulted in suicidal ideation, a total inability to function, and a two week psychiatric hospitalization. She is only now getting re-stabilized.

Please reconsider your decision and reinstate her benefits in as timely a fashion as possible as this patient is not benefited by additional stress.

The letter from my insurance company shot all my secure feelings to hell and reactivated my homicidal rage. On June 14th I called Maria and told her I wanted to kill myself. She arranged for me to be admitted back into PI the next morning.

My anxiety was higher than it had ever been since that night in 1964 when I thought I was being strangled to death. I was leaping out of my skin.

Maria met me in the front lobby of the hospital, and I collapsed on the couch. As she tried to comfort me, my pupils were dilated and I kept saying over and over again, "I need a massive tranquilizer." After I was checked in and taken to my hospital room, I was given a shot. I didn't wake up until later that afternoon. The staff was very kind and told me I needed to take it slow.

I felt a profound sense of betrayal by the Company, a fear and sense of loss of all I had ever worked for. I was in shock. I felt hopeless. I was highly anxious and devastated.

I was also back in a psychiatric hospital.

The uncertainty about my life was now in the hands of someone in a far-off cubicle looking at a computer screen. Knowing that that person was going to be making decisions about my future based on a policy and procedures manual, instead of heeding the wisdom and training of my doctors, was the last straw. I was losing all hope.

Chapter 32

Hope Restored

While in the hospital, a new alter came out. I named this part Neglectful Person.

(Neglectful Person): I don't show or express my feelings because I'm afraid of being put-down, humiliated, or abandoned. I neglect myself in terms of physical health and isolate. I also deny myself opportunities for fun and don't have people over to my house. It is a vicious and painful cycle I want to dismantle.

My attending psychiatrist at PI said, "I can see you are ready to get some of this out. Let's go to the Quiet room." She was accompanied by the head nurse.

After I lay down on my back, the psychiatrist gently pressed her hand on my stomach. I didn't know what was happening, but I could feel enormous energy rumbling near her hand.

She then gently touched each shoulder, and the energy flowed upward. When she touched my neck, I let out a tremendous scream as if I were exhaling all the pain I had been carrying around. It started from my stomach until the scream was full throttle in my throat. I felt tremendous relief and thanked her. It was very therapeutic and healing. Afterwards, I went to my room and rested. It was amazing to me that her simple technique provided the catalyst for the release of my pent-up anxiety and rage.

After that enormous release, I was able to see that my thinking had been seriously impaired with my suicidal and homicidal thoughts. I had always loved life too much to have my life destroyed forever.

A friend of mine called to tell me a Company disability check was in my mailbox. Yeah! I was overwhelmed.

Both my attorney and Maria had impressed upon the Company the seriousness of their actions. Knowing that the Company had reversed their decision finally enabled me to stabilize and prepare for discharge.

Before I left the hospital, I got a newspaper and found a service job paying $160 per week. I had to put aside my pride and realize that this was what was best for me while I finished recovering. I was discharged soon afterwards and went home.

I was starting a new life and had to keep working with my alters.

> (Neglectful Person): I was so beaten down the first 21 years of my life and brainwashed by both parents, I don't feel I deserve good things. All the frustration and losses I've endured over the last 11 years have only reinforced those feelings. The letter from the insurance company stretched my endurance to its limits.

In August I met with Michael, an Episcopal priest highly recommended to me by someone at the hospital. My first impression of him was very favorable. He was soft-spoken and loving in his demeanor. I explained what I had been through, my therapy and diagnoses, and what I was looking for spiritually.

He wanted to understand Dissociative Identity Disorder (DID—the new name for Multiple Personality Disorder) better and how he would know if I dissociated. I said I would be "here and not here." He said he had worked with people who, while they were talking, would seem to "drift away."

He said, "I haven't met anyone in a long time that has your courage and commitment."

We prayed before we started talking and again when we ended. Before I left, he had to wipe away tears.

I felt hopeful.

In therapy the next day, Maria asked if any other parts of me had any ideas about helping all of us work together. I asked parts of me to express how they felt.

(Reporter): It is very difficult for me to ignore my rage when something or someone reminds me of how good I used to have it financially, where I could possibly be if I weren't saddled with the trauma from my past, or how it would have helped to have had a supportive manager at the Company all along like Daryl. Those memories send me into orbit, and then I obsess about it all day long. When other parts of me try to silence my rage, I start getting worse and very angry. I really don't know how to function in a group.

(Despair Person): **I don't believe my life will get better. Something major happens every fucking year. Just like when growing up, it never stops. It's going to be hard for me to have faith things will get better, but I'm tired of being so unhappy.**

(One Deep Inside): I can withstand almost anything. I'm that strong. I see my major role as the one who protects and supports all my child parts, including the infant. When the adult parts are at odds with each other, it affects them, and then I get angry. We need to work together, and I will extend that same love and support to everyone.

(Neglectful Person): I burst forth out of the box while in the hospital and am trying very hard to change. I want happiness. What sets me off is the *deprivation*. I lived with that throughout my entire childhood and the first 10 years I was married. I was determined to make something of myself and now look at me, living month-to-month.

(Free Person): I want to be free. I'm the one pushing so hard to let go of the past. But as I've said before, negativism drains me, and I can't let that happen. I play a very important role for Diane, so their infighting drives me away.

I was trying to function with all of that going through my head. It was indeed a tremendous struggle, but I was determined to recover and have an enjoyable life. I couldn't do it by myself. Everyone had to pitch in on the inside and help or it wouldn't work.

The middle of September I saw Michael again. He gave me a lot to think about. When I talked about my loss of strength, he said that rather than trying to place my burdens on Christ, it might be helpful to look at it another way. He thought my waning strength must be frightening to Spirit Person. He proposed that I focus on where my true strength comes from, God, and that His is truly inexhaustible. Rather than asking God to give me strength, he suggested that I think about accepting and relying on God's strength that was available to me. That was very helpful.

Everything seemed to settle down. My attorneys had straightened things out with the Company, my insurance had been reinstated, and I had a low-stress part-time job. I didn't realize, though, there would be more pain and confusion before I could finally live a normal life.

Part 7

Recovery
1996—2002

Chapter 33

Self-Validation

By February 1996 I was beginning to understand the dynamics of my family in a way that provided more insight into my self-blame and self-hate.

My parents had never validated me as a human being. Because of that, I fought very hard all my life against anyone either tearing me or others down. I was now turning toward validating myself.

Instead of adjusting my behavior in a way that would produce positive responses from others, in any form I could get them, I was shifting toward looking at people as to who they were, what their agenda was, and their character, and whether or not I wanted to associate with them or not. That was a monumental shift.

What was most critical at this point was the work we were doing at challenging my belief system. The work continued to be with my child parts and teenage years.

The following therapy session, I came close to looking at my most crucial dilemma, the fact that I, as a child, had to constantly sublimate my version of the truth for the greater need of feeling loved.

That was the underlying battle between my intellect and emotions and formed the core of my belief system that I was not lovable.

By now, I was extremely frustrated, conflicted, angry, sad, stifled, lonely and confused. I had worked so hard at pulling myself together, controlling my impulses, creating balance, not taking care of other people or stuffing myself with food even though I had gotten very angry at times, deepening my spirituality, listening to my different selves, etc. No wonder I constantly felt overwhelmed.

By this point, my mental health bills had totaled around $231,850 of which I had paid $63,000 out-of-pocket. While in my corporate job, I could afford paying my share. After I lost my job, my therapist, out of the goodness of her heart, reduced her personal fee by one-third.

In spite of all my pain and confusion, I was learning more and more about my perceptions, motivations, reactions, and internal thought processes. It was arduous work, but I could see all the progress I had made.

What gnawed at me was the realization that I had the capability to have a fun, exciting, rewarding life and career, but I was psychologically incapacitated. I lived with the growing fear that I would never be able to function at a high capacity again, that I was living a pipedream for even thinking I could do better.

(Reporter): I have been filled with rage and hatred toward Diane and the other parts of us because I've been locked up and held back all these years. With good reason—they have been afraid of how out of control I can be with my rage. But what they haven't realized is I have exercised extreme control.

Knowing that I could potentially become lethal, and being unsure about what I might say or do, Diane locked me up inside and that's why I became ballistic and took it out on her and the other parts. Then our whole system was incapacitated until we stabilized again.

It wasn't until this morning that Diane finally put together the connection between feeling enraged and my uncontrolled abuse towards parts on the inside. That is what was set as a model for me throughout my early childhood and culminated with my formation as a separate part, because Diane always disowned me.

I've now stopped that behavior. I want peace because it has made me miserable too.

I was beginning to see Reporter's point of view and was much more empathic toward her. I was at another major turning point. My foundation was coming together at the core, but it was very fragile.

I now understood why the work to put the blame on my parents had been so difficult. Until Reporter and the rest of us were reconciled on the inside, we couldn't truly evaluate the past and make substantial judgments.

What needed to be done at this point was to totally focus positively on teaching Reporter how to express her anger in an effective but acceptable manner. We had done a lot of anger work in the past. Now that Reporter and I were both more empathic toward each other, the real teaching could begin.

By April I was monitoring and trying to anticipate anything that would trigger my illness. I was not going to suffer anymore because of other people's ignorance, stupidity or spiteful anger.

I had been afraid of my feelings and reactions for a long time and was at the point where I just wanted to practice expressing them. I was tired of fitting into other people's lives. I wanted to create my own world.

Now that Teenager trusted Maria deeply, more of my inner conflicts during those earlier years were beginning to surface.

I realized I had been carrying around my parents' shame, blame, and anger. I was tired of it. I wasn't responsible for their problems, but they made me feel that way. Also, just because those two people didn't know how to be intimate in a healthy way didn't mean I was unlovable.

By that summer, I was experiencing tremendous conflict, but that signaled to me that growth was occurring. I was trying to create boundaries around my developing identity based on my values. I was learning to be interdependent both inside and out in such a way that I was loving and serving others instead of trying to build myself up based on a past need of protection, control, approval and sustenance.

During a fitful night's sleep, I screamed until I was exhausted as a release from the conflict. Then later, I was filled with rage and anger. While lying on my back in a semi-fetal position, I began a hammering motion, starting from over my head to my feet. I felt like I was trying to break out of a giant egg.

The profound shifts in consciousness I was experiencing were overwhelming to the extent that I became very quiet and reflective. This identity building stuff was pretty powerful. Everything Maria and I had been working on all those years was finally coming together.

I was very focused on balance in my life and taking care of myself. I was aware of what would upset that balance but needed a lot more practice in managing it. As I became more and more my own person, I believed life would become easier for me because my feelings would be based more soundly on internal recognition of truths rather than fears. I would be able to be more proactive in attaining peace and harmony for myself than ever before.

I was able to piece together for myself my distorted thought processes that had developed as a result of decades of abuse and the struggles I had endured afterword.

From the terror-induced hellhole I grew up in, I had developed a way of coping with life (dissociating) that allowed me to keep my sanity and protect my spirit. By constantly splitting off distressful material, I never had the opportunity to develop emotionally or psychologically, so I felt totally unsafe and lived in constant fear. My perpetual state of mind became that of a well-oiled dissociative machine that got tighter and stronger every year. That spirit of mine, though, was always fighting to be free. But to get to it would mean facing all my childhood monsters, something impossible for a child to do alone. It took a grown-up with enormous courage, love, perseverance, strength and dedication (Maria) to walk beside me, open the closet door and help me look at everything.

I had loving, supportive qualities, could empathize with people, was trustworthy and dependable but, whenever I felt afraid or threatened or angry at people, I dissociated from them, split them off, which had been my way of coping.

All of those childhood responses needed to be changed into adult responses.

I had to give myself permission to let go of my old way of life and start anew. I finally saw the possibility of having a happy life by stopping the self-abuse, being true to myself and at last, entering the human race. All of this meant that I was changing my entire self-concept.

Maria had gone through an incredible journey with me. Our work together was monumental in how I was being transformed from a terrified person filled with rage and an extremely hurt inner child-state into a balanced, stable and peaceful adult. I would be forever grateful.

Chapter 34

Centered Within Myself

I was starting to look at the fact that I had spent most of my life dissociated. I was just now entering the human world because I felt safe enough with Maria to try.

My intelligence and survival skills had served me well as I had learned how to function, hold a job, interact with people and support myself. But by not allowing myself to fail or be weak, I had never learned or experienced the everyday run-of-the-mill life. I functioned, regrouped, functioned, regrouped, never just experiencing moments for what they were as they were happening. I wasn't alive in my own body. My parents dehumanized me that much.

I read *A Bright Shining Lie*, the award-winning book on Vietnam. It detailed the life of a man who was deeply neglected as a child, sexually abused and lived though severe deprivation. It described his military career, how it gave him a sense of accomplishment, self-respect, and admiration; his marriage and blatant sexual addictiveness with other women; his desire to go overseas or schooling in the service rather than be home; and the nature of the times during the 1940's—1960's. It was especially interesting in how it described Japan after the war where sex was easily available with submissive women.

My father went to Japan a lot in those early years.

The wife in the book grew angry, bitter, and resentful but felt trapped. With no skills, how would she financially support herself and four kids? Also military life at that time viewed families as unnecessary, except that it looked good for promotions.

All of that rang true for me, and it helped me put my parents' lives in the past. It didn't excuse my parents' behavior but continued to put them in context.

I was starting to feel more stable. I was not blocking my feelings but acknowledging them and was much easier on myself.

In October, another new alter came out during a therapy session.

(Deprived Person): I am using this name, Deprived Person, because it bests describes me. I have wanted to talk for a long time but have been too ashamed to do so. A lot of rage I've felt about a current financial episode is what has finally brought me out.

I have been the primary deterrent in Diane not being able to do things for herself. I've seen how you've treated the other personalities, Maria, so I feel it is safe to come out. I want help too.

A whole bunch of us internally embraced Deprived Person. She didn't have to hide anymore. She needed to be loved and part of the group. She was right. I was not aware that she existed. It was one more piece to the puzzle.

I was beginning to see that people didn't have a right to expect me to sacrifice myself to comfort them or maintain their ability to cope (similar to my experiences with my parents and Joanne). I had a right to choose what I would or would not do regardless of what they thought. If they couldn't or wouldn't accept me for who I was, that did not mean there was something wrong with me. It was not my fault or responsibility they couldn't cope.

Big change.

Taking care of my needs first was my new priority. Various alters were pairing up for support internally while I was expressing my needs externally. My inner world was finally coming together.

Teenager was coming more and more into the forefront. The right side of my head had hurt for weeks. I knew my feelings were always heightened at Christmastime. This was when Teenager was threatened the most, hurt, raped and made to feel like a zombie.

(Teenager): The psychological pain is excruciating. My head hurts a lot. I know I'm not in the past, so why is it causing me so much pain? I've been accompanying Diane and see she is opening up more to friends and handling things in an adult way.

All the feelings I'm experiencing now I felt when growing up but had no one to talk to about them. I need for Diane and Maria to continue acknowledging how horrible it was for me then, even though it's over now.

I am beginning to grasp this is how I felt back then most of the time, to acknowledge those feelings but to focus on how I'm experiencing them today.

I need to know this pain and the torture I went through have been heard and acknowledged by someone other than myself. I know this has been done all along, but I'm experiencing it differently now.

The task for me was to normalize my reactions because other people's responses, while hurtful, were not tortuous or as abusive as my parents. That was what I really had to work on, and to not turn the anger against myself in the form of self-hate. That was not fair to me either.

(Teenager): This morning Diane pointed out all the Christmas cards we had received and read them to me. She reminded me I never had any friends, never got any cards or had anyone to talk to when growing up. She said I'm safe in my home, have two cats to keep me company and a Christmas tree with ornaments from my friends.

One Deep Inside is giving me a big hug and telling me I'm loved and that this, too, shall pass.

Reporter has been great. She has let me know she is
there for me, will not let anyone hurt me, and has not
been abusive toward me or Diane. I want to start enjoying Christmas.

The only person's happiness I was responsible for was my
own. This was not something I hadn't heard before. It was just
finally sinking in. My happiness did not depend upon how others
treated me or watching how people treated each other; it
depended upon how I treated myself.

I needed to respect myself—physically, mentally, emotionally
and spiritually. I would do that by establishing and managing my
boundaries, standing up for myself, not depriving myself of fun or
comfort, respecting and taking care of my personalities, doing
the inside work, and living a balanced life.

When the New Year started in 1997, I realized I had to com-
mit daily to overcoming my cravings and fears through deliberate
self-management. My needs came first. I knew self-management
and self-acceptance were the keys to success. I had to keep working at it.

Chapter 35

Self-Management

It was difficult living in a world of feelings. I was changing a lot. I was becoming quieter, more tolerant, independent and less afraid. I was integrating, making extensive perception changes, looking directly at teenage issues, seeing how much shame I had carried around, letting go of control, socializing more, letting in feelings/compliments from others, embracing and teaching my inner parts, and grieving big time for what I had been put through and my lost potential.

I reread the "Boundaries" book Maria had recommended. What I began to understand was when my boundaries were not made clear to other people, especially when I felt violated, my internal boundary system started to crumble. If it went too far, I turned on myself and then didn't function. I had some very angry, fearful and wounded child parts within who needed to be protected, nurtured and cared for.

As I continued my immense struggle to integrate my alters, Paul McHugh, the Johns Hopkins psychiatrist who was earlier referred to by Dr. Charles Whitfield as a founding member of the False Memory Foundation, was interviewed on *60 Minutes* by Mike Wallace. His hurtful denunciation of Dissociative Identity Disorder was a disgrace. He compared the diagnosis to a fad like the hula hoop, a fad that would eventually fade away.

To make matters worse, he postulated that DID was induced by therapists. I said to Marie, "You're good, but you aren't that good." I wondered what his agenda was and wanted to say to him,

"Shame on you." And, "I'm glad you aren't my doctor. I would never heal."

Christmas 1997 was much better. I was a lot less isolated and was enjoying myself more. I had hopes that 1998 would be a more fulfilling year.

The two owners of the service company I now worked for were arrogant and dismissive. They had boundary problems, were constantly looking for what I might have done wrong, couldn't say anything positive about my work, were accusatory and condescending with their feedback, and were always trying to catch me in a lie. Great working conditions.

I started reading the "Boundaries" book again. What jumped out for me was a discussion about "ownership." I was only responsible for myself, not for other's out-of-control behavior.

I woke up the next morning saying to myself, *I view the world in context of what happened to me when growing up.* I needed to experience things in the present moment, take care of myself, focus on operating my boundaries as to when to let people in or out, and my words would be the fence that outlined my boundaries.

That was the first time I had been able to connect that sequence within my own mind. Whenever anything happened that upset me, I needed to deal with it as soon as possible and catch that sequence up-front. I also had to explain to each personality why that was necessary.

As Maria kept working and re-working with me all I had learned, I got very angry. I realized I had been held back all my life because of *conditioning*. I had fought other people's control over me all my life in one way or another. And I had fought against ignorance. I had had enough.

Trying to broaden my support system, I started attending another new church. (Sadly for me, Michael had been transferred out-of-state.) The next Sunday in Bible school, I sat there like a bump on a log while listening to someone say, "All you have to do is pray about it. It's our job to teach others Christ's Word so they can live better lives." Blah. Blah. Blah.

Just once I wanted to hear, "I don't have all the answers, but through living my faith and modeling Christ's truth, as I've learned it, I can be there for others in ways that may be helpful for them."

I was defining my world and living within that. I was going to live by the principles I believed in. I just couldn't take being preached at anymore.

After a blowup at work where one of the owners accused me of something I had not done, I went home very anxious and upset. The next morning my chest felt very tight. I did mental exercises to relax, but I still found it hard to concentrate at work.

That night my dreams were awful, and once again, I woke up with a heaviness and tightness in my chest. I suspected those feelings had been there when I had been anxious in the past.

It was becoming much more obvious to me that maintaining low stress levels in my environment was essential to my well-being. I had an internal set point, an automatic barometer, as to the desired stress level I needed to be able to function.

I needed to feel responded to as a human being. I knew how to give to people. I knew how to receive from people, so I was very confused as to why I was having problems making more friends.

(Perspective Person): We are all unique people trying to get our needs met to feel fulfilled. We cannot judge each other's needs. We can ask for what we want, and it is entirely up to the other person whether they can or want to meet them. For the most part, we have to determine on our own how to get our individual needs met without expecting other people to do it for us.

When I got home, I thought about my experiences that year. I discovered I didn't know how to just "be." Before therapy, I was totally cut off from any knowledge of myself, focused only out-wardly with the need to protect myself, and used my conditioning to lead and take care of others. Now, I knew myself very well, was taking responsibility for my needs more than ever, did not want to take care of others, did not want to lead everyone, and was looking for mutual relationships—but I still didn't feel like I fit in, and I continued to have problems with just living my life. It was difficult to sit with all of that and believe things would get better.

My task was to gain better control over my reactions so that they wouldn't be so debilitating. To do that, I focused on what happened every time I had a severe reaction.

Something would happen in the present which, in turn, would activate past painful memories, and my reaction to the present-day event would be extreme. I would try to ignore my distressing memories, busy myself, and hope the feelings would go away. They wouldn't evaporate, and I'd start to feel drugged.

At that stage, I couldn't do anything no matter how hard I tried. My higher functioning would shut down, and I was only capable of the very basics. There was no higher reasoning or abil-ity to perform any tasks that required energy or concentration. That usually lasted three to four days. After that, my depression would set in, and I would feel miserable until the sick memories and feelings went away, usually three to four more days.

That was the cycle of my reactions. I didn't want to go through that whole procedure over and over again. I needed to catch it up-front, expend the energy from the reaction, and then nurture myself a lot until it passed. This was another new skill to practice.

The abandonment, neglect, isolation and abuse all con-tributed to my actual helplessness which evolved into a belief that I was all alone and must protect myself. I didn't realize how active a role Despair Person had been playing in keeping me isolated. I knew there had been a big reluctance to having people come over to my home, but I didn't totally understand why.

I had no idea until Despair Person told me she associated our home with the closet, the one I hid in when growing up, and her fears around keeping it as our last vestige of safety. That helped explain why efforts to move forward had been thwarted, particularly around my need to isolate myself.

(Despair Person): My home has to be a safe place. I do see Diane being a lot more assertive about what she will or will not put up with. That's good. Last night I was very upset and afraid because I had told Maria my secret (about my home being the closet I hid in while growing up).

I focused on including Despair Person in whatever I was doing to show her I could make things better. Even if it was taking a bath, doing my nails, painting, reading a book, whatever, there was always something I could do. This was a good way to follow Maria's advice of "One bite at a time."

(Despair Person): It helps when Diane and Perspective Person tell me we are in control of who comes into our home. This is our home, and we are in charge. I feel safer knowing this.

One of the women Diane used to work with at the Company called. She told Diane that Connie has been informed she needs to find another job. They are focused more on marketing now, and she can't deliver what they need. What goes around comes around. This knowledge helps us put closure around our loss.

What I'm struggling with is my *individuation* and how I fit into the world. Metaphorically, I am psychologically beating down my parents' stone wall of conditioning with a sledge hammer. Instead of focusing on how I should react *to* people in my environment, I am learning how to live *in* my environment and figure out how people in my environment can help me.

I was experiencing another big step. I didn't feel inhuman anymore. I didn't feel like a robot. Instead, I knew I was a thinking, feeling, caring, spiritual person who was struggling to recover from and manage the manifestations from my illnesses. That was quite a switch. I was making a conscientious effort everyday to break away from my old conditioning.

Putting myself first and practicing effective boundaries while still caring about others was a major shift. My self-protection came before taking care of others. This was perhaps the most difficult and yet most healing step I could take.

Chapter 36

Avoidant Attachment

I felt like I had changed overnight. It was odd. It was like a switch had been flipped, and I no longer cared what other people thought. I was now more than ever focused on my needs.

All my work with Maria had finally driven home the point that I could feel hurt, be afraid and angry. I could tell her how I felt, and she wouldn't walk out on me. She would discuss things with me, but she wouldn't leave me. That gave me a sense of confidence I had never felt before.

I was working very hard on experiencing things as they happened and letting them go. I was not letting others dump on me. The task for me now was to increase my tolerance of other people's insensitive behaviors and to not internalize them or connect them to my past. I was forming space in my psyche to handle all my ups and downs and then move on.

I felt like all the new connections in my brain were holding. My personalities were integrating. It seemed like there were a million tiny nerve endings knitting together in my head, and I didn't want to upset the applecart. It was critical I maintained this psychological assertion that I could take control of my life. It had taken my continual, methodical striving for almost two decades to turn it around.

What I was working on was taking a lot of brain processing power. I was struggling very hard to push that psychological closet door wide-open. Being openly authentic took a lot of courage.

One night during the Christmas holidays, there rose up a mighty chorus among Spirit Person, Teenager, Perspective Person, and Reporter expressing the need to leave the old system I had lived in all my life and to switch to the new one I had been building. At that point, in my head, I had the sensation of a large egg cracking in half. It was a strange but powerful feeling.

I had the best Christmas ever. I felt optimistic. Everything was coming together. I could sense it in my mind. It was a great feeling, and I felt hopeful. I really believed the year 2000 would be a great one.

I was on a roll at work, but then went through another hell week, something I hadn't gone through in about six months. I felt taken advantage of. I was yelled at and unfairly dressed down a lot without any apology or acknowledgement from the owners. The following day nothing was said, and everyone acted like nothing had happened. The same old shit I grew up with.

A few days later after being put-down at work again, I woke up around 12:30 AM with sharp pains in my chest and my mouth filling up with water. I went to the emergency room. They did a chest x-ray, an EKG and blood work. My heart was fine, but my esophagus was going into spasms. I realized I was internalizing more stress than I had been aware of, so I immediately found another service job.

I accepted a position in a small business where I was told I would be in a supportive back-office job doing paperwork. I misinterpreted that to mean low stress. Once I reported to work, I was told I would be a customer service representative. That job meant taking an unending stream of phone calls, payments and talking to customers.

After several months of receiving excuses about why I wasn't being put into the position for which I was hired, I appealed to the owners. I explained I was diagnosed with PTSD and needed the less stressful job they had promised as I was not functioning well.

The wife said, "We all have to do things we don't want to do. I know I am being brutal, but if you can't perform this job, perhaps you might need to do something else. Do you understand me?"

The husband chimed in with, "If you aren't happy here, why don't you just go somewhere else?"

When I offered to work a little longer to allow me to slowly transition into the other job, the husband stood up and yelled, "This discussion is over! I'm tired of this HUMANISTIC CRAP!"

I left and found another part-time job.

A relative mailed my father's obituary printed in the *Snakeville Times*. It stated:

> *Lt. Cmdr. Samuel R. Chambreaux (retired) was a man of honor with many service decorations and citations. He loved God and his fellow man. He was a decorated husband, father and grandfather. He was dearly loved and will be greatly missed.*

I said to myself, *the person who had created so much havoc and damage to so many lives is now dead.* I felt a great sense of relief but no remorse.

The significant shift I was making at this point was phenomenal. I was accepting all that had happened in my life and all the parts of my psyche. I was not pretending parts of me didn't exist, was honoring my struggle, and understood that some of my wounds would probably never heal. I knew I had the capabilities to attain a happier life and to contribute to other people's lives. I was not sacrificing parts of myself so that other parts could survive. And I was embracing all my parts and choosing behaviors which would be beneficial to everyone.

Teenager had suffered enough. She deserved a warm, comfortable home, a loving, caring partner, supportive and trusted friends and her voice to express herself, all of it, not just the pain. I was going to work very hard to make that happen.

After a lot of reflection, I had another major insight. I realized I was continually projecting onto others my reactions to their willingness or unwillingness to help me. I had looked at people with suspicion, hatred, and jealousy, all because I had given up on my life. I had taken myself out of the picture. I needed to put myself back into action. I had to do this for myself. No one was going to do it for me.

I went to the library and found information that pulled everything together for me. I read about *avoidant attachments*. I discovered that I had been emotionally starved after experiencing a full range of negative feelings on a daily basis when growing up. The book talked about avoidant kids who were highly dependent. It described my behavior perfectly.

I had an expectation I would be rejected when in distress, a self-fulfilling prophesy. It said avoidant children frequently tended to be sulking or oppositional, and because of that came across as arrogantly self-sufficient and were least likely to elicit concern.

One book described how the person who expected to get rejected gave little of herself, acted mistrustful, ignored or misread friendly overtures, appeared superior or standoffish, and so others backed away from her. It talked about how mothers of avoidant children tended to downplay or be put off by attachment demands.

Because of my severe neglect I, too, had shut down my attachment behavior. It was a defense mechanism against further disappointment as well as against the destructive power of my rage.

I couldn't believe it. I finally understood my behavior and why I had had so many problems.

I had adapted an avoidant attachment style to survive. I was not going to get what I needed from my parents no matter how hard I tried. I learned I would be rejected if I asked for what I needed and was shamed each time for not handling my problems myself. And if I insisted anyway, I would endure further harm and/or neglect.

Since I was incapable as a child to understand my parents' refusal to attach to me lovingly, I persisted as I got older in trying to gain their love. But any attempts were met by continued molestation from my father and further neglect from my mother.

Unable to intellectually and emotionally reconcile this as a child living in isolation with my parents as my only source of comfort, I developed a defense system of multiple personalities and was depressed. As I grew older and the violence escalated, I developed PTSD. My behavior as an adult was the result of this attachment disorder and my resulting mental illnesses.

While this new information brought fresh new perspectives, I became enraged at the totality of what I had endured all my life. I was so angry I literally almost hit a man walking in a crosswalk while driving to work.

I was going to a stupid job that was a thousand levels below my capabilities, all because of the torture I had endured the first 21 years of my life.

I wished I had never been born.

The Catch 22 I lived with was, "Don't ask for what you need because you are not going to get it, and if you do ask, you will be harmed or rejected" (in addition to not getting my needs met). That message had played itself out my entire life. The message to me when growing up was to *deny myself.*

Society reinforced this message by minimizing my wounds. Society expected me to once again, deny my reality and to do socially acceptable things even though I was famished because of no emotional support.

I knew where all this pain, mistrust and projection originated from, but knowing about it did not stop the pain. Doing things and sharing similar expectations of people without this problem did not stop the pain.

I kept saying, "I'm not asking for a religious, medical, psychological, or work-related response. I am looking for a human response."

As Mother Theresa said, "When a person dies of hunger, it did not happen because God did not take care of them. It happened because neither you nor I wanted to give that person what he or she needed. We had refused to be instruments of love to give them a piece of bread."[4]

I was fed up with the indifference toward human suffering.

With all of this anger surfacing, once again I went through a terrible nosedive with my illness. My thought processes went wild. I had made strong projections of hurt feelings, misunderstandings, hate, rage and pain.

I called to see about entering PI's Day Program because I knew I was decompensating and wanted to catch it before it got worse. I was accepted and started going on a part-time basis in August 2001.

I was confronting the way I had interacted with other humans my whole life. I was filled with rage and grief about how my life had turned out. I was professionally stifled, very lonely, and didn't have much hope of anything changing.

I had a very stressful beginning with the group because my rage was near the surface. My interactions within the group revealed a lot to me about my own behavior and how I related to people. The major change I saw in myself, though, was I no longer dissociated or switched to other personalities. I was centered within myself, knew I had a right to my feelings, and was expressing them directly.

For the first time, I saw that the poker face I had presented to the world was the wall my mother had shown me. I didn't want to be that person. Changing my attitude and viewpoint was the only thing that would change my life. I could think of a million things to do to avoid life, as I had been doing, or I could change.

---

[4] "Mother Theresa: In My Own Words," Mother Theresa, 1989, Gramercy Books

I decided to greet each day with openness, focus on dropping my psychological wall, and to have fun and not take life so seriously. The group helped me realize just how much I pushed people away and didn't let them in. On top of that, I was beginning to realize how terribly frightened I was to open myself up.

I saw that emotionally connecting with others and supporting each other was what it was all about. I had shouldered a lot because I had been too afraid. That behavior had to stop, and I was working to change it.

Chapter 37

Pulling It All Together

Outpatient group therapy was just what I needed. It allowed me to get intense feelings met and to move forward. I could see how much I was loosening up. I was not as rigid. I was not putting people in boxes and did not feel as afraid. I continued to connect what was happening today with what had happened in the past. I allowed myself to feel my anxiety, fear, etc., but went ahead and did what I needed to do. I saw how everyone was different, and that they all didn't think the same way I did. I was more flexible, slower to anger, and slower to judge. I was also not as depressed, just tired.

I was beginning to understand I had inappropriate expectations of other people when I expressed my needs. I was always looking for a response on a loving, caring cognitive level which was what I never got as a child. Nothing else would do. If I didn't get that type of response, I felt like I hadn't communicated my wishes clearly enough. When I kept getting the same response, I got mad at them. I interacted with everyone as though either they were my parent or I was theirs.

I realized I wouldn't be able to go forward with my life until I gave up that dynamic. I needed to be clear about what my needs and boundaries were, and to just love others and receive whatever I got back in whatever way people wanted to respond. That was a big change.

A few days later, a major revelation came to me which put huge puzzle pieces together. I dreamed I was a child and my mother had died. One person gave me some cookies. I pushed them away and cried, "I want my Mommy." Another person tried to give me a glass of milk. I pushed it away and said, "I want my Mommy." Another person tried to do something else for me, and I said the same thing. Then people started telling me "Look, we are doing the best we can in trying to do what your Mommy might do. You don't appreciate anything, so either take what we have to offer or shut up."

Then the image of 1964 came up where right in front of my mother's face, my father wouldn't let me get out of the bed which demonstrated the blatant truth about his sexual behavior toward me. I knew then she had known all along and had done nothing to protect me.

Next, my father's death came up, and I realized everything was final. I focused back on my mother and someone was telling me, "Your mother is dead. She is not coming back." I, as a child, was inconsolable.

I thought about that dream and my father's behavior. He would get into depressive moods and would expect all of us to take care of him. He let all his aggressions rip, and we were supposed to be understanding. I may have been harboring some of those same thoughts and notions.

I wanted to be giving, caring, understanding and loving toward others instead of being combative and angry all the time. As I thought more about my dream, I realized I didn't recognize what nurturing looked like. I had not understood that people responding to me and talking about themselves was a way of connecting their feelings with mine. My parents never responded to the real me. They never responded to my feelings at all. They were too narcissistic.

I projected onto others the same reactions I had directed towards my mother: anger, contempt, shutting them out, resentment, etc. I went from being victimized by people with distorted thinking (my parents and Barry) to being stigmatized by people with distorted thinking (people in the Company, other employers, and the many churches I attended). This revelation was unsettling but helpful.

I had spent over 20 years sorting all that out.

I sat with that new knowledge for several days and finally pulled together the major stepping stones I had experienced in developing a healthy mind.

The first significant discovery on my path to wellness was when I understood my biggest fear was that of being mentally destroyed. When I felt safely connected to Maria psychologically, I opened up more and my alters made themselves known one at a time.

As they came out, the negotiation process began, but I had to learn to manage the amount of trauma which was coming forward from my unconscious mind. This process was very confusing and disorienting. When I understood, though, that all my alters were "me," I was able to make a major shift in how I coped with the world. I became more centered and self-aware of my needs.

Another milestone was when all the dissociated parts recognized and understood the abuse was no longer happening in the present. Even though people were disrespectful, rude, or nonresponsive at times, I understood I was now an adult and could protect myself, unlike when I was a child.

After years of working with Maria to express strong emotions, and not being put-down or hurt, I was able to work on validating my own needs. After a lot of intense reflection, I made peace with and honored all my parts, thus paving the way for integration.

I was no longer afraid of my feelings which allowed my childhood responses overtime to become adult responses. The final result being I could normalize my reactions to people and form mutually respectful relationships. I could get on with my life.

It wasn't until I finished researching all my therapy notes in December 2005 that I understood the main underlining themes I had been working on throughout my therapy.

When I left my parents' home, I had memories of my abuse, but all my emotions had been split off. I had no idea the full impact my parents' behavior had had upon me. The whole time I grew up I acted responsibly, never cried out for help, but was not allowed to function as my true self. Every time we moved to a new town, I split off what had happened to me in the previous city and started a new life, hoping it would get better, but it only got worse. This was how my multiple personalities evolved.

In 1964 after my father nearly strangled me to death, I yelled for my mother, rushed to the bathroom and locked the door. I had reached my limit. I only knew I had to get to my mother. My true self stepped out for the first time in my life hoping my mother would do the right thing and protect me. She didn't. I finally understood that on a gut level my mother had sacrificed me to keep her husband, and there was no hope.

What I didn't realize was that I had been reenacting all those years in therapy the day-to-day trauma I had lived with the first 21 years of my life. When all the barriers were broken down, when my psyche was laid bare, and I finally showed my true self once again, I was reenacting what had happened in 1964 hoping this time it would be different with my mother (Maria).

It was different. Maria never abandoned me. She repeatedly displayed an attitude of respect and kindness which allowed me to grow into my own person and to develop into a fully functioning adult.

Shortly after I left the Day Center, I met someone I really liked. After seeing each other for six months, we both knew we loved each other very much and have been together ever since. We have a strong, healthy, supportive relationship, and I have found peace and contentment at last.

I was finally in a place in my life where I could be authentic with a partner without the overwhelming fear of abandonment. I could truly be myself, and knew that no matter what happened, I would be all right.

Over the next two and a half years after leaving the Day Center, Maria and I wound down the work we had been doing. It was hard to believe that Maria had worked with and supported me for 23 years. It was truly an honor to have been her patient. I was blessed.

In total, my mental health bills came to about $298,000 of which I paid about $100,000 out-of-pocket. Because Sam and Carolyn were never held responsible, their contribution was zero. I, however, ended up paying dearly for the medical conditions they caused.

I have decided to dedicate the rest of my life to writing and speaking publicly about the issues of child abuse and neglect. I hope by doing so other survivors will gain strength from my story that no matter how bad the trauma, it can be worked through.

Epilogue

For most of my life, I intended to use my family's real names in my book. After I completed my manuscript, I decided against it for several reasons. I am in a loving, committed relationship and live in a safe environment. I do not want any contact with my family nor do I want to stimulate anymore of their aggression and have it visited upon my stable home. Members of my family will recognize themselves and hopefully will learn more about their own behavior.

I do not want to hurt innocent victims. I have had no contact with my nieces and nephews, and I do not want them picking up my book and being exposed by name. I am sure they are wrestling with their own demons. I do not need to add to their troubles.

My life continues to blossom. I have integrated all my personalities and manage disruptions when they occasionally arise due to posttraumatic reactions. I remain unable to work full-time, because I can't handle the stress. In fact, my nervous system has been permanently damaged to the point where I pass out after reaching a certain stress level. I have been found lying unconscious in my shower, and on another occasion, I hit my face on a porcelain sink after passing out. I had to be taken to the hospital for stitches.

One aspect of my trauma that still causes problems are times when I am in situations where people exhibit repetitive negative behaviors and sarcastically put me down. If done for a long enough period of time, I decompensate.

I have lost 60 of the 100 pounds I gained and am working hard to lose the rest.

Carolyn still lives behind her wall of denial. Joanne has remarried, again, and continues to tell others not to believe anything I say about our family's abusive history.

Ray changed his name and is a minister. He is working toward building a church. He collects his navy pension as he builds his church membership.

I no longer attend church. I do not believe Christ's message of "tending to the least of these" is met by indoctrination techniques of blind obedience and rigid intolerance which I have encountered all my life in churches. Also, the massive cover-up and movement of child molesters within the Catholic Church, instead of reporting these criminals to the police, has cemented my repugnance for their abandonment of scripture to love and protect children. The vast majority of religious denominations have reported child molesters in their congregations, and thus, children are vulnerable no matter what church they attend.

It is most telling that the Catholic Church hired as a consultant Paul McHugh who, as Dr. Charles Whitfield wrote, sponsors the denial of both accused and convicted child molesters. The Catholic Church selected Paul McHugh to assist them with their pedophile problem instead of experts in the field of treating sexual abuse survivors or healthcare professionals who have dedicated their lives to the protection of children.

Children in American homes are not safe. The magnitude of child abuse and neglect is astronomical because the United States, for all its pronouncements about human rights, still has not placed the protection of children as one of its highest priorities.

We as a nation are so quick to point our fingers at other countries for their lack of civility, and yet millions of adults in the United States terrorize, molest and rape children every day. And most of this sexual abuse occurs in the home, not out on the street where it can be seen by other people. Our government has been glaringly absent in educating the American public about the extent of the problem. It seems like they want to keep it a secret too.

Here are the alarming statistics:

One in four girls and one in six boys will be sexually assaulted before they reach the age of eighteen.[5]

Over a period of five decades 5,148 Roman Catholic Priests have molested more than 10,000 people.[6] Roman Catholic dioceses in the United States have paid an estimated $1.5 billion since 1950 to handle claims of sex abuse by priests.[7] This does not include the number of children abused by other religious institutions.

One in seven youth online (10-17 year olds) have received a sexual solicitation or approach over the Internet.[8]

The U.S. Department of Health and Human Services reported that over 900,000 children under the age of eighteen were victims of child abuse and neglect in 2007.[9] This represents the tip of the iceberg since most children never tell anyone.

The Surgeon General has stated that family violence is now at an epidemic level.[10]

The United States Department of Education stated in 2004: "More than 4.5 million students are subjected to sexual misconduct by an employee of a school sometime between kindergarten and 12th grade. In New York City schools, more than $18.7 million was paid between 1996 and 2001 to students who were sexually abused by educators."[11]

---

[5] http://www.cdc.gov/nccdphp/ace/prevalence.htm "ACE Study - Prevalence - Adverse Childhood Experiences."

[6] "Five Decades of Abuse," The Washington Post, February 28, 2004.

[7] "Victims of abuse, Oregon church settle suit," The Sun, December 12, 2006.

[8] "Online Victimization of Youth: Five Years Later," David Finkelhor, Kimberly J. Mitchell, and Janis Wolak, National Center for Missing and Exploited Children, 2006, pages 7-8, 33.

[9] "Child Health USA," U.S. Department of Health and Human Services, 2008.

[10] "The Surgeon General's Report on Mental Health," 1999.

[11] "Educator Sexual Misconduct: A Synthesis of Existing Literature," U.S. Department of Education, 2004.

The Bureau of Justice Statistics states: "The sexual assaults of young children are a major social concern. Juveniles were the large majority of the victims of forcible fondling (84%), forcible sodomy (79%), and sexual assault with an object (75%). In the case of forcible rape, children below the age of 12 were about half the victims. For victims under age 12, four-year-olds were at the greatest risk of being the victim of a sexual assault.[12]

The United States Advisory Board on Child Abuse and Neglect has concluded that child abuse and neglect in the United States now represents a national emergency.[13]

Roughly 19% of girls and 16% of boys meet the criteria of PTSD, major depressive episode, and substance abuse/ dependence.[14]

Conservative estimates indicate that five children die every day from abuse or neglect by parents or caretakers. The vast majority are under four-years-old.[15]

In military families, rates of marital aggression are considerably higher than civilian rates, three to five times. Between 1980—1992 firearms were used against 35% of female victims. Females were over 10 times more likely than males to be strangled. Relatively few military personnel are prosecuted or administratively sanctioned on charges stemming from domestic violence.[16]

---

[12] "Sexual Assault of Young Children as Reported to Law Enforcement: Victim, Incident, and Offender Characteristics," Bureau of Justice Statistics, National Center for Juvenile Justice, July 2000.

[13] "Protecting Children from Abuse and Neglect, Foundations for a New National Strategy," Edited by Gary B. Melton and Frank D. Barry, 1994.

[14] "High Percentage of Youth in the U.S. Report Symptoms of Posttraumatic Stress and Other Disorders," Journal of Consulting and Clinical Psychology, 2003, Vol. 71, No. 4.

[15] "A Nation's Shame: Fatal Child Abuse and Neglect in the United States," Department of Health and Human Services – Administration for Children and Families, April 1995.

[16] "Facts and Findings," The Miles Foundation, 2006.

Dissociative Disorders are not uncommon. Research has repeatedly demonstrated an appreciable relationship between a history of trauma and dissociation.[17] In fact, a study in 2006 found the prevalence of any type of dissociation to be 9.1% in the population it observed.[18] And yet, the National Institutes of Health has conducted <u>no research</u> to understand its cause or to determine the best way to treat Dissociative Disorders.

Our government spends over $104 billion a year as a result of child abuse and neglect[19] on everything from child welfare, adoption, substance abuse treatment centers, juvenile delinquency, the court system, and police intervention.

In spite of all these statistics, not one President, Secretary of Health and Human Services, or any member of Congress in the history of our country has successfully put child abuse and neglect on the national agenda.

America's response to sexual abuse and neglect has consistently been denial. It took over 100 years after our country was founded to even acknowledge the fact that women and children were being sexually assaulted and abused to legislate against rape and physical abuse. It took another 80 years before America acknowledged children were being battered in their own homes. It has now taken another 60 years for people to openly broach the subject of child sexual abuse, though not willingly. Families still deny the level of violence occurring in their homes.

The bottom line is until the sacrosanct belief in the "right" to parent children without any training, oversight, or accountability

---

[17] "The Need for Inclusion of Psychological Trauma in the Professional Curriculum: A Call to Action," C.A. Courtois, Ph.D., S.N. Gold, Ph.D., Psychology Trauma: Theory, Research, Practice, and Policy, March 2009, Vol. 1, No. 1.

[18] Ibid.

[19] "Total Estimated Cost of Child Abuse and Neglect in the United States," Prevent Child Abuse America 2007 – U.S. Department of Health and Human Services.

is challenged and changed, America will continue to grow home-grown domestic terrorists, who in turn, will go on inflicting physical, emotional, mental, and sexual abuse on millions of innocent children every year. Their silent partners – the ones who are aware of the abuse but don't report or stop it – are just as guilty.

My fight will continue until our country steps-up to this insidious behavior and puts an end to it. I invite other survivors to join me. America's children deserve nothing less.

Appendix

Reprint Permission

Grateful acknowledgment is made to the following for permission to reprint copyrighted material:

"Letter to the Editor" of the Washington Post. Copyright © 1991 by Dr. Charles Whitfield in responding to an article about Multiple Personality Disorder. Reprinted with the permission of Dr. Charles Whitfield, www.cbwhit.com.

Disclaimer

The reader should understand that neither the author nor the publisher renders professional, psychiatric, therapeutic, medical or other expert services. The aim of this book is to discuss the author's personal family history, and make observations about abuse generally, based upon the author's experiences. Neither the author nor the publisher is liable or responsible for any loss or damage caused by this book. The book is NOT intended as a substitute for professional help or treatment. The diagnosis and treatment of medical or psychiatric disorders, sexual abuse-related or otherwise, requires trained professionals. The information provided in this book is for educational purposes only. Neither the author nor the publisher is responsible for claims made or information supplied by medical specialists referenced in the book. If you have experienced sexual abuse or other trauma that requires professional evaluation, you should seek professional help.

Author's Biography

Diane Champé, the Survivors Champion™, is a Subject Matter Expert on child abuse and neglect. Through willpower, 23 years of therapy and five hospitalizations, she overcame a horrific childhood resulting in major depression, PTSD, and Dissociative Identity Disorder. Despite these catastrophes' and hardships, Ms. Champé rose from an entry-level position in the mail room of a Fortune 20 Company to become a Strategic Planner on the Regional VP's staff in only 19 years. Now retired, she is dedicating the rest of her life to speaking out about child abuse and neglect, and to helping adult survivors reclaim their lives. She speaks to legislators, law enforcement, child advocacy centers, and universities. Ms. Champé recently worked on a National Trauma Campaign for SAMHSA – a division of the U.S. Department of Health and Human Services. Her website www.wearesurvivors.org is a national platform to discuss issues affecting adult survivors of child abuse and neglect.